SETTING THE AGENDA FOR GLOBAL PEACE

Gender in a Global/Local World

Series Editors: Jane Parpart, Pauline Gardiner Barber and Marianne H. Marchand

The series *Gender in a Global/Local World* critically explores the uneven and often contradictory ways in which global processes and local identities come together. It is also cognizant of the deeper historical forces at play in this process. Much has been and is being written about globalization and responses to it but rarely from a critical, historical, gendered perspective. Yet, these processes are profoundly gendered albeit in different ways in particular contexts and times. The changes in social, cultural, economic and political institutions and practices alter the conditions under which women and men make and remake their lives. New spaces have been created – economic, political, social – and previously silent voices are being heard. North-South dichotomies are being undermined as more people are exposed to international processes through migration, travel, and communication even as marginalization and poverty intensify for many in all parts of the world. The series welcomes monographs and collections exploring these kinds of tensions in a 'global/local world'. We encourage contributions from all disciplines in recognition that no single approach can capture these complex processes. The series is thus deliberately international and interdisciplinary, and contributions from all relevant disciplines and perspectives are welcome.

Setting the Agenda for Global Peace

Conflict and consensus building

ANNA C. SNYDER
Conflict Resolution Studies Program
Menno Simons College, Canada

ASHGATE

Published by
Ashgate Publishing Limited
Gower House
Croft Road
Aldershot
Hampshire GU11 3HR
England

Ashgate Publishing Company
Suite 420
101 Cherry Street
Burlington, VT 05401-4405
USA

Ashgate website: http://www.ashgate.com

British Library Cataloguing in Publication Data
Snyder, Anna C.
Setting the agenda for global peace : conflict and consensus building. - (Gender in a global/local world)
1. Peaceful change (International relations) 2. Feminism - International cooperation 3. Peace movements 4. Women and peace 5. Conflict management - Sex differences
I. Title
327.1'72'082

Library of Congress Cataloging-in-Publication Data
Snyder, Anna C.
Setting the agenda for global peace : conflict and consensus building / Anna C. Snyder.
p. cm. -- (Gender in a global/local world)
Includes bibliographical references and index.
ISBN 0-7546-1933-8
1.Women and peace. 2. Nongovernmental organizations. 3. Pacific settlement of international disputes. I. Title. II. Series.

JZ5578 .S65 2002
327.1'72--dc21 2002028166

ISBN 0 7546 1933 8

Printed and bound in Great Britain by MPG Books Ltd, Bodmin, Cornwall

Contents

Acknowledgements

My interest in research on transnational conflict and consensus building began in my twenties when I was working with international peace organizations. Two of the four organizations I worked with fell apart due to conflict and another was inactive for over a year. From my experience, the inability of peace organizations to deal with conflict constructively made both the organization and the movement less effective in reaching their goals. As a mediator and a student of peace and conflict resolution studies, I decided I wanted to make a difference.

When I began my graduate study in peace studies, my interest in conflict among peacemakers was combined with an excitement about the role of women in peace and justice movements. Until that time, I had been unaware that women had any kind of leading role in peace movements and I decided that I wanted to learn more about them. As I discovered women's peace organizations, I also discovered feminist theory and began to read about many of the difficulties that women face in organizing around the identity of 'Woman.' This is how I came to study the process by which international non-governmental organizations set agendas for policy formation within the context of the UN and why I focused specifically on the role that conflict played in determining priorities within an international coalition of women's peace organizations.

First and foremost, I would like to thank the women who allowed me into their lives to study how they process conflicts. I would particularly like to thank the women affiliated with the Women's International League for Peace and Freedom, the Sudanese Women's Voice for Peace, and Beneath Paradise. I was deeply inspired by their courage, dedication, and vision.

I would also like to thank everyone at Syracuse University who helped me with my journey, in particular Marjorie Devault, Louis Kriesberg, John Burdick, Lily Ling, and Pramod Parajuli. I appreciated the many hours of laughing and talking about ideas with Ann Marshall, Katalin Fabian, Susan Adair, Michael Messina-Yatze, Margaret Wehrer, Jessica Senehi, and Byeoung-Chul Park. Thanks to Mara Sapon-Shevin, Karen Mihaly, and Beth Broadway for their support all along the way.

Others who have helped me on this path are my colleagues in Winnipeg, especially Brian Rice, Judith Harris, and Deborah Stienstra. I appreciated very much the technical support of my brothers, Steve and Jon. Most of all, I want to thank my parents, Graydon and Lois Snyder, whose undying love and encouragement made this work possible.

List of Abbreviations

BRA	Bougainville Revolutionary Army
CEDAW	Convention on the Elimination of All Forms of Discrimination Against Women
COC	Chinese Organizing Committee
CONGO	Conference of Non-Governmental Organizations in Consultative Status
CSW	UN Committee on the Status of Women
ECOSOC	Economic and Social Council
FLNKS	National Kanak Socialist Liberation Front
FWCW	Fourth UN World Conference on Women
ICR	Interactive Conflict Resolution
IGO	Intergovernmental Organization
IFOR	International Fellowship of Reconciliation
INGO	International Non-governmental Organization
IPB	International Peace Bureau
NAM	Non-Aligned Movement
NCBI	National Coalition Building Institute
NFIP	Nuclear Free and Independent Pacific
NGO	Non-governmental Organization
NIEO	New International Economic Order

PALIKA	Parti de Liberation Kanak
PfA	Platform for Action
PNG	Papua New Guinea
PrepCom	Preparatory Committee
SPLM	Sudan People's Liberation Movement
SWVP	Sudanese Women's Voice for Peace
TSMO	Transnational Social Movement Organizations
UNHCR	UN High Commission on Refugees
UNIFEM	United Nations Development Fund for Women
WEDO	Women's Environment and Development Organization
WILPF	Women's International League for Peace and Freedom

To my parents, Lois and Graydon Snyder,
whose dedication to peace has inspired me.

Chapter 1

Introduction

In preparation for the 1995 4th UN World Conference on Women (FWCW) in Beijing, China, women peace activists met together at regional and global preparatory conferences to develop global agendas for peace. Given their diverse local and regional interests, it was a difficult task even though they were all working towards a common goal. Civil war, nuclear weapons testing, de-colonization, self-determination, military budgets, police brutality, conflict resolution education and training, land rights, women's involvement in peace negotiations, military prostitution, rape during war-time—these were all issues that were important to the women. As they attempted to identify priorities for their budding network, conflicts arose as to whose agenda would become the focus of the lobbying efforts of the group. According to one participant:

> I'm coming here as a black activist and I want to put the issues for myself and my community on the political agenda. This peace train is not just about trying to be cozy and nice. If we want to change the world, we've gotta change ourselves. In order to change ourselves, that's not an easy process. And so there are going to be difficulties. I want us to be able to deal, really deal with some of those conflicts. Not walk away.

How they dealt with those conflicts was critical to the formation of their network.

Conflicts within transnational networks over issue priorities and frames are not uncommon. One of the main challenges non-governmental organizations (NGOs) face in building transnational movements is that of developing a 'common frame of meaning' among culturally, ethnically or ideologically diverse groups of people.[1] Framing is defined as 'the conscious strategic efforts by groups of people to fashion shared understandings of the world and of themselves that legitimate and motivate collective action.' (McAdam et al., 1996, p.6). Participants construct the substantive content of particular issues; it is not inherent in the issues themselves. Struggles over meaning tend to be a part of the early formation of advocacy networks (Snow and Benford, 1992; Tarrow, 1992). Transnational networks of NGOs use these frames to help launch global campaigns intended to change the behavior of states and/or international organizations.

[1] My research at the FWCW included non-governmental organizations (NGOs) or voluntary agencies, international NGOs (INGOs), social movement organizations (SMOs), and transnational social movement organizations (TSMOs). In order to simplify the discussion, I will use the most inclusive category—NGOs. For an analysis of the differences between these types of organizations see Smith, Chatfield, and Pagnucco (1997).

Within NGO networks, some frames succeed and others fail and as a result, some issues and perspectives gain attention while others do not. At the FWCW, some of the women's peace organizations tried to gain attention for issues relating to armed conflict by embedding peace issues in human rights and development discourse, the most prominent frames at the conference. 'Peace is a human right' and 'Peace is a pre-requisite to development' are two examples of slogans used by most Northern (and some African) peace activists to elicit more support for peace issues from NGO representatives and government delegates. By contrast, a Pacific Island NGO representative introduced the slogan 'De-nuclearization, De-militarization, and De-colonization' as she struggled to put de-colonization on the women's peace agenda by making sure it was included in the transnational framing process. The frames defined by the Northern peace NGOs nonetheless tended to dominate among the women's peace NGOs gathered. As a consequence, some of the representatives from peace NGOs in the South felt their issues had been marginalized. Some challenged the agenda and strengthened their ties within the coalition; other activists dropped out of the peace activities and looked elsewhere for support weakening the budding peace network.

Because they bring together many diverse organizations and movements, global conferences have become a place for NGOs to discover their disagreements. Some of the sharpest divisions among NGOs are between Northern and Southern NGOs because they tend to prioritize different aspects of similar issues. Nevertheless, openly discussing differences within a particular conference, or across several conferences, can further understanding and collaboration among diverse NGOs. In fact, a 1995 survey of NGOs active in international arenas reveals that the organizing and dialogue process were seen as the most valuable aspects of NGO participation in global conferences (Benchmark Environmental Consulting, 1996). This survey shows that NGOs attach more importance to developing processes for working together than to influencing global policy (Smith, 2001). Although the conflicts within the peace network were not necessarily 'resolved,' some of the parties involved expressed some satisfaction with the outcomes of their collaboration and a willingness to work with the network again.

NGOs facilitate the formation and growth of transnational social movements by developing networks or social infrastructures that can process conflicts among diverse organizations and build consensus on global problems and their solutions. However, NGOs face disagreement over goals and means, frames, and resources making resolving conflicts and generating consensus an enormous challenge (McCarthy, 1997; Princen and Finger, 1994; Clark, 1994). NGOs need to learn more about inter-organization cooperation and resist a tendency to 'claim turf' (Boulding, 1997). Heinrich maintains that although the number of non-state actors involved in peace efforts has increased, it has not necessarily led to more effective peace building; instead, 'there is a disturbing shortage of communication, coordination, and cooperation' (Heinrich, 1997, p.10).

Since NGO research tends to focus on policies not process, little is known about which processes NGOs find helpful and why. This book examines the process by which women's peace organizations attempted to reach agreement on common agendas within a network of women gathered for the 4th UN World

Conference on Women (FWCW) held in Beijing, China in 1995. The struggle to set the agenda was one of the most important conflicts at the conferences. During the agenda-setting process, interested parties determined what the substantive areas of their collaboration would be. According to Susskind and Madigan, 'The agenda is often the object of intense debate since some parties will work hard to add or delete issues of special concern' (Susskind and Madigan, 1984, p.185). If some participants believe that the agenda does not reflect their interests, they will lose their commitment to collaboration (Gray, 1991). The FWCW provided an excellent opportunity to study agenda-setting because it drew many NGO representatives with diverse priorities who were determined to influence the conference agenda.

This study shows how non-governmental organizations (NGOs) use conflict constructively to develop transnational social movements and build consensus around issues of common concern. Social movement conflict serves four purposes. Conflicts over NGO network priorities expose inequalities in large scale, non-governmental decision making. Contention arising from policy development increases understanding of regional, ethnic, racial and ideological differences and expand possibilities for collaboration. Deep-rooted, historical conflicts that surface become starting points for dialogue among NGO representatives. Attempts to resolve conflicts strengthen the network and facilitate the construction of transnational activist identities.

In order to study transnational agenda-setting processes, I conducted a two year qualitative study of the process by which women's peace NGOs set agendas at the NGO Forum '95, the FWCW and its preparatory conferences. The UN conferences have become important sites for transnational movement mobilization and construction. I was able to observe and interview 50 peace activists at four preparatory conferences, including regional conferences in Austria and Senegal, two global conferences in New York and then the NGO Forum '95 and the FWCW in Beijing, China. I spent approximately three weeks at each event. In addition, I conducted research travelling on the Women's International League for Peace and Freedom delegation peace train that started in Helsinki, Finland and ended in Beijing for the conference. Attendance at the preparatory conferences was important because much of the agenda appeared to be set before the final conference in Beijing began.

Most NGO literature tends to focus on transnational social movements from a structural perspective (Keck and Sikkink, 1998; Smith, Chatfield, and Pagnucco, 1997; Princen and Finger, 1994; Stienstra, 1994). The literature is missing perspectives from individual NGO representatives on the making of international networks and a day to day view of the practice of international politics. Although transnational networks cannot be reduced to the agency of activists, the experience of NGO representatives contributes to knowledge of how and why international organizing works by addressing ways in which networks deal with internal conflict. Because social movements tend to be seen as collective efforts, transnational social movement theorists rarely focus on network conflict (McCarthy, 1997).

Focusing on how NGO representatives dealt with internal dissension, adds to the understanding of how NGO networks build the social infrastructure of transnational social movements. Concentrating on conflict: 1) increases understanding of contentious issues; 2) explores the problems with current decision making techniques; and 3) shows how conflict resolution methods can be used in the formation of transnational social movements. My research focused on two questions. First, how do NGOs find common agendas? That is, why do certain discourses or frames succeed? The purpose of this question is to examine the process by which NGO participants draw upon, construct, and participate in a transnational discourse on peacemaking. Second, what role does conflict play in the agenda-setting process? Do participants attempt dialogue and, if so, what problems do they encounter? The objective is to analyze how issues of contention emerged among the peace NGOs and how participants addressed them.

Significance of NGOs in Global Arenas

As the number and impact of non-state actors in world politics grows, the importance of understanding how transnational networks of NGOs operate, given their great potential for conflict, will increase commensurately. At the international level, NGOs and social movements are becoming more visible. The growing number of NGOs indicates greater citizen participation in international political life. NGOs often represent people who would be excluded from participation in the formation of transnational policies that shape global and regional activities. Transnational social movements influence regional and global policy providing connections between grassroots movements, governments, and international bodies like the UN. Specifically, transnational social movements help to shape global policy by mobilizing citizen support, broadening public participation, sustaining attention on critical global problems, framing issues, setting agendas, and implementing policies (Kriesberg, 1997).

Those international NGOs that promote institutional and policy changes in the international arena, transnational social movement organizations (TSMO), act as agents of global change (Smith, Chatfield, and Pagnucco, 1997). TSMOs provide the social infrastructure for movement mobilization by developing networks of social relations through which ideas and practices are transmitted. They serve as constituenties for IGOs and in turn, help to foster democracy. TSMOs with access to wealth can offer resources to other NGOs with fewer resources resulting in the redistribution of wealth. Further, TSMOs strengthen transnational identities as people work together to achieve their goals, e.g. human rights advocate. Finally, TSMOs stimulate diverse responses and analyses to transnational sources of common problems (Kriesberg, 1997).

NGO collaboration is important for human security because NGOs have helped to bring about nonviolent social change.[2] For example, using interviews with political leaders, Cortright (1993) documents peace movement influence on the Reagan administration policy during the Cold War. According to Meyer and

---

[2] For a critical analysis of NGO activities and/or relevance see Tarrow (2001), Lewis and Wallace (2000), Edwards and Hulme (1996), and Fisher (1998).

Marullo (1992), social movement organizations contributed to the transformation of Eastern Europe and the former Soviet Union by constraining government activity and supporting alternative policies that helped to create a posture of conciliation from the West which, in turn, gave Eastern reformers room to operate. Even though NGO capabilities are limited, the small shifts that they have achieved can have long-term effects on the large-scale social forces that transform global structures. Furthermore, when NGOs cross-cut national borders and other lines of cleavage, they link the common interests of people across national boundaries helping to mitigate destructive conflicts (Kriesberg, 1982).

Some scholars maintain that an increase in the number of NGOs with shared transnational goals points to the development of a global civil society that is altering or even replacing the state system (Commission on Global Governance, 1995; Benchmark Environmental Consulting, 1996). Others argue that assertions as to the nature and impact of a global civil society are premature (Clark et al., 1998). Whether NGOs have created a global civil society and what constitutes global civic governance is still unclear. However, it is evident that NGOs are more interested in creating direct citizen-to-citizen links at international events than in trying to change the existing inter-governmental system (Smith, 2001). Ninety four per cent of NGOs define the success of an international conference by whether they met and worked with other key NGOs, not by whether government policies have changed (Benchmark Environmental Consulting, 1996). In the 1996 Benchmark study, a high percentage of NGO respondents maintain that they attend intergovernmental events in order to find other NGOs with similar interests and goals.

Constructive Conflict Defined

In the context of my study, conflict is defined as 'an expressed struggle between at least two interdependent parties who perceive incompatible goals, scarce resources, and interference from others in achieving their goals' (Wilmot and Hocker, 2001, p. 41). The concept of perceived conflict is particularly relevant in a setting where there is a very strong norm or ideology of unity, solidarity and common goals. Conflict can occur in a cooperative or a competitive context. For example, the women in my study were working for common objectives such as 'peace' and 'the improvement in the status of women.' Their conflicts tended to be about deciding which issues were most important for women's movements and what strategies to achieve them would be most effective. Concerns about priorities and strategies might be influenced by ideology, culture, race, class, historical context, NGO focus, and so on. Even though not all dissension was expressed in a direct manner, all of the participants were aware of the conflicts to some extent and positioned themselves around them. Many of the women perceived themselves as interdependent because their success depended in part on effective collaboration with other NGOs in lobbying and networking activities.

Dissension within women's organizations has been difficult at times for feminists to handle. With feminist ideologies that emphasize female solidarity and consensus building, conflict and dissension have been stifled because they are perceived to threaten the community. According to Robin Leidner:

> The assumptions of feminism—that the interests of all women are valid and important, that all forms of oppression must be fought, and that solidarity is a feminist responsibility—make disagreement painful (Leidner, 1991, p. 286).

At the same time, feminist organizations face difficulties such as emotional intensity, ideological factionalism, and leadership trashing. Furthermore, conflicts concerning racism, classism, or homophobia have divided women's movements.

This study shows that conflict was useful to the development of women's transnational networks and points to how and why conflicts were processed constructively. Most parties involved in conflict interact in both a productive and destructive manner. It is rare that a conflict is entirely constructive or destructive. As such, when analyzing a conflict, it is important to examine varying degrees of destructiveness and constructiveness by looking at the means by which a conflict is waged and its outcome (Kriesberg, 1998). In constructive conflicts, the participants show flexibility; they engage in a wide variety of behaviors to arrive at an acceptable solution. As a result, parties participate in short cycles of escalation, avoidance and constructive work as their interaction changes. Disputants in destructive conflict often lack flexibility because their goal is to defeat the other. Most often, destructive conflict results in uncontrolled escalation or prolonged avoidance (Folger et al., 2001).

Further, in constructive conflict, parties approach the conflict believing that all sides can reach important goals (Deutsch, 1973). As a result, participants consistently attempt to bridge positions perceived as incompatible. In contrast, parties involved in destructive conflict believe that one side must win and the other side will have to lose and respond accordingly. Productive conflict interaction is sometimes competitive because in order to achieve a satisfactory outcome, both parties must stand up for their own interests (Cahn 1990). Even though disputants exhibit anger and hold strongly to their positions, they are willing to change if it will result in the best outcome. On the other hand, when a conflict is destructive, it becomes more important to the parties to defend their positions than to work out a viable solution.

The outcome of a conflict is considered constructive if the parties find it mutually acceptable. In addition, the extent to which an outcome is constructive is reflected in the degree to which it facilitates an ongoing relationship in which future conflicts can be managed constructively. A destructive outcome results from one party imposing decisions made unilaterally with little or no consideration for the interests and needs of the other party. The outcome may be perceived as oppressive or humiliating and as such requiring further action or revenge. Often destructive outcomes become the basis for a renewed and destructive struggle (Kriesberg, 1998).

Research Methodology for a Global Mega-Conference

The peace activities at the NGO Forum '95 and the FWCW and the NGOs affiliated with those activities were the focal point of my research. I focused my interviews primarily on members of three NGOs from three different regions: the Women's International League for Peace and Freedom (WILPF), The Sudanese Women's Voice for Peace (SWVP) and Beneath Paradise, a network of indigenous women from the Pacific Islands. There were many NGOs involved in the peace events that were not part of my study. Their experience may have been different from the NGOs important to my research. However, given the large number of NGOs, I limited the number to three; I interviewed other peace activists and NGO delegates in order to shed light on the context in which the three organizations operated. In this way, I was able to attend to the NGO agendas and their experiences with the agenda-setting process in more detail.

An ethnographic study of a world conference was difficult because of time pressures, a huge field, and more complexity than any researcher could possibly capture. As such, my study was confined to an analysis of a small segment of conference activities. Nevertheless, during the UN conferences and the NGO meetings, I often worked as a researcher twelve hours a day attending as many as seven meetings. The NGOs worked together on writing resolutions for the Platform for Action, the UN document, coordinated lobbying efforts, and planned activities together like the peace tent, a tent set up in Beijing where workshops on peace issues were held. They marched in demonstrations, presented workshops, and participated in or spoke at plenary meetings. Much of the interesting discussion took place during the informal, unstructured, daily activity such as mealtimes, bathroom breaks and hallway conversations. It was during these events that I observed peace agendas being constructed.

Some of their joint activity took place during what was called the peace caucus. Dozens of caucuses met during the conferences, organized according to topics, such as peace, health, regions and/or identities, such as African or young women. The main focus of the peace caucus was to develop resolutions for the Platform for Action and then to coordinate the lobbying for their inclusion in the document. The peace caucus held gatherings only during the UN meetings in rooms on site so that one had to obtain a UN security pass in order to attend the peace caucus.

Participant observation was central to my study. I found that not only were some of my informants reluctant to talk about conflict but there were discrepancies between their words and their actions. Participant observation allowed me to gather crucial data on how they responded to one another over time. I was able to observe how and if their relations with one another changed during the conferences and from conference to conference.

Discourse and conflict were the central organizing concepts for my data collection. My research questions were concerned primarily with process. What is the process by which diverse women work together to make joint statements and activities? Questions about how people express themselves and what happens when they disagree are important, particularly in a UN setting where there are strong mandates to find consensus and make single statements that apply universally. As a result, when I observed during the workshops, meetings, general sessions and informal conversations, my observations tended to focus on the issues raised, language, both spoken and written, speakers, coalition building, and behavior around conflicts or contention.

In qualitative research, concepts, insights and understanding are developed from patterns of data. A flexible research design was very useful in a setting where current events, particularly current political events, made the conferences unpredictable. For example, the shift of the NGO Forum '95 in March of 1995 from Beijing to Hairou, a small town in the countryside outside of the city, influenced my ability to attend both the NGO Forum '95 and the FWCW at the same time. However, as a participant observer, my struggles with commuting long hours on buses, exhaustion, and rain and mud were similar to those of my informants and simply became more data on the obstacles that NGOs face.

As I conducted my interviews and observed my informants, I was aware that being a European American with middle class heritage played into the dynamics of my relationship to my informants. Some of my informants may not have felt they could speak frankly with me or may have left out important issues. This was to some extent a given in a multi-cultural setting like the World Conference. As a result, the analysis of my data is limited. However, I also found that I was of interest to my Southern informants and to some Northern women of color precisely because they were seeking to gain white/international/Northern allies. Madelaine, an NGO delegate from New Caledonia, was most enthusiastic once I said that I was interested in conflict among women, drawing me aside immediately to talk about her conflicts. Once I explained that I was focusing on conflict, it was some of the white North American/Western European women who were reluctant to talk and who appeared to feel uncomfortable with my very presence. For some, concentrating on conflict meant giving undue attention to the weaknesses in the alliance rather than to the strengths. From their perspective, my research could potentially undermine the credibility of NGOs and the power of the movement in the eyes of the public.

Studying Everyday Activity of Individual Activists

The UN World Conferences on Women are all about 'bringing women together.' This study explores what women coming together means in a concrete embodied way. By observing the women in their everyday activities, listening to them talk about what was of concern to them, and looking at the documents they produced, I was able to explore what happened first-hand. Studying everyday activity often leads to an understanding of social relations intrinsic to and extending beyond them (Smith, 1987). Qualitative methods allowed me to see how women's actual activities are connected (or not) to the formal and abstract formulations or analyses that come out of the UN conferences (Devault, 1995).

A qualitative study contributes what has been missing from previous analyses, that is, a look at the challenges and successes of individual activists working as representatives for their organizations. Historical and/or social movement research has tended to focus on NGOs as units of analysis or on transnational movements as a whole. Greater understanding of the development of transnational social movements can be gained through the perspective of the actors involved. Most of the existing literature written on transnational women's movements tends to concentrate on historical accounts of women's NGOs and their role at the UN, policy content, NGO reports, personal diaries or the development of international relations and feminist theory (Bulbeck, 1998; McClintock et al., 1997; Winslow, 1995; Marchand and Parpart, 1995; Pietila and Vickers, 1994; Mohanty, Russo and Torres, 1991; Fraser, 1987). Through the use of grounded theory, this analysis is more systematic than the personal accounts written by conference participants, but still has the detail and richness of the experience of participation.

Conference Background and History

The FWCW was part of a series of conferences that first began in 1975 in Mexico City during the International Year of the Woman. During the following UN Decade on Women, two more conferences took place, one in Copenhagen, Sweden (1980) and the other in Nairobi, Kenya (1985). Since 1975, when the first World Conference on Women took place, one of the main themes of the conferences has been peace, along with equality and development.

The women's World Conferences are similar to the other mega-conferences that have taken place in the past twenty years on topics like population, environment, disarmament, and human rights. There are two parts to the conferences, a UN conference and a parallel non-governmental forum for interested organizations. The official UN conferences are attended by representatives of nation-states as voting members and observers from various UN agencies and bodies, international governmental organizations, NGOs, and social movements. At each conference and its preparatory meetings, government delegates focus their primary efforts on creating a final conference document to be approved by state participants. Governments develop regional positions on specific issues at regional preparatory meetings. Global meetings of the Preparatory committee (PrepCom) focus specifically on preparing a draft of the conference document. During the PrepComs and the conference itself, the language in the final document is subject to intense negotiations and politicking.

The NGO conferences are parallel forums organized by the Conference of Non-Governmental Organizations in Consultative Status (CONGO). The NGO Forums have no official link to the UN conferences, but consist of general sessions, exhibitions, and workshops organized by non-governmental organizations and other interest groups (Stephenson, 1995). States have far more power in the development of the conference document than do NGOs. However, as soon as official preparations begin, NGOs use the conferences to try to influence the government agenda and to build networks among NGOs with similar priorities. The NGO Forum provides a site for NGOs to set their own policy agenda, coordinate lobbying strategies, and organize various activities among themselves.

NGOs attending the world conferences have expanded their strategies to include not only lobbying but also networking. Both activities represent models of international democratic participation. NGOs using the traditional lobbying model simply extend their domestic lobbying to an international level. The international events provide NGOs with additional opportunities to affect their own governments' policy objectives and increased access to government officials. On the other hand, some NGOs are disillusioned with national politics and find it is more effective to work directly with other representatives of civil society through democratic and non-governmental means. These NGOs would be more likely to make use of the second model of participation, the global civil governance model. In response to the failure of states to address key global problems, citizens are beginning to develop structures by which they can take action at a global level (Benchmark Environmental Consulting, 1996). NGO networking is a central part of the global civil governance model. As NGO participation in both the official conferences and the NGO forums expanded in the 1990s, NGOs became divided as to which model was more important than the other. Some NGOs, however, continue to both lobby and network.

The UN World Conferences on Women are convened by the UN Committee on the Status of Women (CSW). The CSW was created in 1946, after WWII, as a sub-commission of the Commission on Human Rights under the leadership of Eleanor Roosevelt. It was approved by the Economic and Social Council (ECOSOC) as a commission later that year with the purpose to prepare recommendations and report to ECOSOC on promoting women's rights in political, economic, civil, social and educational fields. ECOSOC retained authority over the conduct of business, the selection of members and NGO observers, as well as proposals for action. In Beijing, the task of the CSW was to review progress made to improve the status of women over the past ten years since its last meeting in Nairobi, to develop a new set of proposals, the Platform for Action (PfA); and to formulate strategies to implement those proposals.

During the International Decade for Women, NGOs fought for increased access to and impact on the UN conferences. In March 1995 at the 4th PrepCom in New York, NGOs were excluded from many discussions concerning the conference document. In response to pressure from NGOs, ECOSOC challenged the right of government delegates to exclude NGOs 'in an unprecedented use of its assembly procedures' (Clark et al, 1998). Meeting in New York, ECOSOC adopted a resolution on the matter partway through the fourth PrepCom that extended the NGO application period for accreditation, gave NGOs an opportunity to appeal denials, and declared that the rules for NGO participation at the Beijing conference equivalent to those at the PrepComs (Clark et al, 1998).

NGOs must receive accreditation in order to receive Consultative Status at the UN and to General Assembly conferences and special sessions. Each of the UN World Conferences on Women was a General Assembly conference (Stephenson, 1995). The issue of accreditation is one of growing importance as the number of NGOs applying for consultative status has reached the tens of thousands. At the start of the International Women's Year in 1975, there were roughly fifty women's international non-governmental organizations. By the end of the Decade there were over one thousand women's NGOs seeking access to the UN. As the number of NGOs has skyrocketed, so has the attendance at the NGO forums (which does not require accreditation), meaning that over 30,000 women participated in the 1995 NGO Forum in Hairou, China.

Throughout the Decade, the organization, structure, participants, and size of the NGO Forums changed radically. At the first Conference in 1975, NGOs had little structured activity and collaboration. In Mexico City (1975), NGOs organized and participated in 192 sessions total but in 1995 in Beijing, they held 3,340 sessions at an average of 371 per day. NGOs were not involved in preparatory processes leading up to Mexico City or to Copenhagen (1980); however, they participated in national and regional preparatory conferences for both Nairobi (1985) and Beijing.

By 1995, NGO organization and cooperation had grown to such an extent that the NGOs developed and approved by consensus an NGO-written draft of the Platform for Action based on regional documents, a first in the history of the women's World Conferences. The increased number of NGOs, the skill and expertise of their representatives, the growing diversity of the participants as well as the shared conference history contributed to increased collaboration and expanded dialogue in the hundreds of workshops and meetings held. Furthermore, the women strengthened their UN lobbying strategy and skill using their experience gained at the multiple women's conferences and at UN world conferences such as the 1992 Conference on Environment and Development and the 1993 World Conference on Human Rights. They built coalitions through a caucus mechanism, participated early and in large numbers in the preparatory meetings, and increased their contact with the media and national delegates (Clark et al, 1998).

Women's Peace Organizations at the UN Conferences

Women's peace organizations have participated in the UN World Conferences on Women since the first conference in 1975. Like many other NGOs, the peace organizations are interested primarily in lobbying government delegates in order to influence international policy formation and/or in networking with other NGOs or intergovernmental organizations (IGOs). Some of the organizations, like the Nuclear Free and Independent Pacific, use the global media coverage to gain international attention for their causes. A few, like WILPF, given their long history with the UN as an international peace making body, are concerned with UN reform. Many organizations were eager to increase the legitimacy of their claims and the credibility of their NGOs; the power of the UN, the media attention, and the sheer number of influential international women's organizations present at the World Conference on Women give the conference participants and their proposals a certain legitimacy.

Women's peace organizations are at the forefront of many peace movements. Some women's peace efforts are initiated by women's movements attempting to secure political gains for women through the peace process. The peace table can provide an opportunity to transform institutions and structures and to redress gender inequities as well as other forms of social injustice. Other women take on activist roles in the process of holding together their communities. Women often find themselves assuming the sole responsibility of providing for their families, educating their children, and caring for the wounded.

However, women tend be left out of the decision making processes that influence the direction and duration of the conflict. As peace activists, women often integrate their experience at the grassroots level into peace-building efforts. They are well aware of the many challenges faced by civilian populations and can formulate concrete and effective mechanisms for addressing daily realities on the ground (Anderlini, 2000). Grassroots involvement and ownership is a crucial element of sustainable peace (Lederach, 1997). As such, it is imperative that the voices, concerns and perspectives of women regarding peace and security become an integral part of policymaking processes.

The lobbying efforts of women's peace NGOs at the UN have helped to create what the UN Development Fund for Women (UNIFEM) calls an international mandate to include women in peace processes at national, regional and international levels. The 1979 Convention on the Elimination of All Forms of Discrimination Against Women (CEDAW) specifies that signatories of the international convention raise women's participation in decision-making processes by using temporary measures such as quota systems. In 1982, the UN General Assembly passed a resolution calling for an increase in women's participation in decision making processes related to peace and development by providing opportunities for women to be involved in the diplomatic service, delegations, secretariats of the UN and its agencies (Resolution 37/63 the Declaration on the Participation of Women in Promoting International Peace and Cooperation). The 1996 UN-commissioned study 'The Impact of Armed Conflict on Children' shows that women play important roles during armed conflict and post-conflict reconstruction and calls for the full inclusion of women in relief efforts, peace making, reconciliation and reconstruction programs.

Both the 1985 UN document the Nairobi Forward Looking Strategies and the 1995 Beijing Platform for Action (PfA) highlight the important role of women in peace and development. In the chapter on women and armed conflict, the PfA states that 'full participation [of women] in decision-making, conflict prevention and resolution and all other peace initiatives [is] essential to the realization of lasting peace' (UN Fourth World Conference on Women, 1996, p. 212). Women peace activists refer to these international commitments and policy guidelines to advocate for their participation in peace processes at regional and national levels.

Networking at the UN Conferences has contributed to the growth of transnational coalitions and programs such as the African Federation of Women's Peace Networks, which held its first meeting at the 1994 African Regional Preparatory Conference for the FWCW in Senegal (Snyder, 2000). According to some women, linking with women's peace organizations around the world is a 'two-way street of support and sustenance' (Svirsky, 1998). 'Women in Black,' a peace group started in Israel in 1988 by Palestinian and Israeli women provides an example of how one organization can become a model for international women's organizing. Deutsch maintains that:

> Belonging to the circles of feminist women throughout the world who struggle against violence and who work to promote a political-cultural alternative which will include the experience of women gives me the strength to continue in work that is often perceived as hopeless (Deutsch, 1994, p. 6).

Holding Women in Black vigils all over the world—some in solidarity with the Palestinian/Israeli cause and others taking a stand about local issues—strengthens the impact of each groups' activities. In the words of Asian human rights activists, Women in Black have inspired women around the world to 'stand silently protesting the many forms of violence which are increasingly becoming intrinsic to our everyday realities in our different cultures and communities' (Asian Women's Human Rights Council, 1995, p. 1). At the FWCW, the Women in Black demonstration attracted hundreds of women.

Meeting women who face similar challenges is a source of empowerment. They learn how women in other parts of the world are taking action in powerful ways and using a broad range of strategies. By telling their stories, the women build solidarity regionally which contributes, in turn, to peace building. Peace activists maintain that networking gives them hope that solutions to armed conflict and human rights abuse can be found (International Fellowship of Reconciliation, 1999).

Further, women peace activists strategize and work out practical ways to help each other. By sharing information about their local and regional contexts, the women gain understanding of how their work might connect. Some coalitions have used conferences as opportunities to co-sponsor further education and training in areas such as nonviolent theory and action, peace building skills and fundraising. Peace networks develop international campaigns on specific issues and coordinate international efforts to obtain the release of peace activists who have become political prisoners. They may also find support among other NGOs for community-based programs. For example, the International Fellowship of Reconciliation (IFOR) Women Peacemakers Program is developing ways to facilitate the exchange of resources, such as computers, between peace organizations.

As with other networks, however, women peace activists face many challenges, particularly in the formation of North/South alliances. In their article 'Making Connection: Building an East Asia-U.S. Women's Network against U.S. Militarism,' Gwyn Kirk and Margo Okazawa-Rey (1998) highlight some of the difficulties of building international links around militarism. As a first step, the women acknowledged the complex and layered inequalities among participants and the relationships of domination and oppression that exist between the countries involved: mainland Japan, Korea, Okinawa, the Philippines and the U.S. According to Kirk and Okazawa-Rey, their success in forming a network was due, in part, to their ability to frame issues and questions so as to be able to make connections and to listening carefully to various perspectives and opinions.

Conflict at the UN Women's Conferences

The UN World Conference on Women provides an excellent opportunity to study transnational movement conflict and consensus building. The conferences have increased contact between women around the globe and, as such, increased the potential for both conflict and cooperation. Over the past twenty years, many Southern women have expressed both satisfaction and dissatisfaction regarding their collaboration with Northern women. Feminist scholars tend to focus on the problems of power, difference, and representation that surface as the women determine priorities and strategies for global policy formation. White, middle class, Northern women have been criticized for universalizing their experiences and speaking for others. Early attempts to 'transcend' difference by focusing on 'common' discrimination (Morgan, 1970) have been challenged. Northern women of color and Third World feminists consistently point out the role that white Northern women play in perpetuating racism and imperialism.

Further, the nature of the impact of both the NGO and the government world conferences is hotly disputed, giving voice to important debates. According to some feminists, the conferences have helped women's movements by increasing tension that has, in turn, forced conference participants to develop feminist theory. Most maintain that the four UN World Conferences on Women have played a major part in the development of international women's movements. The non-governmental forums during the Decade for Women were key in setting up an international infrastructure for the continuation of women's movements by bringing NGOs together with social movement organizations (Stephenson, 1995). Margaret Galey argues that:

> These UN activities mobilized a critical mass of women from around the world to formulate strategies and goals to achieve participation as full partners with men in all spheres of decision making and to gain equal access to opportunities offered by their societies. By the 1990s women's issues had become legitimate subjects on the agendas of governments and international organizations and women participated in public activity as never before (Galey, 1995, p.1).

As a result of the conferences, government policies to improve the status of women are now a part of the international agenda.

However, critics have claimed that the conferences have been instrumental in reinforcing essentialized notions of womanhood as well as Northern racist systems of hierarchy. In addition, others argue that the documents create government machineries around women's issues that in some cases have proved to be irrelevant. Moreover, some scholars assert that the conferences merely set up 'elite networks of the marginalized' (Stephenson, 1995; Enloe, 1989; Anderson-Manley, 1991; Davis, 1990).

At the same time, many feminists, North and South, maintain that 'negotiable and partial' collaborations between feminists in different countries are possible – under certain circumstances. First, cooperative ventures must be based on an understanding of historical and cultural differences. For example, concepts of culture, community, and nationalism are more important to Asian interpretations of women's emancipation than Western concepts of individual rights and freedom (Ong, 1997). Without an understanding of how national contexts can effect the construction of feminist issues as they 'cross borders,' issues can become distorted and result in representations of Third World women as 'victims of their culture' (Narayan, 1997).

Second, international feminist theorizing and organizing must be rooted in a clear explanation of how women from different, often unequal societies, are used to sustain world patterns that feminists seek to change (Mies, 1986; Enloe, 1989; Donaldson, 1992). Global feminist movements cannot be based solely on gender analysis. By ignoring geopolitical inequalities, Western women increase the potential of women from postcolonial countries to perceive feminist interventions as cultural imperialism (Ong, 1997).

Third, collaboration must focus more on common agendas and priorities than on assumed identities as women. According to Mohanty:

> It is only by understanding the *contradictions* inherent in women's location within various structures that effective political action and challenges can be devised (Mohanty, 1991, p. 66).

Fourth, to work together effectively, women need to speak openly and face their differences as opposed to trying to erase them or 'get stuck in them' (Anzaldua, 1990; Leidner, 1991; hooks 1997). Women tend to fear disagreement among themselves partly because they imagine women to be the same and deny their many differences. Feminist collaboration requires starting with assumption that there will be conflict and developing processes of talking it through (Childers and hooks, 1990).

Some scholars maintain that women's NGOs are developing an 'enhanced ability to resolve conflicts' (Clark, 1994, p. 181). Before 1985, the conferences were dominated by North-South and capitalist-socialist divides. Northern delegates saw the South's 'structural' agenda (development and imperialism) as a diversion from issues of women's equality and therefore a 'politicization' of the conferences. Feminists from the South rejected the idea that the Northern delegates should decide what was 'political' and what was a 'women's issue.' The North's proposal to limit the agenda to women's issues, narrowly defined (equality) was perceived as self-serving because it left Western economic and neocolonial domination unchallenged. Furthermore, for many women from the South, the struggle to improve their lives was seen not only in male versus female terms. At the UN conference in Copenhagen (1980), government and NGO representatives argued as to whether Zionism was a form of racism. The ensuing debate over the nature of Zionism was so divisive that some government delegates, particularly US delegates, refused to participate in future conferences unless political issues were removed from the agenda.

In Nairobi (1985), the UN delegates passed a document on the status of women by consensus—an important step in finding common language and common ground for the development of an international movement (Friedlander, 1996).

This conference differed from the past two because of the dominance of Southern delegates. The delegates represented diverse NGOs and grassroots movements who were able to speak for themselves in their own way and about the issues most important to them (Antrobus, 1985). During the Nairobi conference, peace became a major issue and the peace tent, a gathering place at the 1985 NGO Forum, the focus of intense debate and dialogue. A growing network of Southern women and an increasing number of Northern NGOs challenged the development paradigm calling for a new approach to women's development. Southern women formed several new research groups in response to conversations highlighting the important role of women from the South in the area of development (Marchand and Parpart, 1995). By the end of the Decade, NGOs were able to build on their connections and come to more agreement on issues of common concern (Friedlander, 1996).

Organization of the Book

The following pages highlight the stories of women peace activists and their interactions during a series of international events. Studying the everyday experiences of NGO delegates at international events reveals some of the challenges they face and how they respond to those difficulties. Chapter two introduces the three organizations featured in my study. The members, the background of the organizations, the resources available to them, and an overview of their participation will be discussed. Chapter three will delve into the decision making process for the network agenda. Conflicts over the agenda will be explored in Chapter four and attempts at dialogue and conflict resolution in Chapter five. Chapter six contains a summary of my findings and a discussion of recommendations.

Chapter 2

Stories From Transnational Peacemakers: An Introduction to the Organizations

Thirty thousand NGO delegates convened at the NGO Forum 1995 in Beijing. Some of them had spent years preparing for their participation in the event. They each had their own story. The focus of this chapter is the stories of the NGO delegates. Why did they come? What was important to them? What did they do while they were there? Story telling is particularly important for the study of conflict. Social conflict emerges and develops on the basis of the meaning and interpretation people involved attach to action and events (Lederach, 1995). As such, storytelling or narrative is a window into how the women perceived themselves, each other, and their interaction.

The following chapter introduces the three organizations that became the focus of my research: 1) the U.S. and Western European members of WILPF; 2) the Sudanese Women's Voice for Peace (SWVP); and 3) Beneath Paradise. I will describe the background of each organization and begin to present the stories of some of their members. In addition, I will discuss the different types of resources available to them. Finally, I will sketch an overview of each organization's participation at the PrepComs, the NGO Forum '95, and the FWCW, if they attended. Because of their positions, the identity of some of my informants will be obvious. However, in order to take the attention off the individuals involved in the study, I followed standard qualitative practice and gave all of the women pseudonyms.

Why Focus on Three NGOs?

My decision to focus on particular organizations was an attempt to look closely at participant involvement and at the same time to maintain a sense of the coherence of participants' experiences at the conferences. That is, I wanted to trace how they approached the conference, what happened as they prepared and what they did once they got there. In addition, choosing three organizations from different parts of the world was an attempt to build into the study an awareness of the global power issues that influence their interactions.

The NGOs were chosen because of their differences rather than their similarities. Each NGO comes from a different region of the world. Each of the organizations has a different relationship to international and domestic conflict: WILPF members are trying to change highly militarized societies in the West; the

Sudanese women are trying to halt the civil war between Northern and Southern Sudan; and Beneath Paradise is concerned with the de-nuclearization and de-colonization of the Pacific Islands. Their size, age, resource pool and scope are unequal. However, the variety of NGOs chosen reflects the variety of NGOs represented at the conference. Furthermore, the three NGOs represent the types of organizations taking part in the peace events: there were a few large international NGOs (INGOs), often but not always Northern, with many representatives, and many smaller NGOs, typically from the South, with few representatives.

Sudanese Women's Voice for Peace (SWVP) was the first NGO that I chose. Its leadership was very visible to me at the African regional preparatory conference. They spent most of their time at the peace tent, speaking on panels, developing proposals, and participating in the creation of a peace federation. Furthermore, they were involved in stopping a war currently in progress, unlike the other two organizations. I thought their perspective as activists during war-time and as refugees would be important. I found their commitment and their stories compelling. In addition, they were very open to talking to me and began to seek me out whenever they saw me.

I chose Women's International League for Peace and Freedom (WILPF) as the Northern NGO central to my study. Given my own location as a North American woman, I wanted to include a Northern NGO so that I could gain more understanding of North American participation in the agenda-setting process. WILPF was very prominent as the NGO organizing most of the peace activities. They would most likely have an important role in the agenda-setting process. In addition, given their years of involvement in disarmament at the UN, they offered a historical perspective. I had heard of WILPF for many years, had a great deal of respect for the organization's work, and was delighted to have an opportunity to learn more about them. Furthermore, it had many representatives, all of whom were very willing to speak to me.

Beneath Paradise representative, Madelaine, caught my attention because I was studying conflict and from the first day I saw Madelaine at the peace caucus meeting in New York, she was in conflict with other conference participants and she wanted to talk about it. Furthermore, she was from a different region than the other organizations—one of my criteria—and she was indigenous to Kanaky, her home. Plus, her political context varied from the others; for example she was struggling with the issue of colonization. As such, I thought her perspective would be helpful. Finally, it seemed likely that all three organizations would actually make it to the FWCW in China.

My intention was not to compare the three NGOs but to use them to analyze some part of the range of experiences that NGOs have at such conferences. My goal was not the kind of variable-based analysis that would examine the role of framing, for example, holding resources and other factors constant. Instead, I was interested in how various kinds of NGOs approach this kind of opportunity for activism and how they attempt to collaborate, despite their differences.

These kinds of conferences inevitably bring together groups that vary in many ways. Therefore, diversity is a condition of their interaction and the backdrop for any collaboration. It may have allowed for a cleaner analysis to consider organizations that are similar in most ways (as it would perhaps make for easier collaboration), but, in this kind of international work, the situation is not characterized by similarity. Therefore, what I sacrificed in comparability, I gained in fit with the actual circumstance of NGO work.

Beneath Paradise

Background

Beneath Paradise is a coalition of indigenous women's organizations in the Pacific Islands that was formed in preparation for the 1995 FWCW. Beneath Paradise members were trained as a part of the Pacific Women's Documentation Project to tell their own stories, in their own words, to an international audience. The result was a multi-media exhibit including life-stories, photo-essays, case studies, testimonials, soundscapes, slideshows, poetry and prose. Under the sponsorship of the International Women's Development Agency and AusAID, twenty-one Pacific NGOs in nine Pacific countries documented hundreds of stories, songs and poems. According to the project overview:

> In the last three World Women's Conferences, the lack of Pacific women's involvement meant that the events and their outcomes had little impact on the day to day working of Pacific countries. Beneath Paradise wanted to involve and inform many more Pacific women so that they too could use the event and its outcomes to change women's lives for the better (p.1).

For many of the women, it was the first time that they had viewed their own story, picture, or poetry in print.

The Pacific NGOs involved in Beneath Paradise provided educational, health, economic, political and legal services at a grassroots level. In the literature prepared for the FWCW, the coalition chose four critical areas of concern to focus on: unequal access to inadequate educational opportunities; violence against women; inequality between men and women in the sharing of power and decision making at all levels; and lack of adequate recognition and support for women's contribution to managing natural resources and safeguarding the environment. Many of the NGOs featured were women's centers that have programs for women who have been battered or raped.

Madelaine, Director of the Decolonisation Desk of the Pacific Concerns Resource Centre/Nuclear Free and Independent Pacific (NFIP), Fiji, was my informant from Beneath Paradise. She attended one global preparatory meeting where she was the sole Beneath Paradise representative and I was unable to attend the regional PrepCom for Asia in Indonesia. Madelaine describes herself as a Kanak woman from Kanaky (New Caledonia). She has been involved in the political struggle of her people against French colonialism for more than two decades.

Kanaky has been a French colony since 1853. It became a French Overseas Territory in 1946. Since French colonization began, the indigenous population has made attempts to free themselves of French rule against the wishes of many French-descended settlers. The majority of the Kanaks (Melanesians) now support the National Kanak Socialist Liberation Front (FLNKS) which was started in 1984 and was led, until his assassination in 1989, by Jean-Marie Tjibaou. Tjibaou negotiated an agreement called the Matignon Accord in 1988 that divided New Caledonia into three distinct regions. Each region was to elect a Provincial Assembly to manage internal administration until a national referendum was held—not later than the end of 1998. Since 1960, France has conducted approximately 149 nuclear weapons tests in the Pacific Islands—what is called nuclear colonialism (Alexander, 1994).

In an interview, Madelaine said that she became an activist at a young age:

> No one will believe me that when I was twelve years old, I was dreaming about Black movement against white movement. Because, you know, when you live injustice everyday being treated dirty Kanak, dirty popony, dirty ponos. This is colonization given to us, to discriminate us, to put us down, to make us ashamed everyday. And I grew up with those words like Kanak, it is really pejorative, really low. And our grandfathers and grandmothers, when they colonized them and our mothers and fathers have grown up being ashamed of themselves. When I was twelve being in that situation I saw how they humiliated my parents.
>
> When I was twelve I fought one day and I came back from school, I was with my bag, really upset because I was already destroyed by the teacher who punished me everyday because I used to punch those little whites who called me Kanak especially those little demoiselles we would have a fight. And my mother believed the teacher was right. I should calm down. A girl is not supposed to fight with boys and things like that. Those white boys and white girls not many tried to fight with me, I was mostly having fights with white boys. And when I was twelve after I had been punished one day because I was being punished everyday and I thought one day there will be a black movement against those whites who are not good. I didn't know anything about politics. I was a child at twelve.

Her conviction led her into politics in Kanaky and later international activism.

Madelaine was one of the first women to gain a leadership position with the Kanak Political Party when she became an official in the Parti de Liberation Kanak or PALIKA Coordinating bureau in 1976. However, because of her political actions against the French government, she lost her job seven years later, in 1983. The following year, she left the country for New Zealand where she traveled widely, learning English and raising international awareness of the Kanak independence struggle. She also studied at the University of Canterbury in Aoteaoa where she finished a BA in Sociology.

In 1994, Madelaine began her work with the Pacific Concerns Resource Centre/NFIP. Established in 1974 in Suva, Fiji, the Centre works for decolonization and demilitarization of the Pacific region, especially the colonies of West Papua, East Timor, Kanaky, Tahiti and the US Trust Territories, by lobbying governments and educating community members. In addition, the Centre focuses on land violations by multi-nationals. NFIP is also involved in the struggle against nuclear colonialism in the Pacific which is, according to Alexander, 'based on absolute faith in nuclear strategy and the strategic importance of the Pacific Islands' (Alexander, 1994, p. 133).

I met Madelaine at the New York PrepCom in March of 1995. She told me she had heard about the program only the week before, and that private sponsors had made her trip possible. I learned that she had participated in the Third UN World Conference on Women in Nairobi in 1985. After the 1985 conference, Madelaine was motivated to initiate a coalition of women from the Pacific Colonies called Omomo Melen Pacific or 'Women, Lifeblood of the Pacific.' Omomo Melen Pacific met in advance of the FWCW to document their experiences of colonialism. Madelaine said that her fight for women's rights began when she was in jail after being arrested in a peaceful action against French colonialism. Once she left jail she began to work on women's liberation and against oppression by Kanak men. Madelaine represented Omomo Melen Pacific, NFIP and Beneath Paradise at the FWCW.

Although I interviewed but one member of Beneath Paradise, I gathered additional information on their members from the documents I collected. Two of the women featured in the Beneath Paradise information packet, Sarah and Harriet were both active in the peace process in Bougainville. Civil war broke out in the late 1980s between the Papua New Guinea Defense Forces and the Bougainville Revolutionary Army (BRA). Sarah and Harriet attribute one of the causes of the war to the massive environmental and cultural destruction caused by the Panguna Copper Mine. Since the air and sea blockade imposed by the Government of Papua New Guinea (PNG) in 1990, there have been 5,000 deaths from preventable disease in central Bougainville.

According to Sarah and Harriet, women have played an important role in bringing peace to Bougainville. They are quoted in their literature as saying:

> Throughout the war, women have consistently pressured their husbands, sons and brothers to lay down arms and seek a political solution to the crisis. In the late 1980s they planned a peace settlement between secessionists and the PNG government through traditional negotiations. In 1990, they attempted peace marches on the island. The fragile peace negotiated in 1994 at the Bougainville Peace Conference owes much of its success to the amazing work of Bougainville women.

They report that women from both BRA and Government-controlled areas are united in their desire to end the fighting.

In reference to their participation at the FWCW, both Sarah and Harriet agree that:

> The NGO Forum is the ultimate meeting we are going to. We are going to present women's stories at the Forum so that women of other parts of the world can know what the effects of armed conflict and violence are like and so all of the women of the world can strive for peace. Many women are raped at gunpoint. Many husbands were killed in the fighting.

The war and blockade affected their participation in the three year long documentation project making it possible for them to join the project just months before the FWCW.

Harriet, secretary and former coordinator of the Bougainville Catholic Women's Association, was a high school teacher until her village of a thousand people was burnt to the ground in 1990, the first village to go in the nearly six years of fighting. Soon after the 1994 peace conference, Harriet helped organize a reunion of two thousand Catholic women on the island which for many women, was the first time they felt safe to emerge from hiding. It was also a first step towards normalization of their daily lives after six years of war and isolation behind the blockade. The Catholic Women's Association provides counseling for couples, conflict resolution, family planning and moral support for women affected by the war.

Sarah is President of the First Provincial Council of Women, Bougainville, which she founded in 1979. The Council was set up to improve women's lives through more political participation, more educational opportunities and better working conditions for women. She provided leadership in the initiation and negotiation of the peace process that resulted in the Peace Meeting in Arawa in October of 1994. After the peace agreement was reached, the Council was re-established and Sarah was appointed to the Bougainville Transitional Government that administered reconstruction and continued political negotiations for peace. One of her goals was to make grassroots women's needs visible in the peace and restoration process. Ellen participated in the 1985 conference in Nairobi as well as the FWCW.

Another activist featured in the Beneath Paradise literature is Lemalesep, President of Tuatu Te Natura, an environmental association belonging to the Hiti Tua network of (French) Polynesia in Tahiti. Lemalesep states: 'I am a grandmother, and I am not afraid to do whatever it takes to protect my land.' She has organized protests on her island, Bora Bora, around the use of resources for tourism and nuclear weapons testing. Lemalesep explains that:

> Maohi people live on seafood. So this tourism is killing us—it is not helping us at all. And all of the businesses here on Bora Bora are geared to the hotels—not the Maohi. We have to pay water and electricity bills bigger than anywhere else in the world. So I organised the people to stop paying. The company cut off our water. But I turned the taps back on. They threatened to throw me and my husband in gaol (jail). But we fought back.

Hiti Tua, a broad based umbrella organization, works to represent the interests of indigenous people in Tahiti, particularly around issues of land rights, anti-nuclear activities, sustainable development and the rights of women.

Beneath Paradise Resources

Madelaine had a great deal of personal strength. As a leader, she had years of experience as an activist in a resistance/independence movement. Her level of energy and commitment to her issues was very high. As a representative, Madelaine had credibility because she had worked for many years at the grassroots level and was chosen by her constituency to represent them. Madelaine also had a strong sense of cultural and ethnic pride as a source of strength to draw on. During the NGO Forum '95 even as the French nuclear test was exploded, Beneath Paradise women danced and sang and talked about their lives with the women at the conference. Given the suppression of their culture and way of life, the dancing and singing was a powerful expression of resistance.

Madelaine had some familiarity with international settings, having lived and studied in Australia where she learned to speak English. She was able to use both her English language skills and her 'Western Style' education as resources in her struggle to gain attention for her agenda. Furthermore, her previous experience at the Nairobi conference was training that she used later at the FWCW. Her attendance at the Nairobi Conference and the New York PrepCom may have led to connections within UN networks that facilitated her visibility. As a result, she was asked to speak at the NGO Forum '95 plenary.

Not only did Madelaine bring her resources as an individual but the power of several movements behind her. She was part of three larger international movements: the Nuclear Free and Independent Pacific movement, the indigenous movement and the movement for Kanak independence. Some of the women in the peace caucus were already familiar with her issues because of the international work done by these movements. Her strong base also helped her to gain the attention of the international media as well as financial support.

In addition, Madelaine's arguments were compelling because of the urgency of her situation—the nuclear explosions actually took place during the FWCW. She held some moral power; the people on her tiny island were quite clearly being oppressed by a colonial superpower. Embarrassment was one of the cards that she held in her hand as a grassroots indigenous woman exposing the hypocrisy of the women around her who ignored her agenda.

Beneath Paradise did not have the same access to information that other NGOs did. For example, Madelaine did not receive word about the New York conference until one week ahead of time. She was unable to rally a group around her, nor did she have time to prepare strategies, literature, etc. As a result, she was alone at the conference, representing indigenous people from many different countries with similar but different issues as well as three different coalitions.

Furthermore, Madelaine's funding sources were unstable. She received private funding to attend the PrepCom. As a coalition, Beneath Paradise members may have received a one-time grant from International Women's Development Agency and AusAID to attend the conference. Omomo Melen Pacific was another coalition that Madelaine had initiated and she never referred to funding sources, if any. NFIP, her place of employment, was perhaps her most stable financial base.

Overview of Beneath Paradise Participation

To some extent, Beneath Paradise and its delegate Madelaine could be seen as the most successful of the three NGOs. Madelaine had no preparation time for the global PrepCom she attended in New York in 1995. She was informed about and given funding to participate in the PrepCom by a personal contact. There was no time to organize a delegation for the PrepCom. On her own, Madelaine was always on the run, going to meeting after meeting and to interviews. She had been asked to represent many different issues brought up by the women in her coalition. Nevertheless, she was able to influence both government and NGO conference discourse so that delegates began to speak of the issues important to her people, insert a proposal into the PfA, and gain media attention during her stay in the USA. Rather than giving up when she was ignored, Madelaine confronted the women around her, both NGO and government affiliated, and struggled to make an impact on the official agenda with partial success.

In the meantime, Beneath Paradise NGOs secured a grant to document their work. They prepared literature, presentations, and displays that included their quotes, poetry, and music. They held their own meetings to talk about what issues were important to them and to chose delegates. Madelaine, who also worked with NFIP, continued to try to halt the French nuclear testing that was scheduled to begin during the FWCW.

At the NGO Forum '95, Madelaine was accompanied by at least 15 of her colleagues, a success in itself. She was asked to speak at the NGO Forum '95 plenary as was another of her colleagues from New Caledonia giving them excellent exposure—the plenary was the largest forum at the NGO conference. They did not stop the nuclear testing at that point in time but Madelaine and her colleagues gained further international allies including the WILPF leadership. Ellen, the former secretary general of WILPF, managed to gain access to the general assembly of the FWCW to read a letter of protest against the French testing. Furthermore, the protest demonstration that Beneath Paradise organized during the NGO Forum '95 was attended heavily by Japanese women representing Japanese NGOs. Although when I saw Madelaine she was exhausted, she did not appear defeated.

Women's International League for Peace and Freedom (WILPF)

Background

The history of WILPF began in 1915, during World War I, when more than one thousand women from 12 countries crossed the borders of their warring countries to meet together in the Hague, the Netherlands. The foundation for an international women's peace organization was laid at that meeting. WILPF was formed by women who split off from the suffragist movement. It was the suffragist movement along with women involved in leadership of various national independence movements around the world that scholars speculate initiated the first international cooperation of women peace activists (Carroll, 1989; Karl, 1995). Some of the suffragists felt that as women they should oppose the war, while others felt that they were bound, as women, to support their state.

WILPF has focused its campaign to a great extent on influencing government leaders and on UN development and reform. Early WILPF members participated in and followed the development of the League of Nations and later the UN. I noticed that some members tended to evaluate their success as an organization based on how extensively they have influenced UN discourse. Given their commitment to the UN, it is not surprising that WILPF has coordinated the working groups, workshops and policy recommendations on peace of every UN World Conference on Women to date, including the FWCW. At four of the five conferences I attended, I met no less than 10-15 WILPF representatives who seemed to be mostly self-sponsored.

Disarmament and nuclear non-proliferation have been WILPF's most recent priorities as they have lobbied government officials around the world in an effort to influence international relations. However, political economy issues are increasingly on their agenda as they have become aware that issues of political economy are integral to issues of peace. Anti-racism work, violence against women, and US foreign intervention are other concerns. They organize around concepts like the unequal distribution of power and economic goods, equal rights, and human rights.

WILPF members have not only worked at the UN over the years but have interacted with both feminist and peace organizations to achieve their goals. The organization has strategically supported and its members have participated in mass protests on related issues. For example, many of the US women I interviewed had taken part in the civil rights movement in the 1960s or militant nuclear protests in the 1980s. Most of their European membership have histories of involvement in socialist and Marxist movements. Further, WILPF has made many attempts to reach out to women peace activists in countries involved in armed conflict throughout its 80 year history.

WILPF has set up chapters in 47 countries, based on their contacts with other women's groups in those countries. The organization appears to attract mostly middle class and working class European and European American women in their sixties and seventies, with long histories of peace and/or civil rights activism. There are relatively few young women and women of color. Although their numbers have dwindled over the years, WILPF maintains many chapters throughout the US and Europe. Their structure is based on volunteer elected boards and directors who oversee the hiring of the few paid staff. WILPF has been directed by such notables as Nobel Peace Prize winners Jane Addams and Emily Greene Balch, and, more recently, Elise Boulding.

One of my member interviews was with Ellen, WILPF's international president and former secretary general, who has also been nominated for the Nobel Peace Prize. Ellen's international work began in 1945 as a radio announcer for an overseas radio program in Montreal, Canada. Later, she moved to Geneva with her husband, an employee of the international labor office and began her work with the World Health Organization in the editorial department. Ellen did not actually become involved with WILPF until the 1960s when she had finished raising her family. However, she first came into contact with WILPF as a young refugee in Canada.

Ellen and her family escaped from the German part of Czechoslovakia, her birthplace, when she was sixteen. Her family had been active in the anti-fascist movement in Europe; through an agreement between Chamberlain and Hitler they were among the 100,000 anti-fascist activists to be allowed out of Czechoslovakia before part of Bohemia was incorporated by Germany. Ellen's family fled first to Britain, where they lived in refugee camps and then to Canada where they became settlers for the Canadian Pacific Railroad (CPR). Unable to make a living, Ellen and some of her family members were forced to move to Toronto where they were expected to find work in the war industry. It was in Toronto that Ellen met women from WILPF.

Ellen told the story of how WILPF helped her when she became a housemaid at age 19 in Toronto, unable to speak English or advocate for herself. WILPF members intervened to try to better her harsh working conditions. Ellen was forced to take over the jobs of three employees of a wealthy family—the cook, the nannie, and the maid—with no time off, no idea where she was or where her family members had been relocated to:

> So one morning there was this knock on the door and the woman introduced herself as, I can't even remember, something. She was from WILPF and they were trying to make contact with all the refugees, mainly from the CPR because they had followed and were threatening if they didn't tell them where to find these people. It was really almost, kind of a slave-like situation. They were going to have an evening to bring all the speaking Germans that they could contact together. She spoke German quite well and I said well, I would certainly like to come but I don't know where I am in the city and anyway, never mind and she insisted on speaking to my mistress and explained to her that I was entitled to one evening out and one every other Sunday, these were my hours. This was 1940, '41 and that they had to give me that evening to go. So they showed me how to get there and that evening there was my father and brother. Then they were just so wonderful.
>
> They were very much engaged in the sort of Jane Addams type of helping what they called new Canadians, Canadians who came in to help them find their rights and help them in every other way. Well then the WILPF women, there were a lot of retired teachers as members so they took on, you know, to teach one or two, to help to teach English and help them generally. I was taken by a few women and they taught me English and helped me all along. Then after six months we decided well that was enough of this kind of exploitation and that they would try to find another work for me and they did. Then eventually I ended up in the office of the provincial Canadian Commonwealth Federation.
>
> So if I am here, it was really what the WILPF women did, they helped me but above all they helped me feel like a human being again and hope for the future because I really felt this was my life and I would be kind of slaving away in some household somewhere. So this was how I got in touch.

It was sheer coincidence that a friend introduced her to WILPF in Geneva almost 20 years later.

Ellen was present at all four of the conferences I attended except for the African Regional Conference in Senegal. She had attended all past UN World Conferences on Women, beginning in 1975 in Mexico City. Her leadership and experience was looked to not only by women involved in the peace activities but those organizing the FWCW. She appeared to be well respected; I noted her speaking in plenaries, on committees, and drafting proposals for the NGO document.

Bettina, WILPF secretary general, told me that WILPF is an 'ideal combination' for her. She had not found a women's organization that was progressive and dealt seriously with international politics until she came into contact with WILPF. Her educational background and work experience is in social work as well as political science:

> Well, I was a student, studying social work and I turned to a feminist group at the university and then I finished my studies and I started working and I had not so much time to do political activity. At the same time I was always very interested in international policy kind of an anti-imperialist movement because Germany was quite radical. So when I looked for a group who could combine my two interests, international policy and feminist or women's issues and I read in the newspaper there was a group called the WILPF was celebrating its 75th anniversary. So I thought with this name, at least in the name, it was a very ideal combination. I went there and at first I was a little bit shocked. I was at that time, director for the home for elderly people. So I came to the meeting and the average age was 60—average, I thought, oh, no, I can't do this in the evening. (laughter) It's too much. Well then I attended another meeting and I found out the women are quite radical in their thinking. Not feminists perhaps but quite radical. It helped me very much to continue and to find relatively quickly the goal of WILPF.
>
> I worked—involved in more thinking the party politics is also necessary—I worked for the Green party. After I finished my social work and I found in WILPF it's much more inspiring, that it's not like the party. In the party you spend a good 60% of your time in power deals and in WILPF you have a relatively loose set-up in which you can devote much more time to issues. So I got involved with them in the small section in Munich even though they were old, older people but there are some of them who are young in their hearts and in their minds and they were very open. So I could come in, take on a lot of work, of course, but also be creative.

Bettina served as personal advisor to Eleanor Romberg, a Green Party representative in The German Parliament, and as the WILPF international president, before taking on the job as secretary general of WILPF.

Anita, a US citizen who staffed the WILPF UN office in New York City, felt it was her international heritage that drew her to activism on an international level. In an interview, she explained how she got started in social movements:

> Anna: So how did you get involved in activism and then in WILPF?
>
> Anita: I was interested in the Civil Rights movement when I was in school and went to some marches on Washington. At that time, that was in the 60s, in the late 60s and then I was an opponent of the Vietnam War. When Angela Davis was imprisoned I became part of a movement to free Angela Davis.
>
> Anna: When was that?
>
> Anita: 1970—1972, before you were around...And in '72 is when I became really politically involved in my community, in Southern Africa, and in Middle East solidarity work in the peace movement. My background is kind of mixed. I came from a working class family in a city where immigrants came to work in factories. So I grew up

> surrounded by people who came from the same part of the world as my family did. Armenians, Greeks, Asyrian, Syrian, Lebanese and Irish. We all had nice talks together growing up dancing to Middle Eastern music and singing our songs.
>
> And so I've always had with me a sense of being part of an international community. My family is Asyrian. I grew up with Armenians and Kurds in Eastern Turkey. I grew up with the occupation of the West Bank in Gaza and the formation of Israel. So all of this has made me very close to what what's happening in other parts of the world. It's really through my grassroots activity that I have many skills that I use here at the UN doing international work. They form the basis of everything I brought to this.

Anita continued, saying that she had been an art teacher before obtaining a graduate degree in textile design and opening up her own studio. For many years she divided her time between studio work and political work until she decided to apply for the New York position with WILPF. Her first work with WILPF was organizing a rally in Brussels to protest the deployment of Cruise 2 and Pershing missiles in Europe.

Lois, president of WILPF region three (the southeast), one of the four regions in the US section, was influenced by her church experience to become an activist. In her interview, she told me the story of how she became involved in peace activism and later joined WILPF:

> Well, I was influenced by a member of WILFP who was a member of our church, United Methodist Church, Christ Church in Washington, DC. Her name was Anna Lee Stuart. She was a very long time activist and was at that time the legislative coordinator/director. She worked with the Congress, living in Washington, DC. So she was the strong influence on my life about WILPF. I guess I should say the United Methodist church was a strong influence on my life as a youth. Even dating back to 1940s and 1950 and the youth director for our conference at the church was a great activist, peace person. I did go through that. I did go to the Brethren Service Center, I should say (laughter at my surprise—she knows I am Church of the Brethren, a historic peace church) and I met all the peace people there. And then I worked for a while in Frederick, Maryland as the director of youth activities when I got out of college. I met there some people who were Church of the Brethren people who influenced me. It was actually through a conference that the United Methodist Church held in Washington, DC on security, national security. I guess this was in the 1970s, late 1970s and it was at that time that I decided I needed to do something more than just monitoring demonstrations and wearing buttons and I joined WILPF after Anna Lee had encouraged me to sign up.

Later in the interview, Lois mentioned her involvement in the civil rights movement. When I met her, she introduced herself as a retired schoolteacher.

I met many WILPF members at the conferences—so many that I do not have the space to introduce all of them. These four women are WILPF members who will appear frequently in the following text. Other WILPF members I will introduce as I go along. All four of these women participated in the two global PrepComs in New York and the Beijing conference.

WILPF's Resources

As an NGO, WILPF had a tremendous amount of resources. It had 80 years of history as an organization and hundreds of members in branches around the world. WILPF had connections to the UN and familiarity with UN procedures. It had been involved in the UN since its inception and had established offices at two of the three UN headquarters in New York and in Geneva. Many of their members had the financial resources to fund their own travel to the conferences and those who did not had enough connections to raise the funds. This meant that WILPF was represented in large numbers at the conferences, often with 15-20 members attending.

WILPF's many years of experience at the UN and with UN conferences meant that its members could organize quickly and effectively. As the organizers of the peace section at the FWCW, they were in charge of coordinating which activities took place when, what would be talked about and who would serve on which committees. Furthermore, as mostly Western women, they were advantaged by the dominance of Western cultural norms in UN procedures. The procedures were not completely unfamiliar to them.

The credibility of the NGO and its leadership was also a source of power. WILPF had made a name for itself at the UN and its leadership, particularly Ellen, was very well respected. Ellen had been nominated for the Nobel Peace Prize. Two of the former WILPF directors had won Nobel Peace Prizes in the past—Jane Addams and Karen Greene Balch. Ellen appeared to have earned access to most of what went on at the UN. When Ellen was praised for giving her time in front of the government assembly to a WILPF leader from Sri Lanka, she responded modestly that she 'could speak at the UN any time.' Ellen's off-hand remark indicates the kind of power she had within the UN structure. WILPF had connections with individuals who were well placed politically, e.g. from ministers in various governments to the organizers of the FWCW, as well as financially.

Each of the NGOs also experienced threats to its power. WILPF, which had gained so much credibility, had more to lose than the others did. Their proposals, although relevant, were not as grounded or concrete as those of SWVP and Beneath Paradise. Furthermore, some WILPF members seemed to lack an understanding of the consequences of their dominance as a culture and as an NGO, making it difficult for them to build the political coalitions that they had hoped to.

In addition, WILPF members struggled with a tremendous sense of powerlessness as women resisting against the military-industrial complexes in Western superpowers. This 'powerlessness' was illustrated in a confrontation that took place during a peace caucus meeting when several African women challenged US women saying: 'You have to stop US arms sales and production!' The African challenge was met with silence and bent heads by the many US women present. They did not know how to respond. Many of the US women had spent years working on this very issue with few measurable results.

Not all of the women who traveled with WILPF on the peace train to the FWCW were WILPF members. Quite a few of the women of color, for example, were not members, nor had they previously been affiliated with WILPF. Many of them, like Geraldine, a British activist of African descent, traveled alone under the umbrella of WILPF. Some of these women did not have the same personal or organizational resources that WILPF members did. For example, Geraldine was able to participate in the FWCW and the peace train only because of the scholarship that WILPF gave to her. Several of the women of color found each other and built up a small community based on some common interests as they traveled to the conference and at the NGO Forum '95.

Overview of WILPF Participation at Conferences

WILPF invested a tremendous amount of energy in preparing for and attending the FWCW. First, they prepared their own membership calling meetings and organizing conferences to develop proposals for the PfA. The Minnesota branch of WILPF USA actually built a coalition of women's organizations that then wrote a collective mini-document of their own. Then WILPF recruited their members to attend the preparatory conferences and the FWCW. Each of the PrepComs was attended by ten to fifteen WILPF leaders and members. WILPF representatives traveled to the global PrepComs in New York City, the regional North American/European PrepCom in Austria, and participated in both the NGO Forum and the FWCW. Although the WILPF international leadership may not have been able to attend some of the other regional PrepComs, WILPF members from their chapters around the world were able to report to the regional conferences.

At the PrepComs, WILPF members took part in the conference activities much like the other NGOs and INGOs networking with other organizations and lobbying government delegates for acceptance of their proposals. I would see WILPF members engaged in conversation with NGO representatives from around the world. Often they were discussing the organization of the NGO Forum '95 and the FWCW peace activities. On one occasion, I joined a WILPF member at lunch who was meeting with a delegate from Vietnam. She presented the Vietnamese woman with peace buttons from her participation in the anti-war movement. The buttons were to be displayed in a Vietnamese peace museum. Ellen, as well-respected leader, regularly spoke to the NGO Forum leadership and other veterans of the UN system. She was not only consulted for her advice but she often had the latest information on the inside stories at the conference.

Frequently I would observe WILPF members working together in small groups discussing the document or sitting at the computer typing out the latest version of a proposal for the PfA. Some attended the national NGO briefings or receptions in an attempt to reach government officials and to learn more about their country's position on specific issues. During the peace caucus, WILPF members would report on their efforts to speak personally to government delegates about their proposals.

Unlike many NGOs, WILPF had an office in New York across from the UN. Their members gathered at the offices everyday to report on their activities, exchange information and plan for the next day. Given their large delegation, WILPF members were able to attend a wide range of activities. For example, one delegate was designated to follow the meetings that took place on the topic of development, a topic that was of great interest to WILPF but not a high priority like disarmament.

Peace Tent Planning WILPF played a central role in the organization of the NGO Forum peace tent. The peace tent was literally a tent, which was conceptualized as a 'peaceful' space where women could report on their peacemaking efforts and where conflict resolution of different types—personal, group, and international—was attempted. (During the NGO Forums in Senegal and in China, my main data collection sites were the peace tents.) At the Nairobi NGO World Conference in 1985, the peace tent was a hot spot. It became a place where people could voice their dissent during open-mike periods. The tent was so controversial that the NGO conference organizers shut it down, though it was re-opened after a public statement from the Secretary General of the government conference, Dame Nita Barrow.

WILPF's former secretary general, Ellen, explained the origin to me during an interview:

> See this table? This table used to be in the other room. We sat, you know (three women named). This was in '84, early '84. You know when we had the planning committee for the NGO Forum. Everything was in place and we had a peace caucus and we worked on peace issues. We were very concerned because there was a constant kind of resistance to giving peace an importance in this conference and in the NGO Forum. Even though it was one of the three themes because women kept saying well we need to work on the advancement of women step by step and if we start talking about peace then we get into a confrontational discussion and the women's issues will be left behind. So we had this resistance on the part of our own colleagues. And that was certainly also on the part of governments except for the socialist and quite a few of the non-aligned governments.
>
> So we said what do we do. We need to raise the flag. You know, peace is a women's issue and this sort of thing and begin to really work on documents and develop good workshops on peace. And R. said, you know in '83 we were at the big peace conference in Prague and we, as women participants, being in the organizing committee, insisted that the women's issues were going to be given some importance at that peace conference because we saw it as an important part of peace to advance the status of women and the rights of women and the participation of women. So we convinced ourselves but also the other organizers that there should be a women's center within the peace conference. We had a fantastic women's center... So she said, you know we had this women's center in the peace conference, why don't we have a peace center in the women's conference. So this is how it started.

She added later in her interview that the peace tent became the symbol of the whole Forum, being very close to the center of all activity.

Preparation for the peace tent in Beijing began years in advance. WILPF set up planning meetings during the PrepComs, organized an opening ceremony for the tent focused on the culture of peace, set up daily themes for the workshops they coordinated, made sure the tent was operational during the Forum, and planned a closing ceremony with music and farewell speeches. During the peace tent planning meetings a US artist introduced the idea for the 'fountain of tears,' a symbolic fountain made of women's tears to heal the wounds of war and violence.

WILPF members did their best to gather input for the tent activities from other NGOs represented at the conferences but there were many challenges. Ellen commented in an interview that there were some problems with organizing the tent in a way that was 'a little exclusive' when their goal was to have 'the tent there for everyone.' In the past, the funders had also been the organizers. The first peace tent was organized by WILPF and another NGO founded by the US woman who single-handedly paid for the tent. Ellen hoped to involve more women in the tent planning by obtaining funding from the NGO Forum committee for the tent in Beijing. WILPF also held peace tent meetings during the New York PrepCom in 1995 and sent out questionnaires to gather input from women around the globe.

According to Tamara, a volunteer at the International Peace Bureau (IPB), Geneva, Switzerland, there continued to be difficulties in organizing the tent globally:

> …like trying to take into account the many wishes the people expressed from NGOs in New York for the peace tent. One frustration was that many people signed up on a big list of wanting to help out—the NGOs put their names down in New York—but many of them gave no addresses, no contact information whatsoever. So if we didn't happen to know them, we had no way to get a hold of them. We tried but in some cases it was absolutely impossible. We tried to delegate out the process as much as possible to keep it decentralized but at the end of the day, it was IPB and WILPF who did most of the work in bringing a lot of the schedule together for the tent (Interview in Beijing, 1995).

In the end, again a couple of NGOs took on the major responsibility of planning the peace tent program, though with some input from women outside those organizations.

Once the NGO Forum '95 began in Hairou, WILPF was pre-occupied with different problems. They were informed that there were not enough microphones for all of the tents and so conference organizers had decided the 'peace' tent—which would be peaceful—would not need them. (It was never quite clear to me whether 'they' were the Chinese Organizing Committee (COC) or the New York-based NGO Forum planning committee.) This explanation did not pacify some of the WILPF organizers who felt that they were being silenced, given the controversial nature of the Nairobi tent. The large empty tent next door, which was fully equipped with a sound system, added fuel to the fire. Eventually, after many conversations, the peace tent was given microphones and the battle was won. In the meantime, some of the peace tent workshop leaders moved their programs next door. Others held their programs without microphones and with diminished audiences.

During the NGO Forum '95, the tent organizers led by WILPF would meet to discuss problems or issues concerning the peace tent program. For the first couple of days, the microphones and a controversial 'altar to the feminine,' which took up a lot of space, were on the agenda. Because it was so difficult to hear the planned program, the planning committee decided to ask those selling goods, namely the groups from Rwanda and the Philippines, only to sell in between programs. Then it was discovered that some of the small groups of women meeting in the tent were sharing religious experiences. Some of the women felt this expanded the definition of peace a little too far and wanted to send the religious women and the altar to the feminine off to the spirituality tent. Those who wanted to keep the tent open for everyone prevailed and they decided to ask the religious women to be quiet when there was a workshop taking place. The planning group then came up with the idea of a 'Day Mom,' a coordinator for the tent who would help keep the focus of the tent as she dealt with daily logistical decisions.

Peace Train The WILPF peace train involved a tremendous amount of preparation. WILPF's history began with women crossing borders to advocate for peace, cooperation, justice and freedom. Eight decades after that historic crossing of borders, WILPF organized another crossing of borders—the peace train. WILPF had arranged the train route, which had never been traveled before, to set up or strengthen ties with women's groups in Eastern Europe. The train traveled through Russia, Ukraine, Romania, Bulgaria, Turkey and back around the Black Sea to the Ukraine, then up to Moscow and down to Kazakhstan through to China. Every two or three days, the train would stop and the passengers would disembark and head for hotels where we would spend the night. Talks with women's groups were organized for these brief stopovers in addition to whirlwind sightseeing tours.

We were 232 passengers from 42 countries and 70 Russian staff in 17 cars—3 dining cars and 2 empty cars for workshops and meetings. (The group used a Russian train for two weeks and then a Chinese train for the last leg of our journey.) One third of the passengers were North American, one third were WILPF members, and there were a dozen male passengers. I found that many of the passengers were retired women who had been and/or continued to be peace activists. There were also many independent media women; besides a number of journalists, three film crews traveled on the train documenting the journey.

During the train ride, days were filled with workshops, wagon meetings, meal shifts, interviews, exercise hours, singing and sewing groups, writing in journals, briefings on our stopovers, attempts to do laundry, endless border control, packing for the next stopover, and long talks or parties in the train cabins that lasted until the early morning hours. Some of the students on board took part in the 'rolling school,' a university level course taught on the train.

Organizing the peace train also took a great deal of staff and volunteer energy and resources. The political difficulties in putting together a train trip traveling through eight different countries with passengers from 42 countries to a politically charged conference were enormous. For example, the Chinese Embassies in New York and in Washington were saying no visas for the Beijing Conference participants until mid-August, and the peace train left Helsinki on August 6th. With the hard work and politicking of the WILPF staff and the German travel agency hired to organize the train tour, the peace train passengers obtained a group visa for China at the Chinese Embassy in Helsinki.

The political struggles continued throughout the journey. We arrived in Odessa to find that the Chinese railway authority had contacted both the Kazakhstan and the Ukrainian railway and rearranged our trip for us so that we would stay longer in the Ukraine, not stop in China as we had planned, and, most importantly, arrive two days late for the World Conference in Beijing. WILPF used their new contacts in the Ukrainian Parliament to negotiate with the Ukrainian railway and peace train participants faxed their various Embassies in China to request that they lobby the Chinese. In the end, we did not stop in northwest China and we were forced to stay longer in the Ukraine and in Russia. However, the peace train did enter the country and arrived on time for the conference.

Throughout the conferences, WILPF members expressed disappointment at how difficult it was to gain attention for peace issues, but by the end of the FWCW, they were pleased with at least some of the results of their efforts. In 1985 in Nairobi, Kenya, peace issues were more prominent, especially at the government level, than in 1995. Women from North America and Western Europe were joined by women from socialist countries in their concern about the arms race. The conflict in the Middle East was also hotly debated, but in 1995 the political situation had shifted enough that WILPF members found themselves struggling to make sure that issues relating to armed conflict and women would be included in the PfA.

Sudanese Women's Voice for Peace (SWVP)

Background

The Sudanese Women's Voice for Peace (SWVP) is a young organization in comparison to WILPF. It was founded in 1994 to address the conflict in the Sudan between the predominantly Arab/Muslim North and an African/Christian or Animist South which has been joined by the people of the Nuba Mountains and the Ingessa Hills. The civil war in Sudan results from unresolved cultural and religious differences between the North and the South exacerbated by government policies that reinforce Northern access to power and resources at the expense of the resource rich South. Since 1962, the Sudanese have experienced two civil wars that have severely limited food production and access to education and healthcare in the South. Over two million people have died because of war-related factors and over four million people have been displaced (UN/WFP-Sudan, 1993; The Washington Post, 1990). Furthermore, the South also lives with violent conflict between factions of the Sudan People's Liberation Movement (SPLM).

The women were particularly outraged by and fearful of the imposition of Sharia Law by the Northern Sudanese government. In 1983, President Omar Basheir decreed Islamic Laws to be the source of legislation for the country, confirming for many that the North is determined to create a Muslim State in the Sudan. Since the Sharia Laws have been institutionalized, Southerners have become legally unequal to Northerners. The social, political, cultural and economic rights denied them in the past now have a constitutional basis. For example, a non-Muslim's evidence is legally not admissible in court. Two women must testify in order to qualify as one witness. A number of times, the SWVP women spoke about the penal code that calls for the amputation of limbs and public flogging. Most important, a non-Muslim must pay a tax (Gizya) in exchange for services and protection provided by the Islamic State, effectively relegating Southerners to the status of squatters on their own land.

SWVP was also vocal about the government's treatment of the people of the Nuba Mountains. Under President Ja'far Numayri, an ethnic cleansing policy known as 'Kasha' (get rid of) was begun with the goal of removing people from their ancestral land to leave room for the settlement of Arabs from the North (Facing Genocide: The Nuba of Sudan, African Rights, 1995). During their workshops in Beijing, the SWVP played a video that showed how the Sudanese army is systematically destroying the Nuba by burning, raiding and looting the villages. They alleged that the genocidal policy of the Sudanese Government encourages army units and abduction squads to abduct thousands of villagers from their homes, fields, and wells. Villagers are then taken to 'peace camps' where they are terrorized, abused, and forced to change their culture (African Rights, 1995).

SWVP supports the right of all citizens of Southern Sudan to choose their destiny. SWVP represents a variety of viewpoints within their constituency so although they focused primarily on self-determination or a separate state, they would also discuss a 'just peace,' which refers indirectly to a confederation. According to Loretta, an SWVP leader, 'The SWVP will promote respect for existing geographical boundaries and cultures in Southern Sudan. It will also promote forgiveness and tolerance.' (Speech at African Women for Conflict Resolution and Peace Conference, Kampala, Uganda, 1994.) The organization has a number of goals outlined in their literature, including: networking and reconciling with grassroots organizations; promoting peace negotiations; carrying out educational peace campaigns and developing information banks on the suffering of Southern Sudanese; and initiating self-help projects to enable women to attain self-sufficiency in food production, health-care delivery and income generation.

SWVP can be seen as part of a larger movement for self-determination of the people of Southern Sudan. Their agenda is political—a just resolution to the civil war in Sudan. They are also interested in the involvement of women in that process. Although they are not explicitly a feminist organization, they are very aware of the obstacles women face as they take on a leadership role in the peace negotiations.

SWVP works with other Sudanese NGOs to build a grassroots alternative to the war. Their difficulties in forming coalitions and alliances with other Sudanese groups do not seem to be unique in a society torn apart by war. Deng (1993) maintains that Sudanese organizations have failed to offer sustainable political solutions in Sudan. The notable exception was the Alliance for National Salvation that helped to overthrow the political leader Numayri and managed to keep peace for several years, the Kola Dam Declaration being their major accomplishment However, grassroots participation in the peace process is critical.

SWVP members have a strong commitment to dialogue, so they organize and attend many conferences. They tend to target leaders of the warring factions, chiefs and village elders, and women in refugee camps. I gathered quite a bit of information about them from the literature they handed out at the conferences, specifically magazines, newsletters, and pamphlets. Their literature gave detailed accounts of the seminars and meetings they had held. SWVP members also distributed what they called their 'concept papers,' which outlined steps towards a peaceful resolution of the Sudanese conflict.

SWVP met with traditional women's groups in order to increase the women's skill as influential leaders, train them in peacemaking and encourage women to stand up and speak out against the atrocities committed during the war. Assisted by the United Nations Development Fund for Women (Unifem) and Life and Peace, two international agencies, SWVP had held talks with women from the North. SWVP also gathered together community leaders, particularly chiefs, to support their leadership as elders in local communities. Traditionally, disputes between ethnic groups were settled by chiefs, not by armed conflict. They asked the chiefs to speak to the rebel leaders and demand that they stop disturbing the people. In addition, SWVP brought together representatives from hostile liberation factions along with other influential community leaders to formulate an action plan concerning the role of rural communities in the process of peace and reconciliation. On a national level, SWVP had participated in peace conferences, and had led workshop discussions on how to persuade people that women could be facilitators of peace. In the future, they hoped to enlist the aid of women from other countries who would act as peace ambassadors, visiting refugee camps and talking with faction leaders to lend support to their efforts.

In Senegal, at the African Regional PrepCom where I first encountered SWVP, there were five SWVP representatives whose attendance was sponsored by the Swedish foundation, Life and Peace, and by Unifem, their major funders. All of the women were professionals living as refugees outside the country. They were also all black African and Christian. In an interview, Lisa, a SWVP member explained how the organization started and its structure:

> We actually live together because in our community we know each other. As a group, we live together. We found ourselves as educated, the few educated Sudanese women who feel that we should do something. We should contact our women in the grassroots. We have almost 30 members in this working group. We have two representatives from all the faction leaders that should carry the message inside the Sudan because the country is divided according to the factions, headed by different factions. So we have asked the rebel leaders to give us two representatives from women who they feel they can work with. These women work with us on the technical committee. So that when we have meetings and we have the resolutions passed, they will carry this message to our women in the grassroots.

The women were eventually able to set up an office in Nairobi, Kenya where many of them had settled as refugees.

Melissa, the only SWVP representative who relocated to Egypt, told the story of why the women had been forced to flee the country in a UN radio interview:

> I am from southern Sudan. I have been in Cairo since 1992. Most of us are intellectuals in southern Sudan. We are being persecuted. The government wanted to kill all the intellectuals in the South. So most of them, at that time, attempted to leave the country.

> I was one of them. We left country under very bad conditions because we are not dictating the terms to leave the country. The rest who remained behind are all dead now or they are in prison and they will never be human beings again.

Most of the SWVP did not disclose their personal circumstances. Instead they spoke generally about the plight of Sudanese refugees.

Melissa spoke in detail about the difficulties facing Sudanese refugees in Egypt. The Egyptian government claims 2-4 million Sudanese are living in Egypt. Most of them are northern Sudanese who immigrated to Egypt many years ago. According to Melissa, many of the refugees currently in Egypt are families with students because the Church provides some funding for students. However, the official schools will not accept Sudanese students. Refugees are crowded into inadequate housing without medical treatment, education, and little employment. It is very difficult to obtain financial assistance from the state. The process is slow and the money received does not even cover basic survival needs. Melissa is working with others to gain refugee status from the UN for Sudanese people in Egypt without passports so that someday they can return to the Sudan. Through SWVP, she is attempting to gather support for a referendum for self-determination of southern Sudan.

Rachel, a journalist in charge of SWVP communications, was very active at both the African regional PrepCom and the FWCW. In a joint interview with myself and UN radio, Rachel spoke about her situation and her motivation for participating in SWVP:

> UN: What made you in particular leave?
> Rachel: I would like to highlight first the problem of refugees and the problem of the displaced. A large number of the civilian population has been dispatched from the areas—they have been dislocated. There is a very big number, about 1 million southerners, living on the outskirts of Khartoum, the capital. And they are in a very pathetic situation...The refugees are all over the neighboring countries, the countries that are neighboring Sudan. I am one of them. I am staying in Kenya, temporarily, because I feel that I am still part of my country. I have to work very hard to alleviate the problem of our people. The situation in which we are living is really bad. We are living on charity. Our dignity is not there. But we have to continue begging.

Rachel, like the other SWVP members, felt it was very important for the international community to learn what was going on in south Sudan.

Lucia, the head of the SWVP delegation in Senegal, was also a refugee in Kenya. In her interview, she explained how the decision of the group to become involved in the peace process in the Sudan was empowering to them as women. According to Lucia:

> We are here to represent the specific aims and objectives courtesy of the working group. I come from southern Sudan. But we are in the group from different parts of Sudan. And working for objectives which would actually address the concerns of women, the effects and all sorts of channels that could really help our women on the ground and our women all of us outside Sudan. The aim is that we should actually look at the effects of war with

> positive attitude. And we also felt that it was our own decision and our own initiative to form this group and we are telling ourselves that we are capable to speak for ourselves, to really even educate those men on peacemaking, on peace process, education. We took it as a challenge. I think we have more talent and more knowledge to educate these men.

As the leader of the SWVP delegation, Lucia spoke most often for the group in public presentations.

Lisa, participating in the African regional PrepCom as a SWVP member, was originally from Juba, the capital of southern Sudan. Like Lucia and Rachel, she was currently living in Nairobi, Kenya. She and her family had been forced to flee to Uganda in 1964, until 1972 when it was safe enough for her family to return. However, because of the war, she is again a refugee. She lamented in her interview:

> I am 38 years old. I was born in exile. I grew up in exile. Today my children are also growing up in exile. When will it end? That is the question all the women are asking of themselves. If we continue like this, what will be the future of our children?

Clearly, Lisa had a vested interest in ending the Sudanese civil war so that she could return to her homeland.

In addition to her work with SWVP, Lisa worked with refugees in Nairobi through UNDP. She focused on educating other refugee women, giving them training and counseling after the trauma of the war. Specifically, through UNDP she helped with training in economic development, e.g. training in tailoring. Lisa thought education for people in urban areas was important because the refugees in Nairobi would be the people who would return to the rural areas of southern Sudan and rebuild the country when the war was over. She emphasized that not many agencies give attention to urban refugees.

Lisa was deeply committed to her people even though she had left her country. She took her role as a representative of her people, particularly southern Sudanese refugees, very seriously:

> Now as a refugee I felt that I have to help my people. I am heading an office which is sponsored by UNDP/Unifem which is dealing with the African women in crisis. Today I am representing the SWVP in Dakar to express our voice and bring the voices of the voiceless, of the people of the southern Sudan so that the world will know our problem.

Lisa and other SWVP members were frustrated that their voices as women and as refugees had not been heard. They hoped that by taking part in the UN process, they would finally gain some international assistance for their struggle for peace in the Sudan.

Lisa summed up the philosophy and mission of SWVP in an interview:

> Power cannot be fought by guns. Power can be fought by policy and democracy. This is the most important message we as women we want to put into the heart of Africa. We cannot get power by guns. We have to sit down, we have to teach our children to work

> for themselves, to love one another so that the ethnic conflict should not exist in Africa. That is the only way we can bring peace to the country.

Nonviolence, development, and dialogue were key concepts for the SWVP.

SWVP Resources

The resources available to SWVP were different from those available to WILPF. SWVP had obtained the long-term support of a Swedish foundation, Life and Peace, that funded their participation as a small group in the African Regional PrepCom and in the NGO Forum'95, Beijing. Life and Peace was helping the organization to gain international visibility (and credibility) by funding their participation in FWCW and by providing technical support and training. Additional funding sources included People for Peace in Africa and Unifem.

SWVP members had not participated in earlier UN World Conferences on Women but they had attended a number of African regional conferences focused on the resolution of armed conflict and refugee issues. Their participation in peace negotiations at various levels gave them concrete experience in developing proposals. SWVP did not appear to have a strong international network at the conferences. They were in the process of building one. Their ties with Unifem were particularly helpful in this endeavor.

SWVP leadership was very impressive. They had a sense of pride in their traditional culture and a strong identification with their people in southern Sudan. In addition to some financial and cultural resources, SWVP members were what they called 'intellectuals.' They had educational and class advantages in their society, although as refugees, they had lost some of their connections and position in Sudanese society. As a whole, the women were deeply committed to ending the civil war in the Sudan, they were well educated, they were grounded in their work at the grassroots level, and they were able to speak persuasively in a language not their own.

SWVP also possessed a kind of moral power. They were calling for justice and an end to violence in a situation where genocide was taking place. Every time they spoke publicly as peace activists about the need for justice in southern Sudan, they embarrassed and angered some of the northern Sudanese women who would then try to discredit them. The urgency of their situation—the on going civil war—made their requests for help powerful.

Although they had much strength as an NGO, SWVP faced potential threat from the government and military representatives, both male and female, present at the conferences. SWVP members were going up against the state and the Sudanese State was visible at the conference. I never saw any threats made towards SWVP members; however, knowing that representatives of the government were attending common events may have been intimidating.

Overview of SWVP Participation in the Conferences

Despite the difficult circumstances under which SWVP took part in the conferences, SWVP leadership expressed satisfaction in their participation. SWVP preparations included gaining financial backing for their participation, preparing literature for distribution and discussion, requesting and writing presentations, and seeking media contacts. In addition, they attended key peace conferences related to the negotiation process in the Sudan specifically and women and peace generally. For example, with the support of Unifem/African Women in Crisis, SWVP held a two-day workshop in Nairobi, Kenya bringing together women from both North and South to attempt dialogue on the civil war. The conference was held in December of 1994, in between the African regional conference and the FWCW.

SWVP leadership was particularly pleased with their efforts at the African regional conference. During the conference, the women had several chances to read their call for peace in the peace tent, made presentations on the situation in the Sudan from their perspective, developed proposals for the African regional document in conjunction with their colleagues, spoke with many women from African countries at war, and helped to create the African Women's Peace Network. In addition, SWVP met with the Life and Peace sponsored delegation (Sudanese, Somali and Swedish) every day for meals and occasionally for group reports. Despite tensions with women from northern Sudan and attempts at intimidation from Sudanese government delegates, SWVP carried on their activities. Lucia stated in an interview that she and the other SWVP members had felt heard, had contributed to the formation of an important coalition, had made their proposals, and had generally followed through on their objectives.

SWVP participation in the NGO Forum '95 (the delegation left at the end of the Forum—they did not attend the FWCW) was more complex. Rachel and Lucia attended, as well as a third delegate I did not meet. Rachel told me she was very pleased with the opening ceremony of the peace tent, which focused on building a culture of peace. She appreciated being with women from around the world who were working for peace. SWVP gave five workshops, presented in the African regional tent and spoke on a panel in the peace tent. However, these events were poorly attended. When they spoke in the African regional tent, they were heckled by northern Sudanese women. Furthermore, their attempts at conflict resolution with northern Sudanese women were very frustrating. Nevertheless, SWVP leadership was pleased with the further international contacts they made and the opportunity for international attention.

Conclusion

The following chapters will explore how such varied organizations might find ways to collaborate despite their differences. The diversity of the three organizations will allow me to discuss the problems NGOs encounter as they attempt to cooperate at the conferences. Although the three organizations differed in their history, their cultural context, and their goals, the members had in common their years of activism and their commitment to peace. However, as these women interacted at the conference peace events, they were unaware of each other's stories. In the busy, sometimes frantic pace of the conference activities, I did not notice in depth conversations going on among the members of these three NGOs. As a researcher, I had the time to learn about my informants, conducting interviews and observing their activities. As a result, I may have seen them differently than the other NGO representatives because I had learned about their background and what was important to them. I saw my informants as highly skilled, committed activists but they may have seen each other as yet another unfamiliar face.

Chapter 3

Coalition Consensus Building: An Experiment in Transnational Decision Making*

At global conferences, the dominant discourse of inclusion and acceptance of diversity has generated efforts to create a wide range of opportunities for people to participate. Nevertheless, my research shows that NGOs face unique challenges in designing decision making processes that reflect NGO norms and values. The study of non-governmental transnational movement decision making is important for understanding transnational social movement organizing. An analysis of decision making helps to identify conditions under which processes utilized by social movement organizations can be useful on a large scale. Furthermore, focusing on decision making processes clarifies movement values and priorities and shows how they shape movement strategy. Decision making most often involves conflict. In the context of this study, conflicts over NGO network priorities bring to light inequalities in large-scale, non-governmental decision making.

Based on participant observation and interviews, I will analyze the decision making process of the transnational women's peace coalition that formed during the preparatory conferences for the FWCW and the NGO Forum on Women 1995. The coalition attempted to include all of their constituents in setting the agenda for the coalition but instead ended up marginalizing some of the very participants they hoped to include. To understand this issue, I will focus on the coalition's agenda setting process. The coalition leadership chose to use consensus, a non-hierarchical decision making process, in order to address unequal relations among coalition participants and to maximize participation. However, the use of consensus heightened rather than transformed power imbalances.

I will describe the modified consensus process used by the coalition and explore the norms and values that it reflects. I will then review some of the common limitations of consensual decision making. Central to this chapter is an analysis of how those limitations become manifest within the context of the transnational coalition of women's peace organizations. Finally, I discuss how participants responded to the decision making process.

---

* Parts of this chapter originally appeared in 'Consensus Decision Making, Northern Ireland and Indigenous Movements' in *Research in Social Movements, Conflicts, and Change*, Volume 24, Patrick G. Coy, editor, JAI/Elsevier, 2002.

The Consensus Process

Decision by consensus means that everyone involved has the opportunity to discuss matters of importance until a decision acceptable to everyone is reached (Iannello, 1992). In the consensual decision-making process, after discussing an issue, 'one or more members of the assembly sum up prevailing sentiment, and if no objections are voiced, this becomes agreed upon policy' (Mansbridge, 1980, p. 32). Consensus is conceived as a non-hierarchical process based on equal participation of all participants in collective decisions. In order to promote minimum differentiation between participants in relation to status and power, participants often rotate roles—particularly leadership roles—and share tasks and share specialized knowledge. Authority of the whole, rather than the individual, is most important.

The peace caucus used consensus as a decision making process; however, the process was modified in three ways. First, the consensus process contained hierarchical elements; some authority was centralized. The process was consultative, that is, the leadership solicited suggestions from participants. Nevertheless, in the end, small groups of designated or elected leaders made decisions for the majority of the participants.

The NGO Forum '95 leadership asked WILPF to coordinate the peace caucus and other peace-related events for the NGO Forum '95 (WILPF had organized the peace events for the past three UN conferences on women). The NGO Forum leadership put WILPF in charge because the WILPF leadership had: 1) many years of experience with the UN; 2) credibility within global women's movements and the UN Women's Conferences; 3) contacts around the world with 47 international chapters; and 4) the resources to develop a coalition. Furthermore, it was more efficient for one NGO to coordinate the activities of a budding, constantly changing, global peace coalition.

Second, the consensus process was modified by the fact that representatives made decisions on behalf of organizations, networks, and/or movements. Some of the representatives were chosen by conference organizers, others selected themselves, and some individuals were elected by their constituencies. During the preparatory conferences, the representatives discussed issues, made proposals, and then decided whether to back the proposals under consideration. Some NGOs like WILPF had many representatives. Other delegates represented two or more NGOs like the Pacific Island delegate who came on behalf of the Nuclear Free and Independent Pacific and Beneath Paradise, an umbrella organization for several women's NGOs.

Third, the modified consensus process built on the multi-layered negotiations that the NGO Forum initiated in order to develop a NGO 'consensus' document. The peace caucus attempted to reach consensus on peace agendas within the context of a global process set up to create a NGO consensus document based on local, national, and regional agendas. Women's NGOs held strategic planning meetings with representative cross-sections of women both locally and nationally. At each of the regional PrepComs, the NGO leadership solicited policy proposals from NGO participants. Through NGO lobbying efforts, some of the proposals were incorporated into the UN regional documents. Three days before the March 1995 Committee on the Status of Women (CSW) consultation and global PrepCom in New York, a highly select group of women drafted an NGO document, based on the regional documents, that represented all five regions of the world (as determined by the UN). It was this document that was presented to the 1,200 NGO delegates from around the world for approval in March of 1995. Furthermore, NGOs like the Women's Environment and Development Organization (WEDO) circulated advocacy documents intended to advance gains made by women at prior UN conferences. NGOs expended a tremendous amount of effort to reach agreement on policy issues and the peace caucus tapped into that process.

Rationale for the Consensus Process: 'As Women, We Use Consensus'

WILPF used an informal consensual decision making process in the peace caucus even though, as an organization, they do not value non-hierarchy (conversation with Mary Day Kent 3/2002). Although their organizational structure is hierarchical, WILPF uses consensus decision making primarily (at the international level voting is also utilized) because it reflects their commitment to inclusivity and empowerment - values reinforced by the dominant discourse at the NGO Forum '95 (Alonso, 1993). Both WILPF and the NGO Forum leadership made an effort to include women of many different backgrounds and to provide various opportunities for participation in the conference activities. Consensus decision making was the norm at the NGO conferences. As leaders of the peace caucus, WILPF followed suit.

At the NGO Forum '95 and its preparatory conferences, consensus decision making was used for two reasons. First, some of the conference leadership believed that consensus reflected the values and norms of the 'women's movement.' These collective values included inclusivity, empowerment, and non-hierarchy. Building on perceived norms and values of movements could serve to develop a sense of common identity among very diverse NGOs and social movement organizations. Shared ideology provides sense of collective identity that is a prerequisite for collective action (Buechler, 1990). Second, NGO Forum '95 leaders were attempting to consolidate the power of women's movements in order to gain and retain influence in the UN arena. Bridging ideological and material differences by reaching consensus would be an indication of the strength of the movement. Following is a discussion of the values, norms, and goals that provided a rationale for the use of consensus decision making.

The Value of Inclusion and Diversity

Many women's organizations have claimed to speak for all women. However, their limited success in recruiting a diverse membership, participating in diverse coalitions, and incorporating the policy agenda issues of importance to women of color, lesbians, and working-class women has created tension within women's movements (Spalter-Roth and Schreiber, 1995). Issues of race were marginalized in women's organizations because these issues tended to divide organizations and were sometimes perceived as a threat to their legitimacy with white, middle class male policymakers.

The UN World Conferences on Women have generated many debates on issues of power, difference, and representation in international women's movements (Mohanty, Russo, and Torres, 1991; Davis, 1990; Enloe, 1989; Joseph and Lewis, 1987; Sen and Grown, 1987). Third World feminists maintain that they are misrepresented by Northern feminists who universalize the experiences and conditions of Northern women. Moreover, feminist claims generalizing the shared gender oppression of women around the world justify Northern authority to intervene and to analyze (Chowdry, 1995; Mohanty 1991). In recognition of the importance of diverse locations within transnational movements, many feminist scholars maintain that women need to speak about and understand their differences if they are to collaborate on common projects (Anzaldua, 1990; hooks 1997; Leidner, 1991).

By the end of the 1980s, in the US most women's organizations had developed specific programs designed to address racism (Spalter-Roth and Schreiber, 1995). For example, WILPF USA designed a Racial Justice Campaign to attack racism within both the organization and the 'wider society.' However, marginalized women criticized these programs as too little and too late; in order to create 'diversity,' they were expected to join white-dominated groups. These programmatic attempts at inclusion resulted in challenges to organizational goals, issues, and resources.

Discourse emphasizing the importance of diversity and inclusivity was common at the NGO Forum '95. Friedlander writes about the plenary sessions at the Forum,

> Difference enriches and is responsible for the vitality and creativity that nourish the movement....only inclusiveness can ensure its growth and continuity into the next century for the coming generations (Friedlander, 1996, p.xxviii).

Friedlander goes on to say that women must acknowledge the diversity of women's lives and experiences in order to 'avoid the tyranny of the well-intended, yet often tortuous, imposition of ideas and wills on others.' She is indirectly referencing the 'imposition' of Northern women on Southern women, a dynamic that has become more obvious to Northern feminists through debates generated by the conferences.

As the organizers of the NGO Forum '95 peace activities, WILPF attempted to include participants different from their own membership in the planning process. They sent out a survey to organizations expressing interest in peace issues to find out what were key issues for their constituents. WILPF organized a peace train from Helsinki to Beijing, in part, to build contacts with eastern European women and learn about their concerns. They funded a number of women from marginalized communities to participate in the conferences and the peace train.

Many WILPF leaders developed personal contacts with Southern women from Vietnam, Sudan, Angola and elsewhere.

Furthermore, during the PrepComs and the NGO Forum '95, they held open meetings; any one who wished could participate. At the peace caucus meetings, WILPF solicited input from participants and rotated the facilitation of the peace caucus meetings so that some Southern participants would have a chance to lead. Inclusion of diverse participants was a priority for WILPF.

The Value of Empowerment

Feminist analysis of power relations led to the development of the term 'empowerment' which refers to power as the ability to 'do' or accomplish something (Hartsock, 1990). In organizations based on empowerment, members monitor or control themselves rather than being controlled or managed by administration. When power becomes domination, it supports hierarchical structures in organizations. Decision making is concentrated in the hands of a few at the top of the organization; the majority of workers are subject to 'commands' from those above and are limited in their abilities. Empowerment expands the definition of power to include the ability to accomplish goals which encourages people to maximize their abilities (Carroll, 1971).

On several occasions, Irene Santiago, executive director of the NGO Forum '95, referred to the Forum as an empowering event for the participants. In her words, the conferences were designed as spaces where 'everyone can have voice.' At the NGO Forum and preparatory conferences, all of the women participating would have the chance to speak and, as a result, influence the development of global policies pertaining to women.

According to Supatra Masdit, convenor of the NGO Forum for Women '95:

> One essential approach is the empowerment of grassroots women. The NGO Forum hopes to encourage the idea of women speaking for and among themselves. One such example is the active and meaningful participation of grassroots groups in this NGO Forum. This is the strength of the NGO Forum—its power to inspire women to build equitable and respectful relationships with one another and the world (Masdit, 1996, p. 3).

Masdit is referring to concerns within women's movements that elite leadership creates a self-serving movement that empowers only those women who already have the most relative power. In the context of the Forum, empowerment meant women speaking for themselves—rather than elite women speaking for them—participating actively in policy development, and building equitable relationships within women's movements.

WILPF's commitment to empowerment is reflected in the structure of their organization. WILPF is a membership organization. A primary goal of a membership organization is to educate and mobilize members to participate in the policy process. The staff encourages women to work directly for their own benefit. Through membership surveys and national conventions, the members set the agenda for the organization. The paid staff gain access to decision-makers and provide information for the public. In turn, the membership provides credibility, effectiveness, and financing to the staff (Spalter-Roth and Schreiber, 1995).

Consensus, the Norm

During the conferences, the NGO representatives used an informal consensual process in every small and medium sized meeting of the roughly 150 meetings that I observed. For example, the approximately 200 women attending the first North American/European PrepCom planning meeting at the 1994 global PrepCom employed consensual decision making. The small groups (consisting of 20–50 delegates) that I observed, e.g. the facilitating committee, the global drafting committee, the working groups at regional PrepComs in Austria and Senegal, and the peace caucus meetings in New York and in China, also made decisions in an informal, consensual manner. Some of the small groups like the peace caucus regularly rotated the task of facilitating the meetings. The smaller the group, the more similar the process was to the unmodified consensus process defined above.

In March 1995 at the New York NGO consultation, the NGO leadership used a consensual process to reach 'minimal' consensus among the 1,200 NGO delegates for the proposed Platform for Action (PfA). Although 'minimal' consensus was not clearly defined, it can be best described as an agreement that would satisfy the largest number of people. Resolutions and proposals were passed if no one disagreed strongly. Sometimes, the proposals were passed even if a small minority did disagree. For example, during the large meetings, the facilitator would pass a proposal if the majority supported it but delegates who strongly disagreed were asked to step outside the plenary hall to discuss the issue. They were encouraged to try to understand each other's point of view. Votes were never counted.

Most often the leadership of caucuses and/or meetings simply began the meetings using a consensus process. Occasionally, someone would question how decisions were made but I did not observe strong objections to a consensual process. For example, during the North American/European PrepCom planning meeting in New York, when a participant called for a vote on a logistical issue, she was informed by the European leadership that 'as women, we use consensus' (Fieldnotes, March, 3, 1994). No one disagreed.

Consensus as Identity

Organizational form is central to the construction of a common sense of identity among social movement participants. The type of organizational structure that social movements take on embody its members' collective identity and the meaning they attribute to their actions (Donati, 1984; Gundelach 1984; Melucci, 1989). Furthermore, an organization's structure is a way to actualize the movement's vision of the ideal society through its practices (Arnould, 1995). Non-hierarchy was considered to be part of the women's movement's vision.

For some Northern feminists, rejection of hierarchical forms of organizing and of leadership has been critical in defining the difference of the women's movement from other social movements (Brown, 1992). Consensual decision making demonstrates core feminist values: participation by all; sharing of tasks and skills; and rejection of hierarchical forms.

The movement towards non-hierarchical organization began in the 1960s with a grassroots branch of the women's movement. Students and others who had been forced into traditional women's roles in civil rights organizations started 'consciousness-raising' groups. Women shared experiences of sex discrimination and developed strategies for change. They were committed to non-hierarchy and experimenting with organizational structure as opposed to the formal structure of larger groups in women's movements (Ianello, 1992).

In the radical feminist tradition, feminist process is necessarily collective, participatory, and consensus-based; otherwise, women are selling out to the system. Hierarchical decision making is equated with patriarchy and power-over others. Non-hierarchical decision making is egalitarian; ideally, all participants contribute equally to the development of the organization or collective. In order to alter dominant power relations, leadership positions are rotated and responsibility is shared among group members (Sargent, 1981, p. 116).

Few women's organizations have retained the radical democratic forms developed in the 1960s (Martin, 1990). Not all women value nonhierarchical forms of organization. Liberal feminists maintain that it is necessary to become experts in procedures used by men because equality for women will be achieved through equality in the system itself. Moreover, few will argue that consensual decision making is unproblematic. Instead, women's organizations have modified consensual processes and/or hierarchical structures in order to address some of the tensions and limitations that consensus decision making raises (Ferree and Martin, 1995). Nevertheless, at the FWCW, the NGOs consistently chose consensus.

Consensus as Power

NGOs had worked hard over a period of at least twenty years to consolidate the power of women's movements in the UN. Consensus was an important symbol of a growing international women's movement even though true consensus was declared impossible. Irene Santiago stated on several occasions that consensus was not only unnecessary but impossible (Santiago, 1996). According to Santiago in a speech at the March 1994 PrepCom, 'We can have solidarity without consensus.' In that same talk, she maintained that the women could diffuse the power of the status quo without consensus building. A few days later, in another speech, Santiago stated that her goal was to support the process of finding common ground so that NGOs could influence the UN. However, because the movement was not a homogeneous group, she suggested that the women look for 1% common ground on which to work together.

Nevertheless, a 'minimal' consensus on the proposed NGO PfA was needed in order to make a show of strength. Gertrude Mongella, the Secretary General of the

FWCW, stated in her speech at the opening of the 1995 NGO consultation that achieving consensus was the greatest goal of the women's movement. The women's movement must minimize differences, she maintained. In her speech at the opening, Supatra Masdit proclaimed there would be 'No Moving Back!' Therefore, despite all the contradictions, the consensus process was used.

Although WILPF did not promote non-hierarchy as an organization, they did prioritize empowerment and inclusion. Ideally, the consensus process increases inclusion and empowerment. Furthermore, they shared the vision of consolidating the power of transnational women's movements. WILPF acted within the context of the larger NGO PrepComs and the forum which established norms for the peace caucus. However, consensual decision making has many limitations and it is to those that I now turn. My research illustrates how the consensus process limited the ability of the peace caucus to practice empowerment and inclusion as they set the coalition agenda.

Limitations of Consensus Decision Making

In any setting, consensual decision making has limitations (Rothschild-Whitt, 1979; Mansbridge, 1980; Freeman, 1984; Brown, 1992; Gastil 1993). Studies of consensus decision making have shown that: 1) resolving conflicts are difficult; 2) without a formal structure, informal power structures develop that are more difficult to negotiate than formal ones; 3) homogeneity, rather than diversity is fostered; 4) the process is time consuming; and 5) environmental factors may constrain the consensus process. Reviewing well-documented difficulties with the consensus process will assist in the analysis of the problems that the peace caucus faced.

Suppression of Conflict

Consensus decision making tends to suppress conflict for two reasons. First, unanimity is required in order for the organization or group to function. Rothschild-Whitt maintains that:

> Structural tensions inherent in collectivist organizations render conflict difficult to absorb. ...The norm of consensual decision making in collectives makes the possibility of conflict all the more threatening because unanimity is required (where a majoritarian system can institutionalize and absorb conflicting opinions) (Rothschild-Whitt, 1979, p. 521).

Organizations cannot act until a unanimous decision has been reached; therefore, dissent threatens the ability of the organization to accomplish their goals.

Second, when common interests and values are assumed, participants in a consensus process may find it difficult to disagree. As such, real conflicts of interest are 'masked,' resulting in a 'false or managed consensus' (Mansbridge, 1980). According to Mansbridge, the suppression of conflict often works 'to the detriment of citizens who are already at a disadvantage' in socioeconomic terms (Mansbridge, 1980, p. 15).

Tyranny of Structurelessness/Power Inequities

Power inequities arising from unequal participation and commitment within non-hierarchical organizations are commonplace (Rothschild-Whitt, 1979; Mansbridge, 1980; Freeman, 1972; Brown, 1992; Gastil 1993). Jo Freeman's research on non-hierarchical women's organizations shows that leaderless or non-hierarchical groups may lead to a 'tyranny of structurelessness' whereby an informal structure hides an elite clique that wields 'unchallengeable' power because they have no obligation to the group at large (Freeman, 1972). The power of these informal cliques is difficult to challenge in part because they are self-selected, not elected leaders, and as such there are few formal mechanisms for accountability and regulation. Even when participants do share a commitment to equal participation and nonhierarchical processes, there is still a probability that inequalities of power and influence may persist in spite of efforts to reduce them (Brown, 1992).

Homogeneity

According to Rothschild-Whitt (1979), consensual decision making is not possible without a commitment to common goals and to the values underlying consensual decision making processes. Therefore, the level of homogeneity required for consensual decision making limits its usefulness. Rothschild-Whitt maintains that: Unified action is possible only if individuals substantially agree with the goals and processes of the collective. This implies a level of homogeneity (in terms of values) unaccustomed and unnecessary in bureaucracy (Rothschild-Whitt, 1979, p. 520).

Because collective organizations do not use centralized authority or standardized rules to 'achieve social control,' they must rely on appeals to a moral commitment. The more homogeneous the group, the more effective the appeal. Furthermore, Rothschild-Whitt argues that the values tied to judgements relative to the importance of consensus are cultural. As such, collectivist organizations tend to attract homogeneous populations based on social origins.

Coalitions, like the peace caucus, bring together ideologically diverse groups that maintain their separate identities. The shared assumptions and ties of solidarity necessary for a consensus decision making process do not exist within the context of a coalition. As such, the homogeneous ideals required for consensus are in direct contradiction to the coalition structure that presumes its members are ideologically diverse and self-interested. Studies have shown that the contradiction between ideological diversity and organizational unity will not become an obstacle as long as the coalition deals solely with issues that require a superficial consensus (Arnould, 1995).

Time

Participation in consensus processes is very demanding and time consuming. Because consensual decision making tends to take more time than hierarchical or bureaucratic decision making, inefficiency is often considered a limitation of the consensus process. The time necessary to find true consensus can inhibit the effectiveness of the organization. According to Eisenstein:

> There is still, to me a fundamental issue that remains unresolved for feminists, and that is how we get from the values we hold dear—of collective, non-hierarchical, democratic behavior—to the outcome we seek, of a peaceful world safe for women and others now subject to discrimination, victimization, and oppression, without sacrificing these values in the rush to seize and use power on behalf of feminist ends (Eisenstein, 1991, p. 3).

Many women's organizations struggle with tensions between democratic process and organizational effectiveness (Leidner, 1991; Eisenstein, 1991).

Environmental Constraints

All organizations are subject to external pressures. However, because collective organizations often operate in opposition to mainstream institutions, external constraints on consensus based organizations may be stronger than on hierarchical organizations (Rothschild-Whitt, 1979). Environmental factors limiting the development of collectivist organizations may be legal, economic, political, and/or cultural.

Application of Limitations to the Peace Network

Each of the limiting factors outlined above helps to explain why the peace caucus ended up excluding some of the participants they wished to include. The modified consensus process tended to suppress conflict. As a result, some women did not 'have voice' and others dominated global policy decision making. Rather than nurturing the expression of diversity, all too often the process helped to mask or cover difference. Following is an exploration of the how the limitations of the consensus decision making affected the agenda setting process of the peace caucus. Given these results, the question arises as to whether the consensus process limited the ability of the peace caucus leadership to express their core values.

Suppression of Conflict

Although all of the peace caucus representatives advocated for an end to armed conflict, some of the interests of the NGO representatives differed depending on their location. However, as the women decided on a common political agenda for their coalition, the leadership avoided contention which, in effect, resulted in the suppression of difference. Most often, when interests collided, the leadership simply moved on. The discussion below will show that the participants who lost the most or who challenged the consensus tended to be at a disadvantage in terms of language, culture, information, and resources—like the Pacific Island and the Saharan delegates. The peace caucus leadership resolved conflicts that arose once the agenda had been set. However, their success had little to do with the informal consensual decision making process that they used during their meetings.

For example, the peace caucus reached a managed consensus at the global PrepCom in New York in March 1995. Within a 30 minute meeting, representatives from approximately 30 NGOs agreed upon several priority issues that all the NGOs could support; it was the only peace caucus meeting where a common agenda was discussed. Their goal was to focus and strengthen their lobbying efforts. By the next day, a peace caucus drafting committee had produced a flyer listing the peace caucus priorities. From that point on, the peace caucus participants focused their lobbying strategy on the issues named in the document. By the time the PrepCom ended, two additions to the agenda/flyer had been made but on the whole, the flyer remained the same. This document was distributed at the conference to NGOs and delegates alike (see Appendix—for a copy of the flyers). Lobbying was particularly important at the March 1995 PrepCom because it provided the last opportunity to add resolutions to the PfA.

The following excerpts from my fieldnotes will illustrate how contention tended to be ignored or suppressed during the peace caucus meetings. Moreover, different contexts for common issues were not recognized in the peace caucus main priorities. As a result, the peace caucus agenda was most similar to the regional agenda of the Northern leadership.

At the beginning of the meeting, the facilitator, a North American leader of Women's International League for Peace and Freedom (WILPF), suggested that the caucus pick a few key issues that they could all support in order to focus and strengthen their lobbying efforts. No one disagreed and they began to negotiate the agenda:

> Bettina, a WILPF International leader, felt it was important that peace be recognized as a human right. Maude, a prominent US activist, suggested nuclear disarmament. 'I hope we're all for the abolition of nuclear weapons,' she said. When she tried to speak again soon after, Anita stopped her, asking that others be given a chance to speak. Madelaine spoke up, raising de-colonization as an issue for the caucus. Then Anita recognized a woman representing a large Japanese women's organization. She expressed concern that it was going to take a lot of time to reach consensus on the common issues. Another leader from WILPF USA suggested military budget cuts as a key concern. 'I think there's the most consensus around financial issues on the military. Everybody else depends on our cuts,' she maintained. A US woman from the International Peace Bureau mentioned that her organization had already worked out a peace statement that the group could work from.
>
> Next a representative from Sahara Women for Peace spoke. She began, 'You cannot know the value of peace without knowing the suffering of war, without knowing what it is like living without land.' She proceeded to tell more of her story but Anita cut her off as facilitator, saying there was no time now to tell stories. Later she announced a workshop on women in armed conflict and asked peace caucus participants to bring their

stories. Anita then summarized the issues raised, leaving out de-colonization, suffering in wartime, and land rights. Another WILPF USA member interjected, mentioning that the North American/European peace caucus had a one-page statement they had produced in Vienna.

Next, Anita asked who would be willing to draft a flyer stating the issues the group had chosen in proposal form. Several North American and European women raised their hands. Anita expressed concern that they needed more diverse regional representation. Maude, the prominent US activist, was chosen to head the drafting committee. She restated three issues as the priorities chosen: gender parity, military budget cuts, and peace education (adding two issues that had not been mentioned). Someone called out another suggestion from the audience and Anita responded by instructing her to speak with the head of the committee. The drafting committee was formed, made up mostly of North Americans, and so was the agenda.

Although no one openly disagreed, the group was nowhere near reaching consensus. The Northern leadership chose what they thought would be best for the group without soliciting much feedback. This meant that the peace caucus did not arrive at a real consensus, that is, one in which the decisions made were acceptable to all and were reached after all members had the opportunity to discuss key issues. Difficult issues, like de-colonization and ending military occupation, were avoided in favor of safe topics known to have gained support in the past, e.g. in Nairobi. Military budget cuts had broad support as did women's involvement in peacemaking and peace education; however, these issues were not necessarily top priorities for some of the groups represented in the peace caucus. Instead, their primary concerns were military occupation or de-colonization. When delegates raised issues such as genocide, self-determination, de-colonization, and/or military occupation, the facilitator either cut off the speaker or simply ignored what they had said. As a result, these contentious issues were left off the peace caucus agenda and out of the caucus discourse.

Furthermore, the list of priorities did not reflect different contexts and meanings for common issues. Some of the same issues had different meanings to each of the NGOs. For example, the Beneath Paradise/Nuclear Free Independent Pacific (NFIP) representative from New Caledonia was very clear about her three point agenda—de-colonization, de-militarization, and de-nuclearization. Every time she spoke, she connected one issue to the other; she was fighting French nuclear testing around Pacific Islands that had been colonized and militarized by the French. Some of the Beneath Paradise concerns that Madelaine spoke about were covered in a general way by the peace caucus priorities. In particular, de-nuclearization was included. However, de-nuclearization was not connected with colonization. Nor was militarization connected specifically with occupation or self-determination. Instead, the peace caucus flyer connected militarization with diversion of resources from social programs, a major concern for WILPF and other Northern NGOs.

Power Inequities: The Tyranny of Structurelessness

The consensus process did not eliminate inequalities of power and influence among the conference participants. Some of the women received greater visibility and tended to dominate group decision making. NGO representatives with more skills related to the UN and who attended conferences more frequently or who were most committed to the UN World Conferences on Women tended to wield more influence. These representatives had greater access to knowledge about the conferences and to the creation of that knowledge.

The above description of the peace caucus meeting illustrates how the more powerful organizers and leaders of the peace meetings and events tended to dominate the process with their own agenda, despite the facilitator's attempts to curb that domination. The Northern NGOs had organized the meeting. They spoke the most, they had attended the most conferences in the past, they had statements ready to go, they drafted the flyer to be distributed, and they decided which issues were acceptable and which were not. The facilitator did try to encourage the North Americans in particular to speak less often. Towards the beginning of the meeting, she asked Maude, the prominent US activist, to wait until others had spoken. Furthermore, a couple of times, she called attention to the lack of regional representation in their organizing efforts. Nevertheless, her attempts at self-regulation were not successful.

The peace caucus flyer was based more on the document that the Northern women had produced at the North American and European Regional PrepCom in 1994 rather than on an in-depth discussion of the issues among peace caucus participants. The leadership relied on their shared understandings of what had 'worked' at previous conferences, leaving out issues that in the twenty year history of the conferences had produced bitter divisions. Given their power and resources, the Northern leadership was able to install what they thought was a strategic frame applicable for everyone.

The Northern peace caucus leadership took on the task of representing the other participants. In situations where there is a dominant or 'unmarked' group, the dominant group claims a language of impartiality and 'the common good,' whereas 'marked' groups are seen as self-interested because they pursue group-specific claims (Young, 1990, p. 104). Angela Davis challenges the assumption that 'marked' groups, e.g. African Americans, are only qualified to speak on behalf of their own people and not on the conditions of humanity at large (Davis, 1990).

The Northern frame was based on Northern regional agendas—it was not impartial. The abstract claims of WILPF, for example, calling for general disarmament, global institutions for peace, or reduction of worldwide military budgets were based on regional concerns. They contrasted sharply with the concrete, regional claims of Beneath Paradise and the Sudanese Women's Voice for Peace, e.g. Sudanese peace negotiations or an end to French nuclear testing. However, those regional claims could be generalized as well, as the Pacific Island representative was able to do with her three point agenda, de-colonization, de-nuclearization, and de-militarization.

Homogeneity

Diverse backgrounds The homogenous profile of a collectivist group that Rothschild-Whitt presents differs widely from the reality of the NGO Forum '95. The women who took part in the conferences varied according to race, ethnicity, religion, nationality, ideology, age, physical ability, class, profession and many other factors. The 'social origins' of the conference participants were very diverse. The women did share a commitment to improving the status of women. However, ideas as to what improving the status of women meant and the means by which this goal could be achieved varied enormously among the 30,000 attendees.

Diverse values and cultures Northern cultural assumptions clearly influenced the decision making processes. For example, many peace caucus members did not conform to or were not familiar with the idioms, vocabulary, or narrative forms that were common to the Northern facilitators. As such, the facilitators ignored or did not recognize some of the issues raised because they did not sound like proposals to them. The norms governing communication are not neutral. According to Fraser, what tends to be heard in public forums is a way of speaking 'associated with those who control social, political, and economic institutions' (Fraser, 1989, pp.164-165). In the first peace caucus meeting (described above), the facilitator cut off and passed over the women who used metaphor and stories to explain what was important to them. Their issues went unheard.

Attempts to raise issues in story form were consistently delegated to another arena—the workshops. War stories were not considered appropriate material for discussions of the policy statements required by the UN. During the peace caucus meetings, if the women did not present their issues in a format appropriate to the legal discourse of the UN document, which is based on Northern cultural norms, then they were asked to stop and tell their stories in scheduled workshops. In some cultures, stories are told to give the broad context of the issue (Lederach, 1995). Although they gave information as to what issues were important to them, they were cut off. Perhaps the facilitator feared that the stories, unlike the issue statements, would take more time and care given the emotional content of the narratives, and as such, would not be appropriate for a business meeting. This meant that although some women in situations of armed conflict had many opportunities to speak about their lives in workshops, they had little influence on the priorities for policy proposals or the dominant discourse because their issues went unrecognized in the agenda-setting meetings.

Diverse goals Members of the NGOs I studied spent much of their time advocating for their own agendas. Although the conferences—like social movements—were conceptualized as collective, cooperative efforts at social change, competition was an integral part of the dynamics. As a coalition, the peace NGOs acted in their own self-interest illustrating the contradiction between the homogeneity required for consensus and the diversity of the coalition structure.

Many of the NGO representatives had limited capacity to negotiate common agendas with other NGOs. Some of the NGOs had spent years of preparation consulting with their constituencies on their priorities and strategies. Many had raised thousands of dollars to participate in the conference in order to further their own goals as NGOs. Their concerns were very serious; for some, international support for their agendas was critical for their survival. For example, Beneath Paradise was trying to stop the testing of nuclear weapons in their region and SWVP was attempting to end a civil war. None of my informants shifted their priorities. The 1995 Benchmark Survey found that only half (47%) of the NGOs surveyed reported that they could commit their organization to a joint NGO declaration. Others responded that they were required to communicate with their home office first or could only commit themselves personally. Basically, the majority of the respondents did not feel they had the authority to act on behalf of their organizations in conference decisions. Commitment to integrating the input of non-participating NGO members given in advance of the conferences was high leaving the NGO representatives with little adaptability when it came to making decisions. As representatives, how much flexibility could they exhibit when they had been sent to the conferences to advocate for a limited number of key constituent priorities?

Hegemony The search for acceptance in the UN setting served to further suppress differing agendas. The legal format of the UN documents reinforces the need for single issue statements that apply universally. For example, the peace caucus leadership attempted to fit the UN standard in order for their proposals to gain acceptance at the UN assembly. Not surprisingly, the abstract, generalized statements did not reflect contextual differences. Hegemony levels difference and standardizes contexts (Minh-ha, 1997). At the conferences, hegemony works through the requirement that NGOs adhere to a format for international communication that favors the abstract over the specific.

Time

Given the length of the conferences, the large numbers of participants from all around the world, and the structure of the UN conference process, the NGOs had little time with which to find common ground. The first meeting of the global peace caucus set up to determine the caucus agenda lasted 30 minutes. There was not enough time to try and resolve conflicts, nor was there adequate time to gain understanding of widely divergent views during the consensus decision making process. Within the context of the FWCW, the NGO representatives felt pressured to make quick agreements as to what they would lobby their UN delegates for, since they had a small amount of time in which they hoped to wield a great deal of influence. Furthermore, not all NGOs could afford to fund their representatives to stay in hotels and eat in restaurants for extended periods of time.

Because of the time constraints, the conversations were so brief that it was difficult for the delegates to gain an understanding of what was important to other

NGOs and why if they were not already familiar with the organization. I learned about the concerns of the organizations by reading the literature they passed out at the conferences, going to their workshops and listening to the interviews they gave me. Often the stories that the women told in these settings provided a compelling rationale for why they raised the issues they did in the peace caucus meetings. However, they were unable to present these full explanations in formal public settings where decisions regarding policy were made. As such, the consensus process and agreements made were based more on a desire for solidarity or a fear of conflict than a clear understanding of interests.

During the first peace caucus meeting, a Japanese woman raised the concern that consensus building took a lot of time. If the group had discussed the issue of time and how they would proceed, the meeting might have gone quite differently. They might have decided consensus was not a viable option or they could have made an agreement to lengthen the time or meet again—there were many possibilities.

Environmental Constraints

The participants of the peace caucus struggled to develop a consensual process within the confines of UN structures and procedures. The UN provides an opportunity for bringing together women's movements from around the world with UN representatives. Nevertheless, political events and conflicts within the General Assembly have influenced the ability of the NGOs to set their own agenda and to build relationships between women with divergent viewpoints.

Throughout the history of the conferences, the discussion of peace issues has been strongly influenced by the larger UN political agenda and current events. The theme of peace was originally suggested in the UN General Assembly by Greece and Eastern Europeans so that women's increasing contribution to friendly relations among states and to world peace could be discussed. The first UN document produced in Mexico, the World Plan of Action, reflected the merging of women's agendas with the larger UN political agenda. The document linked women's equality with the elimination of apartheid, the role of women in development in the New International Economic Order (NIEO), and women's contribution to peace through arms control and disarmament.

From the beginning these issues were controversial. At the Mexico conference, Eastern Europeans emphasized de-colonization, détente, and disarmament. The US asserted that such references detracted from the goal of women's equality. China added superpower hegemony to the list of oppressive institutions that women need to fight against. The US and the USSR rebuffed China's proposal. The Soviets charged that China was 'driving a wedge in the anti-imperialist front' and trying to 'weaken the will of the people for a just peace' (Allan, Galey, and Persinger, 1995). In return, China charged the USSR with engaging in arms expansion with other superpowers and making 'huge munitions deals to reap fabulous profits from war' (Allan, Galey, and Persinger, 1995). Eventually the Northern countries consented to refer to various oppressive institutions as among the greatest obstacles to the full emancipation of women (Allan, Galey, and Persinger, 1995).

The conferences were shaped by UN bloc politics throughout the 1960s and 1970s. With the one country-one vote rule in the General Assembly, power shifted to the South, which in turn began to define its own agenda at the UN. New blocs or country alliances were formed, such as the Non-aligned Movement (NAM) which was united by the strength of anti-colonialism movements in Asia and Africa, and the Group of 77 (G-77) which was led by Latin Americans. In addition, during late the 1970s, the North/South confrontation was heightened by political events, e.g. the success of OPEC, US failure in Vietnam, and victories for revolutionary movements in Iran and Nicaragua.

Jane Jaquette (1995) maintains that it was not surprising that the 1980 UN conference was dominated by the Middle East conflict given the background of North/South tension. The General Assembly had been pressuring Israel to negotiate with the PLO. Israel resisted with the backing of the US. At the third PrepCom in April 1980, the controversy arose over a report on the condition of Palestinian women that had been requested by the General Assembly. Israel called the report malicious and inaccurate and argued that Zionism was not racist but a liberation movement. Syria attacked the Camp David Accords and Israel's 'expansionist' policies in South Lebanon. Northern delegates, as they had before, called for these issues to be dealt with in other UN Forums.

The Copenhagen UN conference ended in a deadlock over Middle Eastern politics. Zionism was referred to as a form of oppression in the final document. Government delegates from the United States, Israel, Australia, and Canada refused to support the reference and, as a result, the document did not receive unanimous acceptance (Jaquette, 1995; Foster, 1989). Later, in 1985 in Nairobi, US delegates and their allies threatened to boycott the event and withdraw funding if there were substantive discussions of apartheid, militarism, imperialism, or, particularly, Palestinian issues. This time around, the US and its allies did not carry out their threats and the UN document was passed, based on consensus.

The WILPF leadership was well aware of how divisive the conflict in the Middle East had been at the UN conferences and within the League itself. WILPF may have associated concerns regarding self-determination, land rights and colonization with the conflict in the Middle East and, therefore, attempted to avoid further division by ignoring those issues in the peace caucus. In January 1979, the WILPF International Executive Committee officially disbanded the Israeli section after its policies of hardened nationalism became totally at odds with the League's position. WILPF took the stand that Palestinians have rights as well as the Israelis and 'accommodations must be made for coexistence' (Foster, 1989, p.82). Once the section had been terminated, WILPF cultivated an association with another women's peace group and a new Israeli WILPF section was founded in 1983 (Foster, 1989). Although the Middle East conflict did not dominate the FWCW, the conflicts during previous conferences illustrate the types of external pressures that NGOs may experience as they attempt to build global consensus among women's movements.

Responses to the Peace Caucus Agenda

Resistance

Women who were dissatisfied with the agenda set in the initial peace caucus meeting, responded in three ways. Some challenged the peace caucus leadership directly, bringing important issues to the forefront and offering the opportunity for transformation of the conflict (their struggles are the focus of the next two chapters). Others expressed their dissatisfaction indirectly by talking with peace caucus members on an individual basis. Some participants did not return.

Two of the peace caucus participants did challenge the managed consensus with some success. After the Pacific Island representative confronted the peace caucus members, the caucus leaders added a sentence on de-colonization. It reads as follows, 'Several countries are still under colonial rule and women demand total de-colonization and their full participation in this process.' Madelaine, the Pacific Island delegate, was pleased with the peace caucus response.

In addition, a coalition of women from Africa and the Middle East lobbied the caucus for a resolution against sanctions. They felt that the effects of sanctions could be devastating to the people of a country against whom the sanctions are leveled. The issue of sanctions was raised in a couple of peace caucus meetings, but the subject of sanctions did not appear on the peace caucus flyer until an African woman announced that they had been successful in gaining support for their resolution among UN delegates. By the end of the conference, the peace caucus flyer was just beginning to reflect some of the differences of opinion within the peace caucus.

Although there were no discussions of Northern dominance during caucus meetings, several people spoke to me privately about their concerns and I observed them expressing concerns to others on an individual basis. In a conversation with Christine, a Filipino NGO representative, about the peace tent meetings, she said she thought the peace tent meetings were more interesting. It was a nicer group, Christine said, more international. The peace caucus was often monopolized, she added, not mentioning by whom; but later she gave indications that it was the US women.

In a one-on-one discussion with Rinchen, a Tibetan activist who had attended the peace caucus, Rinchen asked me, 'What do you think about this North/South thing? I didn't think about it before I came but now I do. The Northern women are talking all the time and saying they talk best.' I asked her how she felt about it. 'I don't like it,' she said, her eyes opening wide and her voice rising. 'I feel uncomfortable with it,' she added with feeling. Her statement indicates that some women felt uncomfortable with the Northern dominance; however, they did not choose to confront the Northern leadership with their concerns. For some of the Southern women, it may have been culturally inappropriate to do so. Instead, they expressed their dissent indirectly.

The reduced attendance at further meetings of the peace caucus raises questions as to how satisfied the participants were with the managed consensus. After the first meeting in New York, the average attendance at the peace caucus meetings was fifteen to twenty and the majority of the women were from Northern countries. There are several explanations for this result, the first being that the PrepCom was held in the US and most of the conference participants came from North America and Europe. Second, because many of the Southern NGOs had sent only one delegate, that lone delegate had various demands on her time and with numerous meetings scheduled at the same time, she may not have been able to make any more of the peace caucus meetings. However, a third reason for reduced participation might be that some of the women felt discouraged about their ability to have input at that first meeting.

Acceptance

Generally speaking, the peace caucus members accepted the Northern leadership and the consensus process. Why? First, WILPF and Northern NGOs responded to the challenges and the concerns of which they became aware. (Their responses will be explored in depth in the following chapters). Secondly, the modified consensus process was better than being excluded entirely from any decision making as NGOs had been in the past at UN conferences. As one of the NGO Forum organizers said to me, 'people may be upset but the process is better than having one person write the document like we did in the past.' Despite the resistance to and frustration with how the peace caucus made decisions, there was still some opportunity for more people to participate at some level however unsatisfactory that participation may have been.

Finally, some of the women must have feared that failing to unite as women would weaken the power and influence that they had achieved. Substantial gains had been made in 1985 and in the years following the UN Decade on Women. At each of the world conferences after Nairobi, women made critical connections between the situation of women and the subjects under discussion bringing attention to the complex interrelationship between issues. Women's NGOs were emerging as new, enlarged, and international force with a legitimacy they did not have before. There were fears that conflict could divide and weaken the movement. At the March 1995 PrepCom, a cheer went up from the crowd when the NGO Forum '95 leadership announced that the NGOs had achieved consensus on their draft PfA. At that point in time, the symbolic value of a minimal consensus may have been more important to the participants than actual satisfaction with the document or their ability to participate in decision making.

Conclusion

As leaders of the peace caucus, WILPF made an effort to include as many NGO delegates in the decision making process as possible. They used a modified consensus process, the norm at the women's NGO meetings, with the expectation that non-hierarchical decision making would facilitate the expression of core values. Ideally, the process would promote respect for difference and the empowerment of all participants by making participation truly egalitarian. Instead, the consensus process facilitated the suppression of conflict and difference and reinforced the power of the Northern organizers. The result was a managed consensus that did not reflect issues important to some of the participants who were the most disenfranchised.

This exploration of the practical and theoretical limitations of consensus decision making in the context of the peace caucus shows that consensus did not promote the values and goals that were important to WILPF and other peace caucus participants. The expression of difference became more difficult because consensus was required to make decisions and move forward. Rather than acknowledging differential access to power, power inequities were denied. There was simply not enough time for participants to build agreements based on an understanding of what was important to each other and why it was important. Within the coalition, each NGO acted in its own self-interest without necessarily a commitment to a 'collective.' Finally, the deep-rooted political conflicts that played out at the UN and NGO conferences challenged the consensus process to such an extent that consensus appeared possible only through the denial of painful differences.

As a result, for some, historical divisions and unequal relations within women's movements may have been reinforced, which was the opposite of what the peace caucus leadership had hoped for. Most often, it was the Southern NGO delegates, like Madelaine, Christine, and Rinchen, who did not find their priorities on the peace caucus agenda and who were in the position of having to struggle for visibility. The Northern domination that Rinchen experienced and heard about from other Southern delegates was hurtful to her.

The satisfaction that participants experienced did not appear to have any connection to the consensus process. Through the expression of conflict and difference that took place after and parallel to the consensus decision making, the women began to build trust and understanding. WILPF and other peace caucus members did attempt to respond to some of the conflicts that arose over the agenda. Once differing agendas had been recognized and accepted, possibilities for dialogue and for developing collaborative relationships began. However, the decision making process that WILPF chose did not sufficiently facilitate the expression of diversity and empowerment. Instead, consensus decision-making reinforced inequalities in decision making power among the NGOs.

Chapter 4

Peacemakers In Conflict: Challenges to the Dominant Agenda

This chapter examines the conflicts that arose after and during the structured agenda-setting process in the women and peace arena at the New York PrepCom. At the events surrounding the FWCW what recourse did the women have if they disagreed with the agenda put in place by other NGO representatives? What did NGOs do that came on the scene after the NY global PrepCom had taken place and the agenda was set? Women involved with each of the three NGOs formed strategies to change the prevailing agenda. Despite the limited success of their efforts in changing the network priorities and the deep-rooted conflicts that surfaced in response to the agenda-setting process, many of the NGOs showed interest in continuing to work together in the future. To a large extent, conflicts were processed constructively even though the parties utilized many competitive tactics. In order to study this issue, the following chapter focuses on the network framing process. By analyzing their struggles to develop strategic frames, information on how the NGOs negotiated their agenda-setting conflicts and attempted to find common ground, is revealed. Studying how NGOs process conflicts among diverse organizations and build agreement on global issues contributes to the understanding of how NGOs develop social infrastructures that facilitate the formation of transnational social movements.

The conflicts that developed reflected unease with the dominant agenda. The women of color involved with WILPF, the members of SWVP, and Madelaine, the Beneath Paradise representative, all felt that their concerns had been marginalized in some way. In some cases, their concern had been named as a priority but the representation of that issue was so different from their own that they felt the issue had not been addressed. There was little discussion of those differences. Conflict escalation was a form of resistance to the leveling of difference (Minh-ha, 1997). Because the NGOs processed the conflicts constructively, the contention arising from the agenda-setting process served to increase understanding of regional, ethnic, racial and ideological differences.

However, in the context of the conferences, declaring difference and exposing inequalities was not enough for the NGOs. Their objectives were to gain support for and build alliances around their issues. As such, their task was very complex. Challenges to the dominant peace agenda in the context of the UN conference were very difficult. Social movement theory characterizes this type of conflict as a strategic framing process, or the struggle to find common meaning. New social meanings are the products of the struggles within social movements—and between them and opponents. Through conflict, NGOs learned more about each other and expanded the possibilities for finding common frames.

One of the main challenges that NGOs face in setting global agendas is to come up with a frame that resonates in diverse cultural and ethnic contexts. Moreover, they compete with other NGOs who are also trying to gain attention for their issues, framed in their own way. Some of the NGOs, particularly an INGO like WILPF, had more resources, experience, access to information, and were supported by dominant cultural norms at the UN making them powerful competitors. Participants' identification as women had drawn them to the same conference to work together but as NGO representatives they competed for resources and for international attention. Research shows that the divisions between newer small grassroots organizations and the larger, older, sometimes more professional NGOs are as volatile as North/South divides (Benchmark Environmental Consulting, 1996).

For some of the NGO delegates at the conferences, the tension arising from the struggle to find common frames triggered deep-rooted conflicts. The conflicts that became visible had long histories; they had gone on for decades, if not centuries, e.g. racism in the North, the civil war in the Sudan, and French colonization of the Pacific Islands. Typically, protracted or deep-rooted conflict is identified as violent conflict between nations or communities over the preservation of cultures and values, such as the armed conflicts in the Middle East and Northern Ireland. Protracted conflict can be distinguished from conflicts over interests, choices and preferences that can be negotiated. Deep-rooted conflict can occur in any relationship where inequality exists and basic needs for identity and participation are frustrated (Burton, 1987). As a result, the conflicts were about more than the particular issue discussed. The power to define, to influence discourse and to shape events was also at stake. Nevertheless, the manifestation of deep-rooted conflicts became a starting point for dialogue among the NGOs.

The following chapter presents the background to each conflict, looks at the NGO responses, and examines the outcomes. The disputes are analyzed using the conceptual tools from social movement theory described below: strategic framing, identity formation, and repertoires of contention. These conceptual tools were developed for studying national movement mobilization. This analysis reinforces the importance of identity formation and strategy to the transnational framing process and reveals successes and failures of various frames in the context of transnational social movements.

Social Movement Tools

Strategic Framing

Strategic framing processes are defined as 'the conscious strategic efforts by groups of people to fashion shared understandings of the world and of themselves that legitimate and motivate collective action' (McAdam et al., 1996, p.6). A master frame, such as the human rights frame, works on a large scale. On a national level, developing a frame that is widely accepted is a lengthy process given the opposition from states, corporations, religious bodies and counter movements that activists encounter. At the transnational level, strategic framing processes are even more difficult. Movements must construct frames that resonate in diverse cultural settings by linking new mobilizing frames with existing cultural perspectives. Each of the NGOs included in my study attempted to frame their agenda in a way that would appeal to the norms and values of conference participants while consistent with their own constituency.

Strategic frames are important to social movements because cycles of protest tend to emerge when movements develop innovative master frames (Snow and Benford, 1992). Cycles of protest can be defined as sequences of collective action (Tarrow, 1983). Mass mobilization may fail, in part, even when structural conditions seem ideal because of the absence of a resonant master frame. Frames organize the experience of movement participants and guide their action by making events or occurrences meaningful (Snow et al., 1986).

Strategic frames are constructed through an interactional process called frame alignment. Frame alignment is the 'linkage of individual and SMO interpretive orientations, such that some set of individual interests, values and beliefs and SMO activities, goals, and ideology are congruent and complementary' (Snow et al., 1986, p.464). Frames must resonate within the movement; in other words, it is essential that a strategic frame relate to existing popular understandings of the target audience (Snow and Benford, 1992). The success of movement depends on maintaining a balance between resonance of the strategic frame with existing political culture and its promise of new opportunities. Frame bridging, a type of frame alignment, involves frame bridging, that is, the linking of new mobilizing frames with existing cultural materials.

Activist identity formation and repertoires of contention or strategies are integral and reciprocal to the process of creating mobilizing frames. Frame alignment is situated within the larger context of collective identity formation (Stoecker, 1995). Social movement organizations align their frames with the orientation or sense of identity of potential participants (Kendrick, 2000). Identities are constructed, reinforced, and transformed by the interactions among movement activists (Hunt and Benford, 1994). However, individual identities are complex and multi-layered, and frames may align with some aspect(s) of individuals' identities but not others. At a transnational level, activist identity formation is effected by globalization processes. Increasing global integration has resulted in increasing personal contact across state boundaries and in transnational communication. As such, transnational activist identity formation is important for transnational frame alignment.

Repertoires of Contention

My research show that activist tactics were integral to frame alignment. Movements can be characterized by the strategies and tactics they utilize, what are referred to as their repertoire of contention. Public education is the strategy most often used by TSMOs (McCarthy, 1997). Social movement analysts have found that movement strategies are contingent upon three variables: framing choices; movement organizational structural configurations; and political opportunity structures (Dalton, 1994; McCarthy et al., 1991).

Activist Identity Formation

Social movement theory has focused on activist identities based on the assumption that the process of identity formation significantly shapes movement mobilization dynamics. Social or collective identity is defined as 'that part of an individual's self-concept which derives from his [sic] knowledge of his membership [in] a social group (or groups) together with the value and emotional significance attached to that membership' (Tajfel, 1982, p.2). As frames, social identities help to define what is right, to identify correct behaviors or attitudes, and to promote certain goals. Social identity is both multifaceted and transient. For example, although some aspects of womanhood are common to all women, the group 'women' includes many sub-groups that may directly contradict one another. Collective identities must be forged and maintained, not taken as a given (Melucci, 1989).

During the course of a conflict, a group's sense of identity in opposition to another group forms and transforms (Kriesberg, 1982). Aspects of social identity evolve and change as a conflict moves in and out of various stages. These changing characteristics include: 1) consciousness of a social identity; 2) salience and solidification of the traits and symbols which accompany it; 3) meaning and centrality of a social identity for group members; and 4) importance of a social identity for security and survival (Kriesberg, 1982). The process of social identity formation and transformation is very complex as it involves the ever-changing context and various layers of conflict and identity.

Specific conflicts cause the significance of the multiple aspects of individual and collective identities to shift. According to Cook-Huffman:

> Social identities are fluid entities which both shift and change and paradoxically serve as static constructs at any given point in a conflict. They become salient and are defined within the conflict while concurrently providing a context and the resources for understanding what is said or what happens (Cook-Huffman, 2000, p.118).

During conflict, the meaning and importance of social identities are constantly negotiated. Although the participants at the FWCW gathered because they identified as women, their identities were multiple and layered. As they came into conflict over the peace agenda, other facets of participants' multiple identities, e.g. indigenous, New Caledonian, black, refugee, became more salient.

When the negotiation process is reciprocal and relatively uncoerced, the shift of social identities may be positive and mutually beneficial for the parties involved. The negotiation process can then be defined as constructive. The conflict becomes destructive when identity needs are belittled and dismissed or violently suppressed (Kriesberg, 1982). Power plays a role in defining social identity; who defines what aspects of a social identity are most relevant? Cross-cutting social categorizations connected to power and influence may serve as basis for distinguishing members who are outside the group (Cook-Huffman, 2000). Disputants may attempt to expand and shape individual's identities in order to provoke and escalate a conflict. This process can lead to positive or negative results.

Positive social identity can be developed through constructive relationships with other groups, as well as through intra-group relations (Williams, 1984). Although individuals value aspects of in-group identity, they may also value relations with members of relevant out-groups. Women are more likely to experience this type of communal identification than men (Skevington and Baker, 1989). Identification based on competition and differentiation from others is 'typically more important for males.'

WILPF

Background of Conflict

WILPF's internal conflict over the issue of racism began in Helsinki, Finland at the WILPF Congress. The conference of approximately 200 was attended primarily by WILPF members but they had made an effort to reach out to non-members, particularly from Southern countries, so that although most of the participants were of European origin, there was a small number of women of color. From the beginning, Geraldine, a key actor in the conflict and a British woman of African descent, felt that she had less power and resources than WILPF members. The only reason she had been able to afford the trip was because she had been awarded a scholarship from WILPF. She took the offer to come to the WILPF Congress and the peace train aware that WILPF's membership was mostly white. From the start, she was afraid that her agenda would be undermined and racism would become invisible.

Geraldine was an experienced activist, particularly in the area of anti-racism. She was a professional organizer with a masters degree from a well-known university in London. She had given many workshops and presentations in her field. Well-informed, she knew where some of the current 'tough spots' were, like the definition of racism in a context where post-modern theory was deconstructing color.

Geraldine did not assume political solidarity with the WILPF women. Within this all-female context, Geraldine strongly identified with the racial aspects of her multi-layered identity. As bell hooks explains:

> Conscious of the privileges white men as well as white women gain as a consequence of racial domination, black women were quick to react to the feminist call for sisterhood by pointing to the contradiction in the idea that we should join with women who exploit us to help liberate them (hooks, 1997, p.400).

Geraldine was open to working with WILPF on particular issues, but she was also prepared to do battle.

Despite her expertise as an activist, Geraldine was not aware that most of the agenda for the Beijing conference had already been set at the preparatory conferences which she had not attended. She assumed that if she could gain the support of a powerful INGO like WILPF, that she could influence the conference agenda through WILPF. Without access to correct information, she also thought that she would have access to government delegates at the FWCW without having gone through the accreditation process. Geraldine felt it was her task to represent the concerns of local and regional black organizations that she had worked with in Britain.

Very quickly, Geraldine found herself in conflict with WILPF over the organization's agenda. As she reflected on her experience in an interview, she made the distinction between racism from a black perspective in contrast to one informed by a white perspective:

> In Helsinki, it was placed on the agenda in a very crude way. It was a debate on racism which was informed by white perspectives, and really there wasn't an attempt to think about black perspectives. It was really a very half-hearted attempt to look at the issues. That left me in position whereby I came into WILPF because of my work around combating racism and because of my experience of looking at that issue then I find myself almost directly in conflict with WILPF because of that.

Although racism was on the WILPF agenda, Geraldine did not feel that her perspective was represented from the very beginning of her contact with WILPF.

Geraldine's perception was based on two conclusions that she formed about WILPF. First, racism was not high on the list of WILPF priorities. She saw a token representation of racism in the literature but she noted little reference to it in the conference discourse. In addition, Geraldine noted that WILPF members assumed that the effects of racism are not as painful as, for example, nuclear radiation, a top priority for the organization. Second, she concluded that the occasional references to racism at the conference were based on a white perspective. Geraldine did not see her black constituency's issues reflected in the WILPF agenda. An agenda that reflected her concerns as a black woman would have dealt with police brutality, immigration and/or citizenship issues. Geraldine did not find what she was searching for on the WILPF agenda and decided to challenge the organization.

The WILPF Congress in Helsinki

Given that Geraldine was traveling alone with few resources under the auspices of a powerful organization she perceived herself to be in conflict with, her first strategy was to try to network and build support for her agenda one-on-one. At an early reception in Helsinki, Geraldine passed around a petition protesting British police brutality in the strangling of a black woman. She was particularly interested in speaking with other women of color/black women present at the Congress. I joined her in a conversation on racism with an African member of WILPF, Georgia, who had been a member and leader in WILPF for many years, and her teenage daughter, Karen. Georgia spoke enthusiastically about WILPF's commitment to taking racism seriously. Specifically, the US branch had organized 'undoing racism' workshops for all of its members. In addition, WILPF USA had formed allies locally with African American groups like the NAACP. The discussion turned to Geraldine's concern about prevailing definitions of ethnic conflict which maintain that racism is not based on color and her fear that confusing ethnic conflict with racism would undermine an anti-racist agenda.

The next day, Geraldine attended a workshop on racism, tribalism, and economics with a small group of young women of color, none of whom she knew previously. Geraldine, Karen, Daba, a WILPF intern in Geneva originally from Senegal, and Jo, a young woman from Hong Kong, had all decided to attend the workshop. The women had connected the evening before and had begun discussions related to race. The workshop was the only one offered on racism and the young women explained afterwards that they had wanted to help out in whatever way they could to make sure that the workshop went well.

Kay, the workshop leader, was a professor in economics at a German university although she originated from the USA. She told me later that she wished she had known that the group of young women of color would be attending—(she would never have offered the workshop given their expertise and standpoint). She felt Geraldine was more qualified than she to lead a workshop on racism. Kay had offered to lead a workshop on racism because no one else had taken the initiative. Her past experience with the mostly white WILPF membership had led her to believe that she would not encounter much resistance to her ideas. The majority of the workshop participants were white Europeans or European Americans although there were a couple of women from Korea and the Philippines.

Key to Kay's presentation was the term 'otherness' and her interpretation of tribalism. She showed how Germans created 'the other' based on bloodlines or German lineage, similar to tribes in Africa, and argued that economic factors can eliminate 'isms' like racism, e.g. middle class and upper middle class people of color do not experience racism. She added that color becomes less important when ethnicity, another form of 'otherism,' comes into play.

Angry, Geraldine confronted Kay. She made it clear that she disagreed and described her frame, explaining to the workshop participants that she defined racism based on color. Color had been used to classify people during colonial times, she said, and it continued to be a way of separating people when 'the pie got smaller.' Racism was not just another form of 'othering' or prejudice. She disagreed that economic status 'changed' racism, insisting that money can 'make it easier' but does not take away racism. Daba spoke as well, saying that tribalism was a uniquely African concept and she did not think it could be applied to the German situation as the circumstances were quite different. Furthermore, she said, with her voice raised, defining tribes in a negative light to illustrate the prejudice behind German lineage was insulting to African culture.

The participants discussed these issues for the remainder of the workshop session but Geraldine confided in me that evening that she had not felt heard. It was very discouraging to her to have to begin the conversation by defining racism, which seemed to her a basic and obvious concept. She changed her strategy.

The next day, the workshop continued—but under the leadership of the group of women of African descent who had attended the day before. The small group decided that they needed to educate the workshop participants about their view of racism and took over the leadership of the workshop. Kay assented. Geraldine, assisted mostly by Karen and Daba, talked and conducted discussions on topics like tools of racism, forms of individual racism, assimilation vs. anti-racism, immigration and the difference between prejudice and racism. Geraldine introduced the phrase 'fortress Europe' to illustrate her points about the difficulty of obtaining citizenship for blacks in Europe. Some of the participants wanted to talk about anti-racist strategies and collaboration with women of color, but Geraldine insisted that they needed to understand racism in its various forms before they could strategize.

During the latter half of the session, Geraldine framed her point of view as a critique of postmodernism. She talked about how racism was 'off the agenda' because race had been deconstructed. Postmodernism, she claimed, beaks down claims of institutional oppression so that only individual stories are legitimate. As an activist, she tried to hang on to collective experience. However, according to Geraldine, the concept of ethnic conflict has made racism invisible. When concept of ethnic conflict is applied, 'there is just this dispute or that dispute,' and racism is no longer discussed. Then she went on to talk about specific examples of racism in Europe related to immigration and colonialization. By giving concrete examples of racism based on color, she hoped to persuade the group that her point of view was correct.

After Geraldine's and her colleagues' presentations, Kay restated her position on othering and tribalism. The ensuing conversation became more and more heated. Geraldine repeated her frame, stating again that racism is based on color. When Kay described tribalism in a European context again, Karen interrupted, saying she had 'had it!' and left the room, crying. Daba and Geraldine followed and did not return. Karen's walk-out was a powerful act that immediately disrupted the workshop and focused the group's attention on the young women of color in a way that their debate had not.

Later, Geraldine and the other women in her group escalated the conflict, drawing it into a public arena. During plenary reports on the workshops, Geraldine, Daba, a young European American woman and I gave a report on the workshop. (Geraldine had approached me, asking me to be an ally by supporting their statements publicly. I agreed.) Kay conceded her authority as workshop leader to the group. In her statement, Geraldine stated her frame, 'racism is based on color,' and implied that what had happened in the workshop was racist. After their plenary report, the group got many responses from the crowd. Some of them they described as racist, others as supportive. Geraldine mentioned to me that she had been called a 'naughty girl' for speaking out. (By the end of the week, the woman who had called her this had apologized.)

The small group of women of color continued to build support for their frame, particularly among the young women at the WILPF Congress. The other young women attending the conference were particularly distressed about what had happened and discussed the conflict at length. During a parallel seminar set up for the younger participants (the Gertrude Baer Seminar), Geraldine built up her allies among the young women. The group managed to reach agreement on a definition of racism proposed by Geraldine. It read, 'Racism is an international system of power that places one group superior and another inferior based on color.' Ellen, the former WILPF secretary general, visited the seminar briefly and listened sympathetically to what the conflict was about.

Next Geraldine and the young women in the Gertrude Baer Seminar reintroduced her frame to the WILPF plenary. The group proposed to the plenary that this definition be written into WILPF's mission statement. This time the WILPF leadership actively supported it. The WILPF plenary session debated the acceptance of the resolution into the mission statement. A number of speakers resisted the idea, suggesting it be tabled for further discussion. Others objected to the frame, complaining that it did not speak to the Jewish situation. Finally, Ellen made an impassioned speech supporting the proposal and the plenary voted in favor of the definition.

In the meantime, using the frame 'the black agenda,' Geraldine tried to put her constituency's issues on the WILPF agenda. It was proving to be a more difficult task than gaining acceptance for the definition of racism. Geraldine had arranged to meet with Anita to discuss the PfA, a meeting that I attended. Her questions for Anita included how could WILPF help her to put Black women's issues on the FWCW agenda? And was racism on the WILPF agenda? Anita responded by explaining that, at the FWCW, no wording would be added to the PfA. The delegates would only discuss whether or not to accept words that had been bracketed for further consideration. She added that Geraldine, representing a non-accredited NGO, would not have access to the government conference. Anita then stated that WILPF covers only peace issues, because nobody else was doing that work but she would support issues on racism in whatever way possible.

After this meeting, Geraldine told me she was 'devastated' by what Anita had to say. She felt that blacks were excluded from the beginning. She would have no access to the government conference. It seemed to her that although white women were marginalized, they still had some access. She thought her best strategy would be to band together with other black women's groups.

Later, Geraldine attempted to disrupt the plenary session on her own in order to gain attention for the black agenda. Geraldine had followed the WILPF procedure for plenary proposals. However, her petition protesting police brutality was not printed up with the rest of the proposals for the WILPF plenary as she had been promised. Geraldine commented to me that 'our agenda gets lost.' She tried to intervene on stage as the proposals were covered in the plenary hall but she was told there was not enough time. Finally, a Philippine woman, who was on stage with the women presiding, stood up and read her petition aloud. Geraldine maintained that because she was Philippine, she had understood the importance of black issues. Geraldine was not as successful as an individual in disrupting the plenary as she had been with a small group.

After a WILFP plenary speech on building a new world order, Geraldine adopted a world order framework. Geraldine maintained that if WILPF was going to build a new world order then it must address racism:

> In Helsinki, we had a debate on racism which was supposed to inform a broader debate about building a new and secure, dependable world or new world order and clearly if you're going to work towards building that world then clearly racism is a priority issue because it's an international system of racism which places the majority of world's people in the kind of social, economic, political position that they are in. So it's really important that that be on the agenda.

WILPF members did not disagree, but at the same time, this framework did not seem to generate action.

The Peace Train

The setting changed dramatically as the women attending the WILPF Congress boarded the peace train to China and racism continued to be a contentious issue. The WILPF leadership had anticipated that the women on board would want to share information and discuss particular issues so they arranged for the train to carry two extra train cars to be used as workshop sites. The leadership had also chosen a WILPF member to coordinate requests for workshops on the train and set up a schedule. Discussions around racism took place in the small group workshops and one-on-one, because there were few, if any, possibilities for large groups to gather during the journey on the train.

During the train ride, WILPF leadership, especially Bettina, initiated and developed proactive strategies for dealing with the conflict rather than just responding as they had in Helsinki. Using their organizational power, WILPF made sure that there were many opportunities to discuss the topic of racism. WILPF's leadership encouraged Geraldine and others to give workshops on racism on the train. Bettina made a point of attending the workshop on fascism and racism led by Barrie, an African American woman, and stood by Geraldine's side to support her statements. Geraldine presented her workshop on racism in the European Union. An African American woman, Angela, led a workshop on bridge-building between women of different races. In addition, a women of color support group met regularly during the three week trip.

Not only had the setting changed but the players changed, too. Although the train participants were mostly white, many women of color from around the world, who had not been present for the WILPF Congress, now joined the peace train. Geraldine was no longer singled out because of her level of leadership, commitment, and expertise in the area of racism.

Conflict around racial issues continued to surface. For example, WILPF provided train passengers with the opportunity to speak about their regional concerns at the meetings with local women during the train stop-overs. At each stop, WILPF leadership asked women representing different regions of the world to speak on the panels addressing the women at the public forums organized by the local women's groups. WILPF varied the panel representation at each location. On one occasion, Angela was invited to be one of the speakers at the Parliament in Odessa, Ukraine, one of the train stops. This gave her the opportunity to gain visibility for her agenda and perspective.

Angela delivered what I thought was a finely crafted speech. She spoke about life as an African American woman in the US. However, as we left the Parliament building, I heard quite a few angry comments from white women about both the length and content of Angela's speech. A number of women, particularly the young women, were then upset at how their friend Angela was treated. In an interview, Sonali, a young British woman of Indian heritage, defended Angela. Sonali was surprised by the racism and cultural domination she had experienced on the train:

> And then there's the kind of ignorance like Angela's speech. Now it was long, I admit. But it was a very direct, to the point speech about life for a woman of color in the United States or any country that is predominantly white but especially in the United States. And I heard things like what an egotistical women she is. How dare she talk about the United States like that in a foreign country. How dare she, how can she go off saying things like that about white people or her society. How dare she take so much time. Who does she think she is. Things like that!
>
> One person says to me, she was talking to me, 'she's preaching to the converted.' And I was just like, and a lot of these comments came from people that gave me my scholarship and I was just like...So I got back on my bus, that was to take us somewhere else, and I just started crying because I just did not know how I was supposed to respond when I get home and have to work with these women that can't even acknowledge their own inherent role [in a racist society].

Given her financial reliance on the white women she was in conflict with, Sonali did not continue to confront them with her perspective on the significance of Angela's talk or on their response to her speech.

WILPF members wanted to give Angela the chance to speak and appreciated the diversity that she represented. Part of the WILPF anti-racist agenda was to give voice and visibility to African Americans. However, once a 'black' perspective became clear in a public setting, it was a source of conflict. Angela's speech escalated the conflict around racism by heightening the difference between herself and her white US compatriots.

Angela challenged the assumptions and values of some white WILPF members. Her statements made some of the women uncomfortable because, on the one hand, it appealed to their sense of social justice but, on the other hand, it prioritized racism in a way that challenged their value system. Sonali gave an example of how Angela had questioned a WILPF member's priorities earlier in on the journey:

> Like one lady said to me about Angela...that she doesn't think Angela is sympathetic towards the people that we have been visiting. And I said oh I don't think so cause Angela is the one who always asks the question so how can we help you? Right? And so this woman said well you know we came out of this workshop where the women had been telling us about Chernoble victims and children of the Chernoble victims and how its really hopeless and I was telling Angela that our problems at home seem miniscule compared to the problems that they have here and Angela disagreed with me. And I was like well I do, too, cause our problems at home are just as big as the problems here. Our children our dying! And this woman said, but at least in the United States they have a possibility of bringing themselves out of it. I was just sitting, I was just kind of like, she did not say that, she did not make that comment, you know?

The woman Sonali spoke of felt that nuclear issues were more important than racism in the USA. When Angela contradicted the woman's viewpoint, she was characterized as selfish for making her priorities and her racial identification known. This encounter illustrates again her anti-racist agenda is different from a 'black' perspective.

Within the diverse context of the peace train, identities continued to splinter making multi-layered identities and loyalties evident. Once the peace train was underway, separate spaces formed with support groups for women of color. However, deciding who qualified as a 'woman of color' was not a simple matter. Conflicts arose over the separate spaces. A number of women of color were shut out by other support group members. They did not qualify because they were not 'black enough'. It was the women who were racially mixed that got caught in the complexity of 'identity'.

Two women, both mixed racially, confided in me their hurt that they did not feel included in the group. One woman from the Netherlands told me that she was told she was 'not black enough' to be a member of the group. Confused and angry, she explained to me that she led women of color activities and support groups in the Netherlands. She went over her ethnic background with me, claiming at least five different heritages, one of which was Caucasian. Jo, who also had mixed racial heritage—Chinese and Italian American, was very hurt that she had not felt accepted in the women of color support group. She cried as she concluded that she was also 'not black enough'. Tonya, on the other hand, was frustrated that as a Guatemalan Indian she was grouped in with Hispanics from Central and South America. She explained to me that she identified herself as indigenous and did not want to be seen as Spanish.

These disagreements about racial identity remained individual complaints. None of the women mentioned above raised their concerns in a public setting. All of them spoke to me one-on-one about their feelings. Perhaps they felt quite isolated in this context. Nor did they wish to risk alienating their companions on the train.

Tensions around racism continued to mount and WILPF leadership responded once again, setting up a dialogue session in a park at a short stop-over in the Ukraine. The leadership of this group meeting included a couple of European American WILPF members and an Indian professor who facilitated the meeting. During the session, the train passengers had an opportunity to talk about some of the reasons why they were uncomfortable traveling with each other, racism being one of the main issues. Some of the women, like Angela and Sonali, were confrontational in this setting; others, like Geraldine, tried to be more diplomatic. Although the conflicts were not resolved, I had the impression that quite a few women thought the community meeting was helpful.

Finally, toward the end of the journey to China, the WILPF leadership, specifically Bettina, initiated meetings to expand WILPF's political priorities. Bettina invited a multi-cultural/multi-racial group to come together and define key areas that had emerged as the result of discussions on the peace train. Geraldine was particularly pleased with this strategy on the part of WILPF. According to

Geraldine, 'If WILPF is to rise to the task of building a new world order, they must restructure their priorities. Racism is the first part of that (restructuring).'

FWCW, Beijing

Once the train arrived in Beijing for the conferences, the setting and the actors changed again significantly. In the context of the NGO Forum, there were thousands of women from around the globe and white women were in the minority. Each day, there were hundreds of events, activities, or forums for the participants to chose from. It was nearly impossible to address the conference as a whole. In an effort to reach groups larger than the workshop forum, the most common event, some women would organize demonstrations and march across the Forum grounds. When the government conference began in Beijing those women who had access to the FWCW had to choose between Hairou and Beijing.

Although women of color were now the majority (Geraldine told me how much at home she felt now that she was part of the majority), some of the Northern women of African descent felt that racism was not on the agenda at the conference. These women tried to raise the level of conflict, bringing their issues and frustration to public places. They networked with other NGO representatives at the Forum to build up their power and resources. Geraldine reported to me that a powerful caucus of women of color, two hundred strong, had started meeting together. At one point they took over one of the tents, stopping the designated program to carry on their own. It seemed to me that this group of women did not feel at home in the spaces created by/for their white compatriots, nor did they feel at home in the spaces where their people of origin—mostly African—gathered. According to Geraldine, the group wanted their own 'women of color' tent. Despite her frustration, meeting with so many exciting, powerful women to form their own space was an empowering experience. Geraldine left for Britain four days after she had arrived in Beijing.

Sue, an African American woman on the WILPF USA staff, approached me to talk about her perspective on the racial tensions. I had met Sue briefly in New York at the 1995 PrepCom and did not see her again until we met in Beijing. Sue was angry that racism had been cut from the PfA except for three references. She was also disgusted that the daily NGO Forum newspaper carried so little coverage on racism after she had worked closely with them. As a result, she and other US women of color were working with the US government delegation to form an alternate group. The US delegation included an African American, Asian American and a Chicana whom they attempted to meet with separately from the white delegates in order to strengthen their lobbying power and make their objectives visible. Given their level of frustration at the NGO Forum, this group of women organized around their identity as US women of color and appealed to US government delegates along racial lines.

Some women of color made a statement in the NGO Briefing toward the end of the conference that they were 'outraged' that racism had been cut from the PfA. Sue mentioned to me that they knew the PfA was impossible to influence at this point. In response to the lack of attention to racism in the PfA, Sue and other US women of color had revised and shortened the Declaration so that it could be used later in the US. The group also wrote up their own separate set of objectives.

Once the women arrived in Beijing, organizational change within WILPF was no longer the avenue for gaining attention for their agendas. Sue and Geraldine centered their work on the PfA and gathering support among NGO representatives. However, I asked Sue if she had appealed to WILPF for support of her concerns around racism. Sue was discouraged by the inconsistency of WILPF's support. She said that she had spoken to Ellen and other WILPF leaders a number of times. They would 'say one thing and do another,' she said. In her opinion, the organization had to 'go beyond the rhetoric of structural violence.'

Outcomes

Geraldine felt positive about the changes she and the small group of women of color had been able to make within WILPF as an organization. They had 'started with nothing' and now she felt WILPF recognized the importance of looking at racism and making initial changes that needed to be made in that area. Racism was beginning to 'creep up on the agenda.' They had changed the WILPF mission statement and started some rich conversations on a complex subject.

Geraldine reported to me in an interview that she felt the WILPF leadership had in some ways dealt with the racial conflict well. Most important, they did not run away from the conflict. Once tension rose, the leadership demonstrated a willingness to deal with the issues rather than covering it up. Ellen's strong support for their proposal to include a definition of racism based on color in the mission statement had been critical for the proposal's success. To Daba and Karen, the acceptance of their definition of racism by the assembly and the visible support of the WILPF leadership was very meaningful. However, Geraldine pointed out that the leadership was also responsible for 'the fact that racism was not on the agenda in any real way.'

In addition to some optimism about initial changes, Geraldine also felt somewhat cynical. The progress that had been made within the organization was made at great personal expense to her and she wondered aloud whether this type of discussion would be maintained once the trip was over.

When the FWCW had ended, I asked Bettina in an interview about her reflections on the conflict around racism and the ensuing dialogue. She responded:

> And with the political demands, I mean, you know, I haven't been through all the workshop reports but of what I heard, there were good workshops on the train. And we will do our political work and follow this up, especially on racism because more detailed suggestions than we were able to get at the Congress because of this incident there. So that is something which we can integrate in our work. But WILPF did not have a bad program that was now changed completely by the train, it was our usual development.
> Anna: They were issues you were already dealing with?
> Bettina: Yes, fascism and racism.

From Bettina's perspective, the conversations that took place during the workshops contributed to the development of WILPF as an organization. They deepened the understanding of an issue, racism, that was already a priority.

Discussion

The Northern women of color, particularly Geraldine, used tactics and frames that were strongly identity based. Many of them came alone as single delegates for their NGOs so their first step was to build up a small network of women of color. They used confrontation, often public confrontation, as well as disruption of planned activities. In addition, the women tried education and persuasive tactics in the many workshops they led or attended. At times, they separated themselves from the white women, forming support groups and caucuses. Finally, they went through the proper channels set up to introduce policy proposals. At each stage, they—Geraldine in particular—felt that the success and/or failure of their strategy was tied to their identity. That is, their ideas were accepted or opposed because of their identities.

The women of color used identity to gather support for their agenda, trying to call other women of color to unite around a common agenda. However, identities fluctuated as the women moved from one setting to another. In the setting of the WILPF Congress in Helsinki, women of color were a minority and some of them pulled together around common interests. On the train, many Southern women joined the group and the phrase 'women of color' became more complex, even a source of tension. At the NGO Forum '95, women of color were in the majority but within this diverse, global context, the Northern women of color found themselves identifying with their regional and national identities.

Geraldine and her allies used several different frames for her agenda, the most successful of which was anti-racism. In the context of WILPF, it was effective because WILPF leadership and members were committed to anti-racism, so that when Geraldine spoke of racism in public settings, it got the attention of the organization's members who then could be embarrassed or persuaded to make time for the issue. Many of the WILPF members and leadership saw themselves as anti-racist activists committed to eliminating racism, so that when Geraldine or others implied that WILPF actions might be racist, they tended to respond.

However, when their audience was more diverse and their target more diffuse, the anti-racism framework became more problematic. In China, the women of color lost interest in WILPF, one NGO among many, and it became much less clear who their adversary was. When the Northern women were dominant/in the majority, Geraldine's frame provided some connection among the 'diaspora,' e.g. specifically Northern and Southern women of color. When Southern women were in the majority, anti-racism was no longer effective as a strategic frame. Racism was not referred to within the context of the peace agenda. My informants felt the topic of racism had all but disappeared. I observed that in other global regions, racism was framed as imperialism, colonization, war, lack of health care or development.

Geraldine's slogan, 'Racism is based on color,' was her most effective frame. Although defining racism was very complex, Geraldine created a slogan that was clear and simple. The slogan worked to some extent—it was accepted by the WILPF plenary for their mission statement even though it was not a comfortable fit. There were so many different understandings of racism and the concepts around it—race, ethnicity, prejudice—that the WILPF members still disagreed among themselves as to the definition of racism. However, Geraldine was successful in initiating a rich discussion of issues that were very important to her and her constituency.

Geraldine attempted to educate WILPF members about academic debates around postmodernism but had little success in rallying support for changing an academic discourse with which they were completely unfamiliar. The new world order framework, on the other hand, was so familiar that it did not propose anything new to the WILPF membership. They simply nodded their assent.

The black agenda frame was not as effective but changing the agenda may have been a more difficult task than changing the mission statement. First, it was a new frame. Many of the WILPF members never seemed to understand the difference between anti-racism from a white perspective and anti-racism from a black perspective. Unfortunately, Geraldine was not successful in developing a frame that communicated the nuances successfully to her audience. Second, by framing her agenda as the 'black agenda', she may have reinforced a perspective that her issues were local and/or identity-based, meaning that her frame had little international appeal. If she had framed the issues within, for example, a human rights abuse framework, a frame that was very prominent at the FWCW, she might have had more success.

Third, although Geraldine explained her priorities in her workshops in detail, in other settings, she would refer broadly to 'the black agenda,' leaving the listener curious and perhaps guilty but uninformed. She had coined the phrase 'fortress Europe' to illustrate her points about the difficulty of obtaining citizenship for blacks in Europe, but without a detailed explanation, 'fortress Europe' had little meaning. Forming a slogan that highlighted a few of her priorities, such as police brutality, citizenship, and economic justice might have made clear to her audience which issues were important to her constituency.

SWVP

Background

SWVP faced unique challenges attending conferences along with government and NGO delegates with whom their people were at war. They developed strategies and frames accordingly. In general, SWVP members did their best to de-escalate conflict. Their people were at war; the situation had already escalated to the point of violence. SWVP members tried not to fan the fire in order to lower the tensions enough so that dialogue could take place. Instead of protesting publicly, SWVP leaders avoided confrontation or making agreements that compromised their principles or goals. They focused on finding solutions for long-term problems rather than becoming caught up in the hatred.

The northern Sudanese delegates disliked the southern women criticizing the Sudanese government.[1] They were also uncomfortable with the southern women representing themselves and their own interests. SWVP's very presence as a southern Sudanese NGO was a reminder to the northern women that many Southerners were demanding self-determination. However, the Sudanese government and northern Sudanese delegates did not represent the concerns of SWVP such as ending the civil war, self-determination, or opposition to Islamic governance (Sharia law). SWVP insisted on the right to represent themselves and quietly went about speaking on panels and in workshops at the conferences.

The Sudanese government delegates and some NGO delegates often tried to discredit SWVP and other southern Sudanese refugees who demanded the right to speak. During the conference in Senegal, at a meeting with a representative of the UN High Commission on Refugees (UNHCR), a refugee from southern Sudan complained that the Sudanese government delegate had told her she could not speak to the assembly because she was a refugee. From the government's perspective, anyone who had left the country was a threat to the state unless they were government employees (Garang Thieu Juac, conversation with author 27 June 2002). She asked the UNHCR representative, 'How can refugee women be heard at this UN conference?' to which UNHCR had no reply. If, as Sudanese refugees, they were able to obtain the proper papers to attend the conference, they then faced government and military delegates representing the state, who had difficulty even acknowledging their existence, much less allowing them to speak at the government conference. A UN agency like UNHCR had little power to intervene.

Some of the Northern women used their power to discredit SWVP presentations and to cajole them into making agreements based on northern terms. The SWVP was a small group of women far outnumbered by northern Sudanese attending the conferences. In addition, the northern women had the backing of the Sudanese state. In fact, given the control of the government over the women, they had little choice but to follow the party line. Some of the northern women were interested in speaking with their southern colleagues about peace. However, their strategy was to develop a peace agreement with SWVP based on the terms of the state.

SWVP members developed their strategies for dealing with conflict in response to northern Sudanese provocation. They created three frames to reach out to the conference participants: a just peace, self-determination, and conflict resolution. SWVP members used their presentations on panels and in workshops, the meetings they attended, and talks with the media and individuals to introduce their frames. SWVP's main goals as an organization were to end the violence in their country and to establish the right to self-determination for their people. At the conferences, they hoped to gain international support for and involvement in their peacemaking efforts. SWVP specifically targeted Western and African NGOs that they thought

[1] For the rest of this section on conflict between the Sudanese women, North refers to northern Sudan and South refers to southern Sudan.

might help them in the peace process. In addition, SWVP attempted to set up dialogue with northern Sudanese women who were also interested in an end to civil war.

Senegal

The following incidents illustrate SWVP's strategy of de-escalation and the frames they adopted in Senegal. I returned to the peace tent after an event to find some of the SWVP women very upset. I asked what was happening. Lucia explained to me with a raised voice that the Sudanese government delegation claimed they did not need to negotiate with the southern Sudanese women because the President had announced that day that they had almost gotten rid of all the Blacks (southern Sudanese). I was shocked and confused but Lucia brought it up again in her interview:

> Actually we got the message even in Dakar now that the government says the Blacks remain very few and soon they will get rid of them. Their objective is to get out of the Black color in the Sudan.
> Anna: They said that here at this conference?
> Lucia: Yes, they said this in this conference and no respond, no reaction because we are here to make peace, to talk peace. We are not government delegation and we don't have access. And we don't want to confront ourselves but we want to address the real issues and these are some of the practical issues many people have here in this tent.

This incident illustrates the intense hatred and mistrust between the women. Lucia clearly stated that SWVP did not wish to confront the northern delegates who had restated the government's policy of genocide. Avoiding confrontation meant they were making 'peace'. They preferred to focus their attention on practical solutions for ending the war rather than grappling with the hatred.

SWVP presented their program a number of times on panels of peacemakers selected by the peace tent organizers. These panels attracted fairly diverse audiences including northern Sudanese. Each time SWVP spoke in this setting, they used a 'just peace' frame. SWVP focused on how women had been silenced for 40 years during the conflict and emphasized the following needs: to have voice, particularly through the media; to identify the constraints of women's participation in the peace process; and to train women leaders in peacemaking. They called for peace with justice and spoke about the suffering of the displaced. SWVP finished by explaining their activities, which included a newsletter, workshops, peacekeeping activities, as well as cultural and traditional conflict resolution in order to promote peace at a local level. They supported a non-violent approach to peace. The SWVP speaker framed her presentation in terms of peacemaking and carefully avoided inflammatory language.

On one occasion, after the SWVP spoke about their situation in southern Sudan, a man from northern Sudan, a government delegate, spoke in disagreement. The male government delegate was most likely sent to carefully observe and control the responses of the northern Sudanese women (Garang Thieu Juac, conversation with author 27 June 2002). He claimed that for the past five years, southern Sudan had been exempt from the Sharia Law, a major source of contention in the civil war. In his opinion, the rebels and their demands for self-determination were to blame for the failure of the peace talks. Next he pointed out what progress women had made under the government, naming a southern Sudanese woman who was a governor and the female minister of peace who was also from southern Sudan. The government delegate stressed the need to be honest and sincere, implying that SWVP had not been. Then he noted that the 'few people talking about self-determination were enjoying life outside the country,' referring to the SWVP members who were refugees.

SWVP members did not confront him but as soon as he had finished, an angry woman who identified herself as from the Sudan, spoke up. She said that she would like to believe that the government of the Sudan was working hard for peace. However, the President has said that the way to end the war is to kill people. In the name of Islam, he imported guns to exterminate the people of the South. In her opinion, no country wanted Sharia Law because it made Africans fight. She had been forced to leave the country because she had talked about peace and her life had been threatened. She called for a 'real peace, not silence.' The governors the speaker had mentioned were appointed to deceive the people. She claimed they had no people to govern. She ended her statement, voice raised and face red, saying the southern Sudanese want a referendum to decide for themselves.

The tension level was high and the facilitator took charge saying it was better to talk and not to keep things down. She did not discourage disagreement. However, again, the SWVP did not respond. It appeared that SWVP was trying to avoid tension. Not only did they not answer the accusations and counter-arguments but they were not the ones to raise the issue of self-determination.

My conversations with northern Sudanese women interested in making peace made clear why SWVP chose to frame their appeal using the word peace. The northern Sudanese women saw themselves as peacemakers. Furthermore, even though they did not bring up a 'just' peace themselves, some type of confederation was more palatable than a separate state. For instance, I met and talked with a northern Sudanese woman, Zachara, who attended the peace caucus off and on during the global PrepCom in New York 1995. As I mentioned earlier in the text, SWVP members were not present at this PrepCom. Zachara, the president of the Sudanese Women's General Union, spoke extensively about the importance of peace in her country. The Sudanese Women's General Union is the only officially recognized women's organization in the Sudan. The peace office, a branch of her large organization, negotiated with different factions, worked with displaced women and children, and promoted a culture of peace.

Zachara was particularly proud of how they had persuaded women in a particular village to become peacemakers. She told the story of how the women would sing songs that 'are very effective socially.' After the death of a young man during a fight between two tribes, the women had sung songs of revenge. Another man was killed and the singers sang that the man murdered was an elder. However, when members of her organization had shown these women how useful and effective they could be for peace, the women began to change their tunes that in turn reversed the situation. They sang ballads for peace instead of for revenge.

Later, in Beijing, I met Sayida, a leader in the women's section of the Sudanese People's Liberation Army, the northern Sudanese army which is supported by the Sudanese state. She felt that, as mothers, it was the duty of women to protect their families. She showed me a picture that she identified as victims of the war in Bosnia and said that it was the responsibility of women to see to it that this would never happen in the Sudan. She also pointed to a photo of the peace initiatives that the women's section of the army had participated in. They had not been successful but she stated very clearly that they were for peace. I asked her before leaving if she knew of the SWVP to which her answer was negative. Both of these northern Sudanese women saw themselves as peacemakers and responded to the idea of women bringing about peace in the Sudan.

During the conference in Senegal, many of the women speaking in the peace tent spoke of African women as peacemakers. They maintained that as women, as mothers, as educators, they held together the fabric of African society and were therefore better peacemakers than men. SWVP seemed to identify with this rhetoric. At the conference, they joined women peace activists from many African nations to form a federation of women's peace movements. Northern Sudanese women were not present at the meetings during which the federation was founded. Lucia reported later that forming the federation was the highlight of the conference for them.

SWVP's just peace frame contrasted sharply with the second frame—self-determination. In a UN radio interview, Rachel emphasized the injustices committed towards her people that justified a separate state. She explained to the interviewer that Northerners and Southerners were 'completely different people' in terms of race, culture and religion. Since most of the development and the seat of the government was in the North, the South felt that they had been left behind. According to Rachel, 'we were made into second class citizens.' Furthermore, the South was not consulted about what was happening when independence came to the Sudan. The Islamic Sharia Law was imposed on her people and a large number of Southern people suffered. 'Their legs were amputated. Women were flogged in public, they were fined, they were killed,' Rachel explained graphically.

Rachel maintained that it was becoming increasingly difficult for the two parts of the country to live together:

> So we feel that it's better instead of crying for unity, which is not for the benefit of the people of south Sudan in particular because the war is raging in the area of south Sudan. We would like our people in south Sudan to be given the right to choose what type of state they want so that they are free. So we want a democratic solution to the problem so that the south Sudan can go its own way if its people so choose.

SWVP was advocating a referendum on self-determination for the people of southern Sudan. Rachel emphasized the need for democratic process in determining the fate of her people.

Beijing

During the NGO Forum '95, SWVP members changed their strategy. Again, northern Sudanese women attacked SWVP publicly for calling attention to their concerns. This time, however, SWVP called for conflict resolution sessions between the Sudanese women, north and south. Instead of calling public attention to the attacks of their northern sisters, SWVP made public their conflict resolution attempts in an effort to get help from international NGOs represented in the peace tent.

The conflict erupted in the African regional tent. The northern Sudanese women were upset that the southern Sudanese women had taken the stage in the African tent and had spoken as black Sudanese. They had told SWVP publicly that they did not think it was appropriate to show that the Sudan is a diverse country. 'But that's how it is!' Lucia exclaimed, 'We are black.' Apparently, some African women had offered to help their Sudanese sisters, but neither the facilitator nor the northern women had showed up at the appointed time.

Lucia announced to the women gathered in the peace tent (they were mostly African, attending reports from African peace activists) that the next day SWVP would hold a conflict resolution session. 'You were there in the African tent,' she appealed to the audience, 'You saw what happened.' When Lucia returned to her seat, she asked me personally to attend the conflict resolution meeting. Lucia made an open invitation to non-nationals, hoping to gain international support and involvement.

SWVP met with women from northern Sudan for conflict resolution sessions three times during the NGO Forum. Each time they announced the sessions publicly in the peace tent and invited everyone to come. During the session that I attended, the participants were almost entirely northern Sudanese. Few, if any non-nationals participated.

The conflict resolution meeting I attended in some ways fueled the conflict. During the session many of the northern women talked of the need for peace in the Sudan. They spoke eloquently about how women were naturally good peacemakers because they were mothers. Women were better peacemakers than men, the northern women agreed among themselves. Rachel, irritated, pushed for concrete proposals. She called for a just peace. In response, a male government representative present fueled Rachel's anger by undermining her credibility. He insinuated that Rachel had no right to speak since she was no longer in the country, and that she had left the Sudan of her own free will. Rachel confronted the male delegate, saying that she was upset that he said some refugees were just having fun outside of the country. The northern women tried to smooth over the conflict, denying that the minister had said anything that Rachel had accused him of. At the end of the session, someone summarized the proposals suggested, mentioning first the need to address the UN, and second, the decision to write a letter to the Sudanese government and the opposition, which would be delivered by her excellency, the minister for peace. The group decided to meet a third time.

This meeting was very frustrating for SWVP; Rachel told me afterwards how angry she was. There was much Rachel could have said to incite both the delegate and the other women whom she felt were insincere. Nevertheless, she restrained herself, criticizing the male delegate only for his personal jab at her as a refugee. In this context, SWVP stuck to their non-confrontative strategy of calling for a just peace and peace proposals. However, I learned later that the SWVP leadership had refused to sign the peace letter that the northern women had produced. The signed peace letter would have been a coup for the northern women, particularly for those employed by the state. However, SWVP did not agree to their terms and had left China without signing the letter.

The SWVP-initiated conflict resolution contrasted sharply with another Sudanese mediation session I attended that took place during a peace caucus meeting at the FWCW. In this case, the southern Sudanese refugee told a story of human rights abuse that she must have known would infuriate the northern Sudanese women present. She said her daughter had been kidnapped and sold into slavery. The refugee did not monitor her language carefully as SWVP had. A fight broke out that grabbed the attention of the peace caucus members. In the context of this international meeting, a team of women from four different countries formed spontaneously and offered to help the women out with their differences. The international team made sure that the northern women did not dominate or intimidate the southern Sudanese woman and the conversation was much more frank than the SWVP conflict resolution session.

In addition to the conflict resolution sessions, SWVP gave several workshops at the NGO Forum '95. I attended one of the last workshops they offered. The subject was genocide. Rachel showed a video on human rights violations and the Nuba who were being killed off or relocated. Rachel also reinforced the need for a separate state. The workshop was not attended by the northern Sudanese women.

Outcomes

SWVP members were particularly pleased with the results of their participation in the African Regional Conference. Lucia, in an interview, spoke about her satisfaction with SWVP participation:

> Up to today, Monday, the 21st, I feel that we have spoken enough and we have done something. Our objective was to see that action must be taken. Our action panel has been done yesterday. We formed African Women's Peace movement and we set up our center which is networking for peace and we put it we must cooperate and collaborate with Femnet. Femnet is coordinating all the NGO women's activities in Africa and outside Africa. We feel that that is a place that our voice, our values could be strongly channeled outside and inside. And we formed, the women's peace movement formed a committee for the grassroots networking. This is based on the countries who have been here for peace and we made very specific recommendations and made objectives and activities.

Lucia implied that she and the other SWVP members had felt heard, had contributed to the formation of an important coalition, had made their proposals, and had generally followed through on their objectives.

Eventually, SWVP's strategy made an impression on WILPF leadership, as they had hoped. Although WILPF members did not attend SWVP workshops or the conflict resolution sessions the Sudanese women set up in Beijing, they noticed the effort the Sudanese women were making to reconcile their differences. WILPF made sure that SWVP had space in the peace tent to conduct their conflict resolution meetings even though many groups were competing for that space. By the end of the conference, the WILPF leadership was interested in working with SWVP. They spoke about a desire to maintain contacts with women from Africa. Ellen, who was moved by the reconciliation efforts of the Sudanese women, suggested that WILPF organize a peace mission to the Sudan.

As a result of their participation in the conferences, SWVP was also able to make some contacts with women from northern Sudan. SWVP and some of the northern Sudanese women seemed to have a strong desire for cooperation but a great deal of mistrust. In addition, the northern women talking about peace in the Sudan appeared to be operating in different circles than the SWVP. When I inquired, some of the women were aware of each other's NGOs but none of them had much contact. Through the conferences, SWVP made contact with the Sudanese Women's Union. SWVP reported to me that they had met with the Women's Union before the conference and they planned to continue their networking after the conference.

Discussion

SWVP's strategy of de-escalation, e.g. avoidance and non-compliance, was linked both to the frames they developed and to their sense of identity. A 'peaceful' strategy may have been reinforced by one of their major financial backers, the Swedish Christian foundation, Life and Peace. Because I observed other southern Sudanese women confronting and challenging their adversaries, I cannot attribute SWVP's strategy to southern Sudanese culture. In addition, SWVP members were not long-time activists. They identified themselves as intellectuals and as such, may have felt that education was more important than confrontation.

All of the Sudanese women obviously identified very strongly with their religious and racial/ethnic backgrounds. Tension around Arab/Black African and Muslim/Christian divides is a major cause of the Sudanese civil war even though the dividing lines, particularly the racial classifications, are very complex (Deng, 1995). Nevertheless, SWVP was attempting to build connections with the women from the North based on gender. In a workshop on the Sudan, when Rachel was asked whether there was much difference between the Sudanese men and the women, she responded that there was not much difference because both men and women were oppressed. Rachel did say, however, that they were attempting dialogue so that they could reach common ground as women.

Given the circumstances, their sense of common identity was fragile. At the African regional conference, SWVP joined in the essentialist rhetoric proclaiming women to be natural or better peacemakers. They participated in the formation of the African Women's Peace Federation. However, at the Forum in China, when the northern women began the conflict resolution sessions with the same rhetoric, it fell flat. Rachel felt the women as peacemakers frame reinforced the insincerity of the northern women because they spoke about an abstract identity as a way of avoiding discussion of concrete proposals for peace or the conflict that had erupted between them at the conference.

SWVP deliberately altered how they framed their issues, depending on their audience. When they were speaking to a general audience that might contain delegates from northern Sudan, they spoke about the need for a 'just peace' and emphasized their peace efforts with women. In contrast, when they spoke to an audience gathered specifically to hear their story, such as an SWVP workshop or a media interview, the SWVP spoke about the need for self-determination. Self-determination was a term that could have been inflammatory and SWVP chose not to incite their northern colleagues. In the global setting of the NGO Forum '95, SWVP added to their strategy by calling for conflict resolution between the northern and southern women. It was their goal to attract international involvement and support for their attempt at peaceful negotiations.

Although 'just peace' had a very specific meaning in the Sudanese context (confederacy with a secular state and equal distribution of resources), it was also a widely-known frame for international NGOs applied to a new context, the Sudan. It appealed to both Western and African allies. It was language these allies were familiar with and would use themselves. In addition, the frame lent the Sudanese women an air of respectability and facilitated their acceptance into the Peace NGO network. 'Just peace' had meaning—peace was not acceptable at any price—but was generic enough to leave the international listener unaware of a specific agenda. For this reason, it was doubly useful. The phrase may have made northern Sudanese women uncomfortable but it did not incite them and international delegates felt an affinity with it. It was a useful frame.

Self-determination, on the other hand, was much more controversial. Nevertheless, it communicated the SWVP agenda clearly in a way that a 'just peace' did not. Self-determination was a particularly effective frame for grabbing the attention of international listeners who knew little about the situation or for rallying support among those who had already made a decision to support the southern Sudanese cause. For some, like the WILPF leadership, it posed a crisis. Through the PrepComs and the peace train, they had made more connections with women from the north of Sudan, who supported unity rather than self-determination. Although I noted references in WILPF literature condemning the foreign intervention and supporting the right of self-determination, the word may have also been perceived as synonymous with war. Furthermore, because women from both sides of the war wanted to take part in the peace events, supporting SWVP may have been perceived as taking sides.

The third frame that the SWVP developed, conflict resolution, gained support from many different participants. Like 'just peace' it was an old frame applied to a new situation. Conflict resolution was central to the mission of the peace tent and the organizers of the peace activities. As a result, conflict resolution appealed enormously to the SWVP's targeted audience, Western and African peace NGOs. Most of these women considered themselves to be peacemakers, as did some of the northern Sudanese women. The northern women advocating for an end to the war wanted to see themselves and to be seen as peacemakers. Moreover, under the watchful eye of the Sudanese government delegates, the northern women could safely advocate for mediation or nonviolent resolution of the war without fear of reprisal—it was safe issue. The northern women agreed to take part in the conflict resolution sessions with the encouragement of the international community, setting the stage for the dialogue that SWVP had worked for.

In the meantime, WILPF was impressed with SWVP's attempts at reconciliation and spoke of strengthening ties with the organization after the conference. Initially, WILPF was cautious with their support. The conflict in the Sudan was not easily understood by potential Western allies. The religious basis for conflict—Arab vs. Christian/Animism—and the murky racial lines drawn in the civil war may have made it difficult for them to know how to support SWVP. Religions in themselves might not be perceived as bad and it might have been difficult for some Westerners, including myself, to distinguish the racial divides. However, eventually WILPF offered their support and the conflict resolution frame was effective in bringing SWVP closer to their goals.

Beneath Paradise

Background

Madelaine's main tactic to gain attention for her agenda was conflict escalation. Her attempts to raise issues, particularly de-colonization, were largely ignored. The power differential was so great between France and New Caledonia (Kanaky) that Madelaine was unable to initiate any kind of discussion with the French government delegates during the conferences. As a result, she resorted to open, public confrontation and embarrassment. The conflicts that she initiated became useful to her because she could then use them to gain more attention for her issues.

As a lone representative of three different NGOs, Madelaine had much ground to cover. Her goals were to stop French nuclear testing in her region, gain self-determination for her people, and end French militarization of New Caledonia. However, at the New York PrepCom in 1995, neither the New Caledonian nor the French government delegates were speaking about these issues in the context of the Pacific Islands. Madelaine's main objective became to alter the conference discourse. She targeted New Caledonian and peace NGOs, NGO representatives in the indigenous and Asia Pacific caucuses, and the media, as well as the New Caledonian and French government representatives.

Madelaine developed a frame that focused attention on three issues: de-colonization, de-militarization, and de-nuclearization. It was important to her that all three issues be recognized—attention for one of the three concerns was not enough because they were inextricably connected. In an interview with UN radio, Madelaine responded to a question put to her on the relationship between colonization and militarization:

> You cannot dissociate the militarization from the colonization. And as I say everywhere because people want to talk only about the militarization but not about colonization, hang on, it's not the angels who came and killed our people and the military is the main instrument of the power. And colonization they hear, they dictate, they say you do this, do that, and on. And when we don't do it, like what happened for example in New Caledonia or wherever, they send the army and we deal directly with the occupation of the army. We are fighting against the army.

Her effort to keep bringing colonization into the conference discourse was the core of her struggle in the conference settings.

Madelaine declared herself in opposition to anyone who did not support her political agenda as a whole, regardless of their identity. She was expecting a battle. She had attended the Nairobi women's conference in 1985 and had been ignored by the French government delegates. Madelaine was an experienced activist in many different arenas, from women's rights to the Kanak struggle for independence. She maintained that she was not afraid to confront anymore. It was the poverty, the suffering of her people that kept her going. 'It makes me strong,' she said, 'What have I to lose?'

New York PrepCom, 1995

As I explained in Chapter three, at the first meeting of the peace caucus at the global precom in New York City, Madelaine raised the issue of de-colonization only to be ignored. Madelaine's next action was to speak at a larger meeting, called the linkage caucus, which was set up to link activities between the various caucuses at the PrepCom. Bettina and another prominent peace caucus member, Maude, were in line to speak at the microphone when I arrived. I then noticed that Madelaine had gotten in line. She told her story to the crowd, saying that she had talked about de-colonization as a peace issue in the peace caucus but it was not 'taken up.' She demanded 'attention for her people.' Maude was the first to start the applause after Madelaine spoke.

Publicly embarrassed, the peace caucus added a sentence about the need for self-determination and de-colonization to the peace caucus priorities. I noted its appearance in the flyer to be distributed around the conference stating the main peace caucus issues. Later, when a Canadian peace group offered to re-type the flyer, I noted that the sentence on de-colonization disappeared. However, it re-appeared in the statement the following day. There was some struggle but the statement remained in the list of peace caucus priorities for the remainder of the conference.

Because of her commitment to her agenda, Madelaine found herself not only in conflict with the peace caucus but the government delegates from New Caledonia and from France as well as NGO representatives from the Pacific Island region. She described disputes with all of them. Her political agenda was absolutely essential to the formation of her alliances. The many facets of her identity—national, gender, and/or racial identification—were important to her but so were her issues.

After a peace caucus meeting, Madelaine agreed to talk with me about her work. She seemed particularly interested that I was studying conflict between women. 'You're studying conflicts between women? Very interesting, very good,' she said. At the PrepCom, she said, she was occupied by trouble with government delegates, intra-group conflicts and trying to get her issues on the agenda of the general session.

Madelaine began to talk about some of her conflicts. Her first concern was the composition of the New Caledonian government delegation at the PrepCom. 'They say they represent the Pacific,' she said, 'but they are elite women with privilege.' Madelaine had confronted them in a regional meeting stating that they would have to represent themselves and no one else because they do not represent the Pacific peoples like she, Madelaine did. Madelaine explained to me that she had 'slept with', fought for, and listened to Pacific women. She had lost 19 family members in the fighting and many friends.

Madelaine complained that the New Caledonian delegates were not raising the issues important to her people. However, she felt that as a result of her actions the delegates were forced to deal with concerns like de-colonization. She was certain that the delegates from New Caledonia would not have talked about colonialism unless she had been there to raise the issue. Madelaine had been raising her issues in all public forums from the beginning of the PrepCom.

In addition to the government delegates, Madelaine was also suspicious of NGO representatives from the Pacific Islands. Although she identified strongly as an indigenous woman and attended the indigenous caucus at the conference, she had conflicted feelings about some of the representatives. Madelaine told me she was unsure of another indigenous woman at the PrepCom. She had told Madelaine that she also represented NGOs, leaving Madelaine somewhat perplexed. She was not familiar with the NGOs, the cooperatives the woman mentioned, nor had she seen the NGO money. 'I don't know where NGO money goes,' she said, frustrated, 'in their pockets?' She feared the NGOs were 'just there to further their own purpose.' Nevertheless, Madelaine did add that she was glad to see people around who 'are like me.'

Most important, Madelaine felt herself at odds with the French government. During the conference, I saw Madelaine in action as she confronted the French government delegates. I met Madelaine at a meeting set up for government delegates representing countries in the European Union to answer NGO questions. Madelaine was recognized by the chair. She asked the French delegates about their position on New Caledonia and Tahiti and de-colonization. She said that the peace caucus had taken up de-militarization and de-nuclearization issues but she hadn't seen those issues in the platform. In addition, she brought up the accreditation process, pointing out that the women from Tibet and from New Caledonia had been prevented from attending the conference. 'Can you defend us?' she asked. She ended her 'question' by calling attention to French immigration policies. The government, she said, was bringing in more and more French citizens to vote against the de-colonization referendum.

Madelaine finished and the French delegates conferred among themselves. Finally, one of the delegates responded to Madelaine's question saying that her concern is not of interest to large numbers of women. At the conference, they were looking at issues that were of interest to most women. She thought Madelaine's question was too general and too specific. They were concerned specifically with women's issues, and de-colonization in New Caledonia was not a women's issue.

I was shocked by this response from the French delegates, but Madelaine reported to me immediately afterwards that she thought it was good to raise the issue. 'Let's not dream on,' she said. She knew what their response would be and would now go and 'make a big deal of the question.' In other words, Madelaine would now use their response to draw attention to her issue in public settings at the conference. She left me and headed off to the Asia Pacific caucus.

The next day, I ran into Madelaine at breakfast at the NGO center across from the UN. I sat down and we began to talk. 'You see why I don't identify with women, with feminism,' she said. She clarified, saying there are big differences between her and 'those French women.' Clearly, Madelaine did not identify with the French women based on gender. Although she added that she was 'used to them,' she declared that she was going to announce the response of the government delegates at the peace caucus press conference. She was not going to let their answer go by.

After telling her story at the Asia Pacific caucus, Madelaine exposed the French response in a radio interview with UN radio and WBAI which she invited me to attend. During the radio interview, she explained the situation as follows:

> But if you are with the idea of de-colonizing, demilitarizing for justice this is no way you will get anywhere as long as you are French. That's why I'm quite happy, that the other day I went to the briefing meeting, those French, European Union, whatever, and when the French started to speak about you know how wonderful they are here to try to look at compromise so everyone will have their place and then a consensus after that to gather everyone.
>
> So I asked, where is our place? What did they think about militarization, colonization and militarization by them in the Pacific and nuclearization of course. And the response was that they are not here to talk about that. It is not a subject. It is exactly like Nairobi. They told me that in Nairobi. I wasn't surprised. And the people around are not interested which is horseshit because I had many people in that audience who came and signed the petition against Mauri. Not against the Mauri but for the Mauri but me personally, I'm taking that responsibility. So I was quite, not shocked but the more disgusted and the more determined that Kanaky has to be free, New Caledonia and Tahiti, of course.

She had had a history of mistrust with the French delegates. Although her agenda had been ignored in 1985, at the 3rd UN World Conference in Nairobi, she continued to raise the issue of de-colonization, using the French hypocrisy as a way to call attention to the subject.

Her next step was to publicize the French insult at the peace caucus press conference. A large crowd and TV crews had gathered to view the human rights caucus press conference, but most of them left when it was over, leaving a small group at the front of the room singing peace songs with the peace ribbons displayed in the background. Madelaine was one of the first to speak. She spoke briefly about the French nuclear testing in the Pacific Islands. She also spoke about how the French delegates had responded to her question on French de-colonization. Her statement was heard not only by the US press but by peace caucus members from around the globe, and Bella Abzug, a prominent figure at the conference who had been persuaded to stay after the human rights press conference.

Before Madelaine left the conference, she was filmed by CNN at a meeting set up by the indigenous caucus. Again, Madelaine highlighted the French hypocrisy. When the meeting facilitator asked Madelaine if she thought the situation would end, Madelaine said angrily that 'white people are crying about people everywhere but what about the Kanak?' She commented that there is a lot of talk about Bosnia, which is good. But, she complained, these same people (whites/French) who show so much concern for Bosnia are hiding the suffering of her people. She emphasized that her people are killed because they talk about their rights.

Beijing

Once the NGO Forum '95 began in Beijing, Madelaine's strategy changed. She was no longer the only representative from her umbrella organization. As Madelaine had hoped, there were at least 16 indigenous women present from the Pacific Island coalition. Furthermore, she and a number of other indigenous women were given the opportunity to speak at the large plenary sessions at the NGO Forum '95. The peace caucus arranged for a panel of speakers from the Pacific Islands to talk about the French nuclear testing. To some extent, it was no longer necessary to gain attention through public embarrassment. However, with a larger constituency present, Beneath Paradise organized a demonstration against the French nuclear testing the morning of the first explosion. The conflicts continued. Each time they publicly protested the French nuclear testing they connected the struggle against nuclear weapons to their struggle for independence.

When I arrived in Beijing, it was several days into the conference before I was able to make contact with Madelaine. In the meantime, one of the first plenary speakers at the NGO Forum '95, Winona LaDuke, a well-known Native American environmentalist, mentioned the French nuclear testing in the Pacific as she was discussing the effects of colonization and imperialism on the planet. Her reference to the French testing was an indication of the networking among transnational indigenous and/or environmental movements.

Madelaine was invited to speak at a plenary session on peace at the NGO Forum '95 on the fifth day of the conference. This was quite an accomplishment, given the thousands of women leaders and activists present at the conference and competing for a chance to speak to the largest forum at the conference. Madelaine described the effects of colonization on the Pacific, speaking openly about the atrocities committed by the French military on Kanaky. Then she elaborated on nuclear testing:

> Nuclear testing is militarism, and the French have decided that their military prowess is more important than our health and safety. But it is equally important to keep in mind that nuclear testing is inseparable from colonialism. The French keep French Polynesia

> as a colony in order to test their weapons because since the independence of Algeria in the 1960s they no longer can test them in the Sahara desert. This is what we mean to them: We are their testing ground. Without colonization there would be no nuclear testing (Ounei-Small, 1996, p.167).

She placed part of the responsibility for the testing on the international community, which she described as complacent.

The next day, a group of women from the Pacific Islands spoke in the peace tent on French nuclear testing in the Pacific. Heidi, a WILPF member from the Pacific Islands, had coordinated the panel. Heidi was currently a member of Parliament but had had lost her job twice because of her outspoken views on French nuclear testing, including a position as a minister in the government. Heidi publicly thanked peace activists, particularly in Europe, for helping to stop the testing. She thought it was possible that this provocation by France could help to develop a stronger global moratorium on nuclear testing. When I inquired, Heidi said she gotten to know Madelaine through NFIP.

Heidi spoke again at a plenary session on Asia Pacific strategies using a frame similar to Madelaine's. When listing the issues important to the Pacific Islands, Heidi began with colonization and nuclear weapons. Like Madelaine, she emphasized that nuclear testing would not stop until colonization had been stopped. If one supported the ban on nuclear weapons testing in the Pacific, then, she stated emphatically, one must support the independence of the islands. She described the UN Convention on Small States and pointed out that the 'instruments' for independence were already in place. What was needed was the commitment to implement them.

I finally met up with Madelaine the morning of the nuclear test and corresponding protest. It was a very important morning. Not only had a nuclear bomb been exploded that morning in the Pacific but U.S. First Lady Hilary Clinton was coming to the NGO Forum '95 to speak. The Beneath Paradise demonstration was held behind the hall where Mrs. Clinton was speaking and the wife of the French President, Madame Chirac, was accompanying Hillary on that day.

At the protest, about 15 indigenous women from the Pacific Islands, accompanied by another 20 women from around the world, walked in a circle shouting, 'Stop French Testing!' and holding colorful banners and umbrellas (it was raining). As I walked the circle, I noted that quite a few Japanese women, who had declared nuclear issues a priority, had joined the demonstration. They were joined by some peace caucus members once the peace caucus demonstration, also staged for Mrs. Clinton's benefit, had finished. The Beneath Paradise protest ended when two black limousines, presumably carrying Hilary Clinton and Madame Chirac, slid through the crowd. Madelaine yelled 'Fascist!' after the cars.

The demonstration did not receive much attention in the wake of Hilary Clinton's visit, but Ellen decided to bring the issue to the FWCW. WILPF composed a letter protesting the nuclear testing, but Ellen was not allowed to read it to the government assembly. A woman loudly supported her, insisting that she be given space to speak and soon people in the assembly began to clap. Ellen was finally given the chance to read the WILPF protest. People stood and applauded when she had finished.

The following is part of the text of the one page letter. It was one of three letters protesting French nuclear testing in the Pacific that I collected. In the letter, WILPF connects colonialism, racism, and nuclear testing:

> In complete disregard of the wish of the majority of the world's peoples and of the majority of its own citizens, the French Government undertook a nuclear weapons test in the early morning of 6 September 1995. This is the first in a series of announced tests. We, the Women's International League for Peace and Freedom, urge the French Government to have the courage to reverse its decision and to renounce any further testing.
>
> We particularly protest the testing by France in the land and seas that is the home of the Polynesian people, a people that has fought for its independence from France for more than thirty years. We consider the nuclear test in this region a colonial and racist act. We call on France to respect the human rights, the well-being and interests of all people in the entire region.

The WILPF letter was not only read in the government assembly but the Women's Environment and Development Organization (WEDO) declared it had been accepted by acclaim at the NGO Plenary Briefing session.

Outcomes

Although I did not note a public response from the French delegates, I did notice that women in both the non-governmental and the governmental sectors began to speak about Madelaine's three issues as a result of her actions. The nuclear concern was given much more attention than de-colonization but both issues were acknowledged. Specifically, Madelaine played a part in the acceptance of a proposal relating to de-colonization, self-determination and women into the PfA. Her strategy of public visibility and confrontation worked particularly well within the context of the New York PrepCom.

Following her public confrontation with the peace caucus, her issues were raised briefly at the peace caucus even though Madelaine herself did not appear. Maude, who had attended the linkage caucus, mentioned that people in the Pacific were very concerned with nuclear issues. Someone else said that nuclear disarmament and de-colonization had been taken up by the Group of 77 who had raised the issue in the general session. Later that week, I heard an African American woman speak up for Pacific Island issues in a caucus on racism. The African American speaker talked about the importance of educating themselves about particular issues. She mentioned specifically that 'we need to know more about our sisters in the Pacific who have had trouble with nuclear testing.'

Moreover, the peace caucus made more of an attempt to include Madelaine in its activities. After the initial peace caucus confrontation over de-colonization, Madelaine returned. This time when she brought up her agenda, some of the women, particularly a Canadian woman, acknowledged her, encouraged and supported her verbally. Both the Canadian and a Nigerian woman supported her in her effort to talk about the Mauri. Anita asked her to chair a meeting. When I asked Madelaine what she thought of the peace caucus, she replied that they were 'doing okay'. She was particularly pleased with the invitation to speak at the peace caucus press conference.

Madelaine was quite successful in getting the attention of the press. During the PrepCom, she was interviewed on two radio stations and CNN, not to mention the peace caucus press conference. Madelaine pursued every opportunity to gain visibility; everywhere Madelaine went, she brought up her agenda. Not only was she an outspoken leader, but she tapped into the resources of the transnational movements she was a part of as well as the urgency of current events happening in the Pacific. In addition, it was clear to many that France's nuclear testing in the Pacific was morally wrong. All of these factors contributed to Madelaine's success with the media in the USA.

Moreover, she and other Beneath Paradise members were successful in rallying the support of NGOs around the French nuclear testing at the FWCW. Quite a few women joined their demonstration, particularly women representing Japanese and North American NGOs. Three letters protesting the French testing in three languages were addressed to the government assembly from international NGOs. By the end of the FWCW, WILPF had decided to use their power and resources to support the Beneath Paradise anti-nuclear agenda.

Discussion

Madelaine used strategies designed to generate conflict and draw the attention of large groups. Her strategy of causing embarrassment and exposing hypocrisy would have been ineffective in small homogeneous groups. She wanted her complaints out in the open where they could be discussed. She raised her three issues in every forum she attended and if she did not receive at least a token recognition of Beneath Paradise priorities, she tended to challenge those in charge. Madelaine had a pre-packaged frame, a slogan that she repeated over and over again. The three d's—de-colonization, de-nuclearization, and demilitarization—were short and easy to remember and to understand. Madelaine made concrete, specific regional claims. Although she framed her issues in general terms that could be understood globally, Madelaine lobbied specifically for ending French nuclear testing in her region and for the independence of New Caledonia.

Madelaine's frame built on familiar concepts that were not normally combined. She inserted de-colonization into the Northern women's peace agenda, which prioritized de-nuclearization and de-militarization. The campaign against nuclear weapons was very important to WILPF, one of their highest priorities. Militarization was the word that WILPF members used to describe their own regional problems. Colonization did not resonate as strongly as nuclearization or militarization but the Northern women were familiar with it in an abstract manner and knew immediately that they were against it. Moreover, when Madelaine pointed out that the peace caucus had ignored her concerns about colonization, they could be embarrassed because they knew they should have supported her.

De-colonization was not new to Madelaine's targeted audience but it was not ordinarily combined with de-nuclearization in a Northern context. She had to confront and embarrass the peace NGOs in order to expand their frame. Her tactics were similar with the New Caledonian and French government delegates. The frame did not resonate at all with the French delegates, but Madelaine had not expected that. She publicized their resistance to her frame to reinforce her de-colonization agenda. Her struggle, then was to keep de-colonization on the peace caucus and conference agenda. She insisted that in her context, the three issues were inextricably connected.

Unlike the civil war in the Sudan, the conflict in the Pacific Islands appeared to be clear cut—a classic case of oppressor/oppressed. France, the big colonial superpower, was oppressing New Caledonia, the tiny island in the Pacific. It was clearly unjust that France would use the Pacific Islands as its nuclear testing grounds, displacing whole peoples, polluting their land and water, and damaging their health for generations to come. Finally, racial lines seemed clearly drawn with the white French and the indigenous Kanak. The 'enemy' was visible to Northern eyes. The frame based on familiar symbols and the clearly marked enemy both facilitated international support of Madelaine's issues.

Madelaine made it very clear that anyone who did not support her political agenda was her adversary, regardless of their identity. She participated in the indigenous caucus but questioned the credibility of the only other NGO delegate from her region because the NGO delegate from Fiji did not openly talk about the three D's. Madelaine participated in the Asia Pacific caucus, but she publicly challenged and cajoled her national government delegates until they finally began to discuss the three D's. She spoke fondly of how she had bonded with a female comrade in jail as they spoke about discrimination against women in the independence movement. However, after the French government delegates had told her publicly that colonization and nuclear issues were not women's issues, she said to me, 'You see why I don't call myself a feminist...I have nothing in common with those women.' Madelaine identified strongly with her people involved in the New Caledonian independence movement. Anyone else, including any of her own people, male or female, was suspect unless s/he embraced Madelaine's political agenda.

Conclusion

In conclusion, challenging the dominant agenda and discourse was difficult and complex. The smaller, local, NGOs fought to gain attention for their agendas and influence the dominant discourse. They competed with and at the same time targeted the larger NGOs. As they negotiated, differences in power to influence the agenda triggered deep-rooted conflicts. By using their repertoires of contention, appealing to activist identities, and experimenting with various strategic frames, the women involved with the three NGOs had limited success in changing the agenda. However, because their struggles tended to be constructive, all of the women drew closer to their goals in the process. This positive sense of how they had processed their conflicts and the outcomes attributed to their struggles contributed to their willingness to continue to be a part of the network.

By focusing on conflicts regarding the NGO framing strategies, the process of transnational frame alignment becomes clearer. The smaller NGOs experimented with frames that they hoped would resonate in global settings revealing how strategic framing processes develop. Within the transnational context, the frames that focused on clearly articulated issues tended to be more successful than the frames based on ethnic, racial, or national identity. The women of color affiliated with WILPF used a frame of 'anti-racism' that built on the values of the white Northern women and at the same time bridged the different experiences of some of the Southern women affiliated with WILPF. Further, Geraldine developed a slogan, 'racism is based on color,' that communicated effectively within the anti-racism frame. Like Madelaine's frame, the three D's, it was short and to the point. In addition, both slogans used some concepts familiar to their target audiences. Under pressure, the frame was accepted by WILPF.

When the white Northern women were dominant in numbers (e.g. at the New York PrepCom and WILPF preliminary activities), anti-racism worked as a mobilizing frame for women who identified as women of color and white women. Everyone was against racism. However, within the context of the NGO Forum '95 and the FWCW, the frame was no longer a rallying point for a broad spectrum of activists. Colonialism, imperialism, self-determination, development, and human rights were all examples of regional or global frames involving racism that motivated larger numbers of conference participants. As such, the anti-racism frame is an example of a frame that lost power in a highly diverse and global setting.

In contrast, Geraldine's 'black agenda' frame did not resonate in either context. It was so localized and identity-based that it did not appeal to the white Northern women or the women of color who lived outside of Britain. Nor did it communicate a specific agenda effectively. Geraldine and the Northern women of color were not alone in their concern about racism. SWVP and Beneath Paradise also spoke about racism as a core issue. It would have been interesting to see what the impact would have been had the three organizations targeted each other and been able to create a joint frame around racism. Unfortunately, although they were all present at the NGO Forum '95, the women most likely never met.

SWVP's efforts to engage international NGOs was particularly difficult because the civil war in the Sudan is complex and relatively unknown. Further, they targeted northern Sudanese women with whom relations were strained, at best. SWVP's 'just peace' frame was useful as a compromise frame that would hint at issues without inciting anger and would presumably build connections. The frame resonated international women unfamiliar with the Sudan because it referred to key values—peace and justice. Although it facilitated conversation and connection, it is an example of a frame that did not mobilize the either of the targeted audience. For the international audience, it was too general or too familiar to motivate action.

The self-determination frame bridged across cultures because of its potential to draw together peoples who identified with struggles for independence and/or self-determination of their ethnic/racial group. However, developing allies through this frame was complicated for SWVP, because the civil war was difficult for outsiders to grasp. The international media had given little attention to the civil war in the Sudan as compared to Somalia, Rwanda, etc. Some outsiders would be cautious in their support until they had decided where they stood on the issue of self-determination for the southern Sudanese. Although the frame itself mobilized few people or resources, the frame did communicate the SWVP goal effectively.

'Conflict resolution' resonated with diverse populations, serving to mobilize or engage quite a few people. With a push (the conflict), the idea of conflict resolution mobilized northern Sudanese NGOs and the Sudanese military personnel. Moreover, potential Western allies, uncertain how to respond to calls for self-determination, were interested in supporting conflict resolution. Resolving conflicts peacefully was one of the highest values of the women taking part in the peace activities at the conference. With the support of the international community, the conflict resolution frame was successful in mobilizing northern Sudanese women and eventually in engaging Western allies.

Madelaine's frame was effective for a number of reasons. First, as a slogan, it communicated quickly and effectively. It was also easy to remember. Second, the frame combined concepts that were already part of an existing frame for the Northern peace NGOs—de-nuclearization and de-militarization—with a concept that was not unfamiliar, that is, de-colonization. As such, with some pressure, the frame was accepted by Madelaine's target constituency. Third, the frame was not quite as identity-based as some of the other frames, focusing instead on issues. Nor was it highly localized. The three 'D's' mobilized women in the highly diverse settings of the FWCW.

Discussion of strategic framing at the conferences also leads to some conclusions about NGO repertoires of contention in transnational contexts. The most successful frames would not have been effective without the pressure tactics used by the NGO representatives. Presenting their issues without competitive strategies was ineffective. Given the power imbalance among the NGOs, conflict escalation served to gain the attention of the larger, more powerful NGOs. The delegates were willing to disrupt, confront and embarrass. On the other hand, SWVP chose a non-confrontational strategy, given the volatile situation that they faced with the northern Sudanese women. Their 'peaceful' strategy appealed to members of the peace caucus.

Activist identity formation was a significant factor in shaping frames and strategies, affirming the assumption that identity is key in mobilizing dynamics on a transnational level as well as the national level. The transnational activist identity 'woman' served to bring the women together. However, as conflicts arose, particularly around agendas, other aspects of their multiple-layered identities became more salient. Some of the women defined themselves in opposition to each other and attempted to organize around their difference. In a group without men, whose presence might help define the collective identity 'woman,' the category splintered. In-group differences were heightened. National and sub-national identities were reinforced. At the conferences, the women's sense of identity shifted as the setting and actors changed and the conflicts unfolded.

Even some sub-categories shifted. For example, the category of women of color changed meaning at the NGO Forum '95 and FWCW, where white women were in the minority. What does it mean to be a woman of color in a diverse international context? Who belongs and who does not? As a result, the mobilizing strength of the strategic frame changed as well. Further, the activist identity essentializing women as peacemakers was useful to the African women until it was challenged by the strong racial/religious identification in the Sudanese war. Nevertheless, it did help to mobilize the Sudanese women around the conflict resolution frame so that they were actually willing to speak to each other.

As a result of the conflicts and the ensuing identity definition and redefinition, the transnational activist identity 'woman' was reinforced. The women activists involved in my study tended to identify with women from other groups to the extent that it was empowering to them, that is, it drew them closer to their goals. There were enough positive outcomes from activities at the conference that all of the women would continue their transnational activism as women. Geraldine, generally, felt that WILPF had responded well to the conflict over racism and was pleased with the actions she had taken. Bettina, on the other hand, was happy with what WILPF had learned as an organization through their contact with one another. Rachel and Lucia were satisfied with their own performance at the conferences and with some of the new international contacts they had made even though the conflict resolution attempts with the Sudanese women were frustrating. Madelaine saw that she made a difference in the conference discourse, gained international allies and media attention and would probably attend the next UN World Conference on Women if she thought it would be useful to her struggle.

During the agenda-setting conflicts, the NGO delegates made their positions known and, as a result, they learned more about their differences and priorities. As they struggled together to find mutually acceptable solutions, they experimented with frames that they thought would resonate with and therefore mobilize the budding alliance. Because most of the NGOs showed some flexibility—in particular the more dominant NGOs—the outcomes were positive enough that the NGOs initially marginalized by the process were open to working with the network in the future. Throughout their negotiations, aspects of their identities shifted and changed. However, in the end, the constructive outcomes served to reinforce their sense of themselves as transnational activists.

Chapter 5

Transnational Activist Conflict Resolution: Dialogue for Deep-Rooted Conflict

As they negotiated areas of common concern and how they would frame their issues, the NGOs used various strategies to resolve conflicts and ease tensions. The WILPF leadership: incorporated some new issues into the peace caucus agenda; included women who had felt marginalized into their discussions of priorities for the future; set up many workshops and forums for women to speak for themselves about their own issues; and, finally, they organized group conflict resolution sessions for the NGO delegates. SWVP initiated a number of conflict resolution meetings with northern Sudanese delegates. Most of these efforts helped to build relations within the network and to create a common identity as transnational activists.

This chapter analyzes different models of group discussion utilized by the NGO delegates to address their conflicts. The basic assumption of cross-cultural conflict resolution is that under the right conditions, members of ethnic groups in conflict can learn to cooperate with each other to solve shared problems. However, not all conversations are constructive. Contact between competing ethnic groups will not always lead to improved relations. My analysis focuses on the question: under what conditions was international discourse instrumental in building common agendas? When did discussion reify divisions and/or when did it assist collaboration?

The women adapted three methods of group interaction for their purposes: debate, prejudice reduction, and dialogue. I will describe the characteristics of each model. Then I will clarify the advantages and disadvantages of each type of discussion for the NGOs within the context of the conferences. I argue that dialogue was the most useful model for processing the deep-rooted conflicts arising from network agenda setting. As such, the major focus of this analysis is the dialogue method.

Using the dialogue process, the peace activists began to develop a desire and a capacity to negotiate even though there was serious disagreement. Dialogue is a way to show variety or difference from stereotypic images; it allows participants to 'differentiate the image of the enemy' (Kelman, 1986; Rothman, 1991). Disputants often dehumanize and stereotype the other in order to maintain the conflict. Through dialogue, differences among participants on the same 'side' are revealed as individual and personal foundations of beliefs and values are explored. Dialogue allows participants to identify problems underlying relationships and to move towards working on those issues identified. Furthermore, the conflict resolution frame through which dialogue was presented had broad appeal to the women's identity as peace activists. As such, dialogue provides a frame within which the participants can challenge the dominant discourse, uncover difference and find common ground with which to build or rebuild transnational activist identities.

Defining Dialogue, Prejudice Reduction and Debate

In the context of this chapter, dialogue refers to a specific type of interactive conflict resolution (ICR). Interactive conflict resolution is broadly defined as 'facilitated face-to-face activities in communication, training, education, or consultation that promote collaborative conflict analysis and problem solving among parties engaged in protracted conflict in a manner that addresses basic human needs and promotes the building of peace, justice, and equality' (Fisher, 1997, p. 8). Scholar-practitioners began developing these methods in small-group discussion for resolving protracted international conflict in the 1960s.

Types of conflict resolution activities can be distinguished by the identity of the participants, the form of intervention, the objectives, and the relationship of the intervention to formal processes (Fisher, 1997). Because many characteristics common to ICR are also common to dialogue interventions, distinctions between them become blurred. Like other applications of ICR, a central assumption of dialogue is that the conflict resolution process requires the assistance of a skilled and knowledgeable third party. Further, the methodology is based on a social-psychological approach; that is, the antagonists must address relationship issues and develop mutually acceptable solutions through direct interaction (Fisher, 1997).

In contrast to other ICR methods like the problem-solving workshops, dialogue interventions tend to focus on ordinary members of groups in conflict. Interactive problem solving workshops frequently involve influential, informal representatives of the parties. Most often, the purpose of dialogue is to increase understanding and trust among the participants with the goal of eventually influencing public opinion. Although the intervention may not focus on generating alternative solutions to the conflict, dialogues sometimes produce ideas that can be used in the policy-making process. Furthermore, dialogue leaders may use a problem-solving process even though the impact of the participants on policy-makers is minimal or unclear (Fisher, 1997).

Increasingly, dialogue intervention has been applied to controversial social issues as a form of democratic process. The process of changing relationships among conflicting groups is thought to be central to the construction of a strong civil society (Slim, 1996). The Charles F. Kettering Foundation, Dayton, Ohio, USA, is an example of an organization that holds public policy forums led by trained dialogue facilitators on issues such as abortion, the environment, school violence, or US foreign policy. Within this context, dialogue is a long-term project. Sustained dialogue is defined as 'a political process in which participants probe the dynamics of even the most destructive relationships and gradually develop a capacity together to design steps to change them' (Saunders and Slim, From Role of Dialogue Leader in a Dialogue Circle, Community Wide Dialogue: Racism, Race Relations, Racial Healing, Inter-religious Council, Syracuse, NY, n.d., p.1). Dialogue has been useful not only in aiding peace negotiations in situations of international conflict or civil war but for engaging citizens in a search for common ground on polarizing policy issues.

Prejudice reduction refers to a workshop format developed by the National Coalition Building Institute (NCBI). The NCBI model was 'designed to assist participants to come to an understanding of the dynamics of institutionalized racism by working through a series of personal and small group explorations' (Brown and Mazza, 1992, p.4). The main goals of prejudice reduction are to: 1) explore the emotional and social impact of discrimination; 2) learn how to remove the hurt, misinformation, and powerlessness that hold prejudice in place; 3) identify one's own experiences with discrimination in order to become a more effective advocate in ending discrimination; and 4) to learn useful strategies for handling prejudicial remarks, slurs, and jokes (NCBI, 2000). Typically, NCBI bridge building focuses specifically on groups 'deadlocked over emotionally charged issues' (NCBI, 2000, p.3). The prejudice reduction model is similar to dialogue in some ways but the differences are significant enough to warrant a separate discussion.

Debate is defined in the Encyclopedia Americana (1998) 'as argumentative processes in which affirmative and negative advocates seek to gain a favorable decision on a formally stated proposition, resolution, or motion.' Debate encompasses discussion, argumentation, and persuasion. Discussion refers to the process by which a small group enters into reflective thinking in order to find a mutually satisfactory solution to a problem. Argumentation, in a formal sense, is defined as a dialectical process that involves the rigid formation and presentation of opposing arguments in a search for the truth. Persuasion takes place when an advocate attempts to gain acceptance for his/her argument and to motivate action through strong appeals to his/her listeners' emotions. Through discussion, argumentation, and persuasion, debate facilitates the exploration and clarification of ideas. During the Middle Ages and the Renaissance, debate became an important educational tool at universities. It differs from dialogue and prejudice reduction because it is not a form of conflict resolution.

Dialogue as a Pre-Negotiation Strategy

Dialogue is helpful to the agenda-setting process because it allows participants to identify deeper motivations and to explore ways of satisfying common human needs when protracted conflict arises. In the process of ICR, action possibilities emerge only when identity issues, historical grievances, and strong emotions have been considered and empathic communication has been established (Volkan and Harris, 1993). According to Volkan and Harris:

> We have found that large groups are profoundly affected by such factors as ethnic or national pride, and by mental representations of historical grievances and triumphs which are transmitted with their accompanying defenses and adaptations, from generation to generation. Underlying these factors is a shared need to belong to a large group and to have a cohesive group identity. Such factors function as 'unseen powers' in relationships between groups (Volkan and Harris, 1992, pp.170-71).

Once third party intervention helps to establish an atmosphere in which it is acceptable to express emotions, antagonists can identify underlying resistances to change. A process in which problems of opposing parties become shared is more important than developing 'logical' or 'quick' answers.

Fisher (1997) maintains that dialogue interventions are most useful in a pre-settlement phase, that is, before negotiations take place. Dialogue allows antagonists to talk again and share their differing perceptions of the conflict and each other. As a pre-negotiation strategy, ICR makes it possible for parties:

1. to connect the social-psychological aspects of their conflict to policy making and public opinion;
2. to obtain more realistic information as opposed to stereotyped information;
3. to change attitudes which lead to less distorted perceptions and more complex views that in turn support consideration of a wider variety of policy options;
4. to reassess intentions and build trust through empathic sharing which may lead to cooperative rather than unilateral strategies;
5. to experience group norms at the workshops that encourage mutuality, reciprocity, and collaboration;
6. to encounter a model for inter-group relations based on respectful interaction and equal status;
7. and to help participants to understand their interactions by examining the nationalism and ethnocentrism expressed (Fisher, 1997:170-71).

Dialogue functions as a foundation for problem solving, negotiation, and reconciliation (Fisher, 1997).

The Dialogue Process

The following discussion will outline the stages, conditions for, characteristics and key elements of the dialogue process. This information is central to the analysis of the dialogue sessions that took place during the conferences. It was not possible to interview all of the participants after these spontaneous sessions. Furthermore, to a large extent, the dialogue sessions took place after the agenda had already been set. Nor did the women refer to their group discussions as dialogue. As such, the assessment of the potential of this model for NGOs is based on the extent to which the discussions met the criteria for the dialogue process. If the NGO meetings were similar to other dialogue models, then it is possible that the goals of the dialogue process were met.

Stages of Dialogue

Many different dialogue models outline stages of the dialogue process that participants complete in order to reach the goal of the group discussion (Rothman, 1997; Saunders, 1999). Harold Saunders (1999), a former US diplomat, breaks the process into five stages. The purpose of the first stage of dialogue is to overcome resistance to dialogue. By the end of the first stage, participants have agreed to take part under certain conditions for particular purposes. The purpose of the second stage is to: 1) get out in the open the main problems that affect the relationships among the participants; and 2) identify the significant relationships that are responsible for creating the problems and what would need to change to resolve them. It is a process of mapping and naming problems and relationships in order to develop a full picture of the situation from as many viewpoints as possible. Stages three and four involve probing the dynamics of the relationships, generating the will to change, and designing ways to change relationships in order to deal with the problems agreed upon. Stage five focuses on assessing and implementing action plans. Saunders has applied his experience in Soviet/US citizen-to-citizen dialogue to domestic conflicts such as race relations.

Given the time and space available and the commitment of the participants, the groups in my study were able to complete the first stage of the dialogue process and begin the first step of the second stage—discussing the main problems that affect the relationships among the participants. As such, they were only able to start the process that has been developed for people involved in international conflict. The dialogue attempts are so short that I refer to them as moments of dialogue. Nevertheless, the moments of dialogue fit some of the conditions necessary for dialogue.

Conditions for Successful Dialogue

Under what conditions did dialogue take place? The moments of dialogue that I will describe in this chapter meet some conditions necessary for successful dialogue but not others (Fisher, 1990). First, the participants were self-selected. Most often, dialogue participants are carefully chosen. They are to be well respected but not too highly placed, to be moderate in their views, and to have equal social status. This condition has come under criticism for restricting the conversation to elite members only (Abu-Nimer, 1999); nevertheless, selecting the participants carefully is a common step. At the conferences, the dialogue leaders had little control over who participated, although one might argue that the women who came to the conference fit the requirements.

Second, the dialogue sessions were spontaneous, in contrast to most sustained dialogue which requires much advance planning and strategy as well as preparation of the participants. For the most part, the moments of dialogue were not part of the planned programming. Participants became interested in taking part in dialogue because of the conflicts described in the previous chapter. People tend to engage in dialogue because they feel a need to build or change a relationship in order to resolve a problem that hurts their interests. Once many of the women started to feel uncomfortable and to recognize that a problem existed, they were ready to talk. When the need was expressed, a few conference participants expressed a willingness to lead the dialogue. They initiated, planned, and organized the dialogue sessions. Without their leadership, the discussions would not have taken place.

Third, the moments of dialogue were short, one-time events. Sustained dialogue groups can continue for years with many of the same participants. Fourth, although the moments of dialogue took place within the context of setting agendas and preparing proposals, the dialogue did not include a specific task. Many dialogue models focus the group on a cooperative task or educational project. As such, the dialogue is often well structured and, in theory, action oriented unlike the moments of dialogue at the conferences.

Although the moments of dialogue did not meet some necessary prerequisites, they did meet others. In the context of the women's conference there were some expectations that dialogue would be a productive and positive interaction, a condition necessary for dialogue. In addition, there were many opportunities for making personal contact and acquaintance within the conference, another prerequisite for successful interaction. Further, the moments of dialogue at the conferences did contain both characteristics and elements of dialogue, which I outline below.

Characteristics of Dialogue

Because it is a specific form of group interaction, dialogue has attributes that distinguish it from other types of conversation. In order to clarify further what dialogue consists of, the characteristics of debate are contrasted to the characteristics of dialogue (Becker, 1995).

Pre-meeting contact Pre-meeting contacts and preparation of participants are essential parts of the dialogue process but largely irrelevant for a debate.

Type of participant Participants in a dialogue are not necessarily outspoken leaders but individuals whose behavior may vary in some degree from stereotypical images. Participants in a debate tend to be leaders known for propounding a carefully constructed position. The leaders may already be known to the public and their behavior tends to conform to stereotypes.

Atmosphere Dialogue nurtures an atmosphere of safety—facilitators propose, get agreement on, and enforce ground rules designed to enhance safety and promote respectful exchange. In contrast, during a debate attacks and interruptions are expected by participants and usually permitted by moderators, resulting in an atmosphere that is threatening.

Location of speaker Dialogue participants speak as individuals from their own unique experience, whereas participants in a debate speak as representatives of groups.

Audience In dialogue, participants speak to each other, but people debating speak most often to their own constituencies and sometimes to the undecided middle.

Individuation Differences among dialogue participants on the same side 'side' become evident as personal beliefs and values are explored. Differences within 'sides' of the debate are denied or minimized.

Positionality During the dialogue process, participants reveal uncertainties as well as deeply held beliefs. However, during a debate, participants express an unswerving commitment to a point of view, approach, or idea.

Function of questions When in dialogue, participants listen to understand and gain insight into the beliefs and issues raised by other participants. Questions are asked from a position of curiosity rather than certainty. In a debate, participants listen in order to refute the opposition's data and expose weaknesses in their arguments.

New information During dialogue, new information comes to light, whereas in debate, statements are predictable and offer little new information.

Complexity A successful dialogue requires exploration of complexities of the issue being discussed. In contrast, a successful debate involves simple, impassioned statements.

Relation to dominant discourse Finally, in a dialogue session, participants are encouraged to question the dominant public discourse by expressing fundamental needs that may or may not be reflected in the discourse and by exploring various options for problem definition and resolution. The participants may find that the language and concepts often used in the public debate are inadequate. Debates, on the other hand, take place within the constraints of the dominant public discourse which defines the problem and the options for resolution. Fundamental needs and values are assumed to be clearly understood (Becker, 1995). The characteristics of the group conflict resolution discussions I observed corresponded more to dialogue than to debate.

Key Elements of the Dialogue Process

There are four elements of dialogue intervention that are particularly important for making it successful: a dialogue leader; an exchange of suffering; confrontation; and a visible or symbolic indication that the speaker has been heard. First, although there is some discussion among theorists as to whether the facilitator or dialogue leader must be an outsider to the issue or whether it works well to use trained participants involved in the controversy, many theorists agree that the dialogue process needs leaders. As the leader, the facilitator is expected to take responsibility for stimulating and moderating the discussion by asking questions, identifying key points, and managing the group process. Further, one of the crucial tasks of the facilitator is to help develop an atmosphere of safety among the participants. In order to help the group feel at ease, the dialogue leader tends not to interject her or his own personal opinions; the facilitator does not act as a teacher or lecturer (From Role of Dialogue Leader in a Dialogue Circle, Community Wide Dialogue: Racism, Race Relations, Racial Healing, Inter-religious Council, Syracuse, NY).

It is important to note that what I have described so far of the dialogue facilitator is based on US cultural norms. The main facilitators of the moments of dialogue at the conference were not from the US and their behavior contrasted sharply with US norms just described. For example, the Indian dialogue leaders did interject their own opinions and did appear to see themselves as teachers. However, the responsibilities that the Indian dialogue leaders took on were similar.

Second, the most important outcome of a successful dialogue is for each side to understand where the other side is coming from. During the dialogue process, the participants learn the reality of each other's suffering, which in turn changes how the participants see each other. Even if one group has clearly perpetrated most of the violence and suffering, all sides must share how they have been hurt. Stereotypes break down as the participants speak as individuals about their lives and beliefs. As a result, a focus on personal experiences is crucial for the dialogue process. This personal 'venting' is an important precursor to the discussion of issues. Storytelling can transform enemies into human beings (Saunders, 1999).

Third, confrontation is an important part of the dialogue process (Gordon, 1986; hooks, 1997). According to Gordon, 'Dialogue will not occur when a person identifies with the Other, instead of confronting him and relating to him as Other' (Gordon, 1996, p.37). Dialogue is not about empathy and love, nor is it about giving up identity. Learning to confront is the most difficult aspect of dialogue, because it involves risk. However, disagreement must be constructive and caring—'expression of hostility as an end in itself is a useless activity, but when it is the catalyst pushing us on to greater clarity and understanding, it serves a meaningful function' (hooks, 1997, p.410). Support, which is often equated with unqualified approval, can create barriers to understanding and inflict emotional damage (Rule, 1981). Real support does not mean the suspension of critical judgement, but self-respect and respect for other people even when they seriously disagree (hooks, 1997).

Specifically, participants must confront the role that certain parties play as oppressors. One of the main goals of dialogue is empowerment. However, without addressing inequities of power, the dialogue process may simply reinforce the asymmetry of the parties involved (Abu-Nimer, 1999). Dialogue can become a form of co-optation and control. Contact with adversarial groups may assuage the conscience of members of the oppressor group so that they feel no need to take further action (Kuttab, 1988). For the oppressed, dialogue can serve as a safety valve for venting frustration. If difficult problems and asymmetric power relations are ignored and similarities are overemphasized, the dialogue process can not contribute to changing relationships.

However, emphasizing individual storytelling should not preclude discussion of collective identities and political context. In this way, dialogue has the potential to address conflict on both individual and collective levels. If the discussion focuses solely on psychological or cultural issues to the exclusion of political issues, then the process may contribute to the escalation of the conflict (Abu-Nimer, 1999).

Fourth, listening and feeling heard is also important for the dialogue process. Some models, such as the Common Ground approach, stress the importance of reflective listening in situations that are polarized. Reflective listening involves repeating back to the speaker what he or she has said without using inflammatory adjectives. Most often:

> The two sides are so sure they know what each other is going to say, that often they do not listen, or they listen with such a thick filter, that only a portion of the message gets through. Active listening can be a key tool in breaking through the stereotypes and in developing real understanding. It is good for a person on one side to have the experience of really being heard by someone on the other side (Common Ground Facilitator Training Packet).

Either the dialogue facilitator or the participants can reflect back to each other.

Reflective listening is a skill commonly taught in US conflict resolution training. Again, it is a culturally constructed approach which most of the international dialogue leaders did not use. However, they did give some indication to the participants that they had been heard.

WILPF

Workshop I: Debate at the WILPF Congress in Helsinki

In this section, I will contrast the characteristics of two workshops, which I would not characterize as dialogue, with one moment of successful dialogue, which occurred in a spontaneous community meeting. I will start with a workshop organized as a debate. In the previous chapter, I described a workshop on tribalism, racism and economics that ended with some of the women of color walking out of the session in tears and in anger. Afterwards the workshop participants discussed their views on what had happened and reverberations rippled throughout the conference. Both the workshop leader, Kay, and the vocal participant, Geraldine, used techniques common to a debate.

As in a debate, the identity of the two leaders was significant. One black and the other white, they both indicated early on that they saw each other as potential opponents. In addition, both had a great deal of experience in presenting their well-constructed arguments. Kay was an insider to WILPF. She was a respected member, as a university professor; she was familiar with the cultural norms of the organization; and she looked like the majority of the WILPF membership, who were older, white women. Geraldine expressed to me later her resentment towards Kay, emphasizing that professionals like her would get their theories on people of color published, furthering their own careers, whereas Geraldine did not have that kind of power or access. Had the workshop leader been a woman of color, the debate might have been very different.

On the other hand, if Geraldine and her allies had been white, Kay might have responded quite differently to their point of view. Kay told me later that she had not expected the politicized, well-informed young women of color to attend the conference. She informed me that she would not have offered the workshop had she known that Geraldine, a professional, would be participating. At past WILPF conferences, her expertise had not been challenged by the rather homogeneous group of WILPF members. Kay may have felt threatened by Geraldine.

As workshop facilitator, Kay modeled intellectual debate (Sather, 1999; Ericson, Murphy and Zeuschner, 1987). Kay presented her argument, then during the discussion posed challenging questions to her opponents and gave examples to strengthen her own position. She provided many opportunities for the opponents of her theory to elaborate on their position and to refute her argument. In the interest of pluralism, she was not afraid of disagreement or conflict in the workshop. Kay asked challenging questions and presented examples to strengthen her own argument, which was quite different from Geraldine's. Both Kay and her opponents attempted to persuade the undecided audience that their argument was the most powerful. At no time did Kay acknowledge common points in their positions. Her technique was effective in exploring positions and ideas.

Geraldine, also unintimidated by conflict, responded in kind by taking over the leadership of the workshop and presenting her position in detail. She spoke passionately about issues important for people of color or 'blacks' in the European Union. Under their leadership, many different ideas about racism and discrimination were contrasted and compared or challenged.

For Kay and several other women in the workshop, it was important to have an atmosphere where it was 'okay' to have different opinions. (Several women mentioned this in the go-round after the young women of color had left.) Kay said that she wanted to be able to say what she thought. It was their problem if the others did not like what she had to say. In her mind, they could disagree and still work together. She could have gone along with Geraldine's arguments or attempted to find a compromise; Kay may have felt under pressure as the workshop leader to resolve the conflict. Instead she encouraged further discussion. She felt it would be condescending to agree when she really disagreed. During the workshop, Kay maintained her position and, in her mind, her integrity.

Kay saw a need for conflict. She felt that she had contributed to the growth of the organization, and to anti-racism, by escalating the conflict. She did not agree nor did she remain silent. As a result, the conflict was not resolved and ended up going to a public arena where it would receive more attention rather than being forgotten. Because of the conflict, Geraldine and the others brought their concerns to the WILPF plenary and the definition of racism was discussed by the organization as a whole.

In an interview, Kay said she was pleased with how the conflict had ended. She maintained that the result of the discussions was very positive and that she had played a role in making it happen:

> Looking back now, I am delighted with that which happened, happened because I think it gave a push to WILPF to look at matters of racism with a focus that hasn't been there

> before. And that may not have happened if we had resolved things within the workshop and put everything nicely on a piece of paper. It might have been filed away and not come into the open the way it did. So at the moment I am delighted things happened the way it did.

In addition, she felt she had responded well in the situation by giving the black women the floor.

The style of the workshop was more congruent with the description of debate outlined above than with dialogue. Several key elements of dialogue were missing. Both Kay and Geraldine focused on issues, not personal experience. They did not explore their own place within a racist society or their own feelings about racism. As a result, they did not have a chance to express their painful experiences to each other. However, the conversation was emotionally charged. Even though Geraldine and the other young women of color did not speak of their personal experiences with racism, they had very strong feelings about the issues and about how the conversation was going. For example, Geraldine's argument for a definition of racism based on color was founded in part on fear and anger that her agenda would become invisible if color was no longer essential in how racism was constructed. She was afraid that anti-racism work could no longer be considered a priority if all hurts or forms of 'otherness' were weighted equally. These emotions were never acknowledged, and in the debate format, there was little room for feelings or personal experience.

Further, Geraldine confided in me after the first day of the workshop that she had not felt 'heard.' Some of the participants thought they had acknowledged, even agreed with, her viewpoint, through the many responses and arguments challenging her viewpoint. After the young women of color had left many of the participants said in the go-round that they were confused, they 'didn't understand what they had done wrong.' They thought they had listened, that they had agreed that racism included color. The conflict must have been a result of miscommunication or a misunderstanding they felt. However, I noted few affirmations, indications of agreement, similar stories, or attempts at summarizing and clarifying, which are often considered indications that one has heard and understood the content of the discussion. For example, Kay expressed to me in an interview that the 'black issue' was important, that is, 'immediately and emotionally,' it made sense to separate out 'the black issue' because it was so much in the forefront. But Kay did not acknowledge this important point to the workshop, a statement of common ground that might have left Geraldine with the sense that she had been heard.

Acknowledging the content of the speaker's words can serve a dual function of affirming the speaker and encouraging the listener to think about what was said on a deeper level. The debate did not appear to promote understanding of each other. After the group of young women had left the workshop, many of the women expressed their confusion as to what had happened, causing me to wonder how much some of the women had comprehended. They had enough understanding of racism on an abstract level to understand and even agree to some extent with the women of color, but they seemed to be confused as to what it meant on an emotional/personal level. They were totally mystified as to why the young women of color would suddenly leave. Why were Geraldine, Karen, and Daba so angry and hurt?

The following statement from Karen clearly illustrates the effects of the debate. In response to the acceptance of the proposal to accept the women of color group's definition of racism. Karen wrote a note for me, at my request, describing the event. It read:

> The overwhelming support of our definition of racism and other resolutions this morning was really encouraging. There were, of course, the inevitable questions, 'What about the holocaust?' 'What about racism on the basis of occupation?' but I think they were a knee-jerk reaction, arguing for the sake of argument. The whole G.B. (Gertrude Baer) seminar went up front and answered questions, once again perfectly spur-of-the-moment organized, and with the support of 'prominent' WILPFers, the resolution passed. I can't believe it! We won, we did it! What's more, I think that the whole Congress has really learned something and WILPF history has been made.

For Karen, the discussion was framed as a win/lose situation and her side had won. She discounted the arguments of the older European or Israeli women arguing that racism was not entirely based on color. Some of these women had lived through World War II and the Holocaust when Hitler based genocide of the Jewish people on his construction of the Jewish race—a racism not based on color. In the debate format, Karen missed an opportunity to gain greater understanding of perceptions of racism different from her own.

The debate reified positions and identities. There was little room to be different. As Geraldine felt more and more alienated from the group, she made more and more attempts to control the situation. The second day of the workshop, she took center stage and started presenting her own workshop on racism in the European Union. I observed that it was out of frustration and desperation, in addition to her own conviction, that she began to insist that there must be one definition of racism, her own. She was not persuaded by the many international examples of racism discussed in the workshop that color might not be the only basis for racial discrimination or oppression. Instead, Geraldine, Karen, and Daba maintained that there was one universal definition of racism based on color, and demanded not only that the workshop participants agree but that WILPF adopt the definition as part of the WILPF mission statement. Their proposal generated much conversation among WILPF, members but it also polarized the positions of those involved in the conflict.

As the discussion became polarized, some women began to feel that if they disagreed with the group's definition, then they would be labeled racist. Later I heard that one young European American woman, Sandy, who had attended the controversial workshop, decided that she would not travel on the peace train because of the conflict (despite the fact that there were no refunds). She told me that after this experience, she felt the underlying atmosphere was 'poison to her system.' Sandy felt that there was no room to disagree. She had not perceived the workshop in the same way as the others, and when the young women had discussed racism in the Gertrude Baer Seminar (a class set up during the WILPF

Congress in Helsinki for the young participants), there was no room for her definition, so she left. In her opinion, everyone experiences oppression or 'otherness,' so she wanted to broaden rather than focus the definition of racism. Sandy decided that she would work better elsewhere and would try to get to the FWCW in some other way.

There were clearly differences of opinion among the women of color that did not come to the forefront. I spoke individually with two young women, both living the US, one a Guatemalan/Mayan refugee and the other an Asian American of mixed racial heritage. The Mayan woman felt that the definition of racism that was passed was 'not quite right.' She did not think the issue was just color, particularly given the discrimination she faced as a Mesquite/Mayan in Guatemala. The Asian American woman agreed that the definition was not complete. She said she understood that 'racism was being co-opted but…' She could not put her finger on why the definition was 'not quite right,' but somehow it did not satisfy her.

Although the debate generated much discussion and gained attention for the issue of racism, it also set people at odds. Many of the women did not feel heard or understood. In addition, as much as Kay talked about an atmosphere where people could disagree, the polarized debate did not promote expression of difference. At the end of the workshop go-round, a couple of women talked about their regret for what had happened. One said that in WILPF they like to intellectualize and that 'we are afraid to acknowledge that we are racist.' Another woman spoke sadly, saying, 'We lost our humanity—we didn't respond to people hurting.' Furthermore, the conflict made cooperation appear out of the question for the group of young women of color. Outraged, they brought the conflict to the organization as a whole, where their position was recognized, but not without personal costs.

Workshop II: Peace Train Prejudice Reduction

During the train ride, the WILPF leadership, in particular Bettina, initiated and developed proactive strategies for addressing the conflict rather than just responding as they had in Helsinki. WILPF provided several opportunities to discuss the topic of racism, particularly in the workshop format. Bettina made a point of attending the workshop on fascism and racism led by Barrie, a professional African American activist and when Geraldine spoke during Barrie's session, Bettina stood by her side to support her statements. Twice, Geraldine presented her workshop on racism in the European Union. An African American woman, Angela, led a workshop on bridge building between women of different races. The topic of racism arose in many other workshops often in connection with development and post-colonialism. Furthermore, Bettina called together a small international group to discuss WILPF global priorities. These meetings took place while the train was in motion on two empty train cars provided expressly for that purpose.

Angela's workshop on bridge building, the focus of my discussion, was based on the prejudice reduction workshop format developed by the National Coalition

Building Institute (NCBI). Although the prejudice reduction workshop is similar in some ways to dialogue, the differences are important enough that I do not categorize it as dialogue. In order to complete the workshop program, the 15 participants met several times. This took a great deal of perseverance on Angela's part, given the scheduling difficulties with the open train cars, but we finally finished the program. One of the reasons the participants continued to attend over a long period of time was the respect that Angela had earned during the journey. She was outspoken, articulate, and showed a willingness to take on leadership. Further, her identity as an African American woman gave her a certain authority in the area of race—the theme of the workshop.

In many ways, Angela's method of facilitation was the opposite of Kay's debate style. First, Angela's method of facilitation was highly structured whereas Kay seemed satisfied with the workshop as long as an interesting conversation was going on. Angela's workshop consisted of group exercises. The first exercise focused on getting to know one another and encouraged racial pride. According to Brown and Mazza, exploring their own racial background allows participants to examine internal stereotypes which function to keep groups divided and powerless. NCBI maintains that 'working through intra-group divisions is one prerequisite for building inter-group coalitions' (Brown and Mazza, 1992, p.5).

The second set of exercises was set up around speak outs. Speak outs focus the attention of the group on predominant forms of institutionalized oppression, such as racism, sexism, anti-Semitism, and homophobia (Brown and Mazza, 1992). The participants were organized into panels according to racial or ethnic groups and then each member of each panel spoke in turn to the larger group about what it was like to be a part of that racial/ethnic group. Speakers were instructed to talk about their personal experiences of discrimination. Specific questions that Angela put to the speakers included 'What is good about being from your racial or ethnic heritage?' and, 'What do you never want said about your racial/ethnic group?' The speak outs took up most of the workshop sessions. As a conclusion, the group exchanged appreciations of each other and of the workshop as a whole.

Second, with the exercises, Angela focused the participant's response on personal experience rather than on intellectual issues. NCBI prejudice reduction is based on the theory that the most effective way of communicating the effect of racism is through personal narrative (Brown and Mazza, 1992). Angela asked each individual to reflect on how race had shaped their lives instead of exploring issues or positions as Kay did. Third, Angela stipulated that the responses to the speakers must be positive and supportive; criticism and confrontation were not allowed. Angela based her workshop on the philosophy that positive affirmation and sharing of personal experience were key to building community. Her techniques differed from Kay's in that they encouraged connection between the women rather than conflict. As they listened to stories of individual suffering and pride, the participants began to empathize with one another.

Fourth, unlike Kay, Angela focused almost entirely on emotional agendas. Participants were asked how they felt about their racial and ethnic identities. Emotions such as anger, frustration, hurt, and confusion were a critical component of the stories told. However, no discussion of these feelings or of related problems were allowed. Fifth, Angela restricted participation in the workshop by requiring those attending to come with a partner who had a different background than their own. Participants then were required to have done some bridge building with someone of a different ethnic or racial background in order to take part.

Angela's workshop did exactly what the title stated the workshop would do—build bridges. Through the speakouts and appreciations, the participants shared their personal experiences and feelings, building upon and strengthening their friendships with each other. For the most part, Angela's workshop was very well received by the participants. At the closing, many of the participants expressed their satisfaction. They had a chance to share their feelings, gained a better understanding of each other, and were drawn closer together. Angela's highly structured techniques seemed to free up the participants to listen actively. Each person would have a turn to speak and they were not required to respond, so that the participants' only job was to listen and try to understand. The atmosphere was relaxed, attentive, and affirming.

However, the workshop did not develop skills for dealing with conflict or criticism, leaving the connections somewhat fragile. The participants did not explore the underlying problems in their relationships to one another nor did they search for common ground across the racial/ethnic identity groups The personal stories told did not necessarily speak to current dynamics or specific issues that concerned the women involved in the workshop.

Furthermore, the participants were not allowed to question or confront one another. Only supportive statements were permitted. Personal experiences were presented for understanding and approval, not discussion. According to Jane Rule:

> Support is a much used word in the women's movement. For too many people it means giving and receiving unqualified approval. Some women are awfully good at withdrawing it at crucial moments. Too many are convinced they can't function without it. It's a false concept which has produced barriers to understanding and done real emotional damage. Suspension of critical judgment is not necessary for offering real support which has to do instead with self-respect and respect for other people even at moments of serious disagreement (Rule, 1981).

If the women had concerns, thoughts, or assumptions about their colleagues, they remained unchallenged. As a result, it was not clear how strong those 'bridges' were and how well they would fare under stormy weather when serious disagreement arose.

Dialogue: Peace Train Community Meeting in Ukraine

Tensions around racism continued to rise during the journey to Beijing. For example, several white women who wanted to join Angela's workshop were turned away because they came alone. They were quite upset and/or embarrassed. In response, a number of white women decided to form a group for white allies but the group turned into a session for venting hurt and resentment at being shut out and labeled racist.

The high level of tension around this situation and other events on the train resulted in a meeting which I would categorize as a moment of dialogue. The following is a discussion of a spontaneous community meeting that took place during a brief stop in a small Ukranian city. One of the filmmakers aboard the train recorded it on video, making it possible for me to quote the women participating (WILPF, 1996). This was the first and only large group meeting (approximately 50 people) that took place around the issue of difference during our journey by train. Unlike the two workshops I described previously, it was not on the schedule. However, this session successfully began the dialogue process.

The Dialogue Leadership

Bhuvana, a woman originally from India but who taught at a University in Canada, facilitated most of the community meeting. By the end of the second week of the peace train, Bhuvana had gained the respect and confidence of many passengers from diverse backgrounds. She was asked many times to lecture in workshops and classes on the train in the areas of development, gender and the UN. In this international setting, Bhuvana had much to offer as a facilitator because she was from the East but worked in the West. In addition to the confidence she inspired, she was very familiar with both 'cultures'; she was a bridge builder.

Bhuvana was part of a group that initiated and facilitated the meeting. The other women on the team were from the USA. Marilyn, a European American leader in the US section of WILPF, Bhuvana, Barrie, and a young European American woman, Kathy, were all part of the planning group. Marilyn and Kathy spoke at the beginning of the meeting and occasionally commented during the session. Marilyn said in her opening comments that she hoped the group would focus not only on the negative but the positive, what unites the group. She gave some examples of issues that the planning group might talk about, like nationalism or racism. Kathy laid some 'ground rules' for the discussion. She requested that the participants talk about 'person to person' issues, not logistical complaints. She emphasized the need for active listening, which she defined as not talking while others were talking and concentrating on what is being said rather that what you would like to say. Kathy added that they wanted everyone to have a chance to speak who wished to so they might cut off long speeches. Barrie closed the session.

Bhuvana's technique as a facilitator differed from the model dialogue leader discussed in the literature and outlined at the beginning of the chapter. As an older Indian woman, her perspective on conflict resolution differed from that of the US author of the dialogue training packet. In societies oriented more towards family and community than the individual, mediators are elders or family members who have some kind of authority because of, for example, their cultural skills (Merry, 1987; Augsburger, 1992). As an elder, Bhuvana did not hesitate to interject her opinion or try to teach the dialogue participants. Further, her attitude was more serious and directive than friendly and facilitative. Nevertheless, Bhuvana accomplished the main goals of the dialogue leader. She took responsibility for stimulating and moderating the discussion by asking questions, identified key points, and managed the group process. Further, she helped to create some safety within the assembled group so that some of the women felt comfortable enough to talk about their personal experiences.

Like Kay, Bhuvana encouraged confrontation, but more on an emotional than an intellectual level. She opened the meeting by saying:

> So we would like to share on what are the issues that unite us and what are the issues that might divide us? Maybe there are no issues that divide us. So we thought that instead of talking to our friends and neighbors perhaps bi-laterally or having some ideas, getting frustrated or getting angry, it might be a good idea for all of us to give expression to our feelings under these nice trees and even if we get angry...But what we'd like to know from you is how do you feel about this experiment, about this metaphorical community that we have become? We would like you therefore to give your feelings as they come, without any restraint, without any constraint.

She and the organizers of the meeting thought that the gossip (they referred to it as whispering) on the train was more destructive to community than an angry face-to-face confrontation.

Bhuvana would ask specific questions related to concrete problems in order to get a frank conversation going. Throughout the meeting, Bhuvana would interject asking the group 'Are you uncomfortable? Why are you uncomfortable?' As a facilitator, Bhuvana strongly encouraged self-reflection. For instance, when a participant asked if Bhuvana thought they had avoided the issue of racism, Bhuvana responded firmly that:

> I don't think we are finished, my friend. We are going to deal with it squarely. We are not going to avoid it. And we are going to face it. We have to face it as we have to face it in the world everyday. Racism is an issue...Why do people feel they are being excluded? Why do they feel cliques are being formed and on the basis of color people are being excluded on our train. Any views on that?

Her response encouraged the participants to face the issue of racism and raised a concrete issue for discussion.

Bhuvana tended to reinforce the points of women who felt discriminated against (because of color, disability, age, language) by summarizing the issue or making suggestions to the group. For example, when the first woman, Sonali, spoke up about her experience with racism, Bhuvana said Sonali had raised an important issue after a couple of women responded by denying the problem. Later, when a German woman said she felt discriminated against because she did not speak English well, Bhuvana responded by encouraging English speaking people to be more sensitive to those for whom English is not a first language. In this way, she indicated to the women who spoke about how they had been hurt that they had been heard and understood.

Bhuvana did not overlook positions which she disagreed with. Frequently, she challenged statements, particularly of the white women who spoke. For the most part, her comments helped the flow of the conversation by challenging assumptions or directing the conversation. At one point, Bhuvana challenged a woman on the team of dialogue leaders. Someone for whom English was not a first language had mentioned language discrimination. Then Kathy told the story of how a tour guide could not keep track of all the Caucasians who look alike. We have to be willing to be uncomfortable, she said. Bhuvana interjected saying:

> Let us not confuse identity and everyday obstacles like language with racism. Language barriers can be crossed by learning the language. Can we learn the language of the other race and cross the barrier? That is a different question. Any views on this question?

Bhuvana inserted her opinion that racism could not be equated with other forms of 'othering.' Nevertheless, she kept the dialogue on the topic of racism.

Occasionally, however, her opinions stopped the conversation. For example, Bhuvana shouted her response when a white Dutch woman said she did not like North American 'colored' people telling Europeans what to do about racism in Europe. The Dutch woman was upset that the definition of racism passed in Helsinki excluded Jews. Bhuvana responded:

> Also who should learn what from whom, we not going to discuss. Whether Europeans tell Americans or Americans tell Latin Americans or Latin Americans tell Africans, we are supposed to be a community. Anyone can tell anybody not to be a racist!

Angry that the Dutch woman apparently wanted to restrict the dialogue, Bhuvana made her views known and the woman did not speak further. However, had Bhuvana explored the Dutch woman's feelings rather than reacting angrily, she might have opened up an interesting topic for discussion. The Dutch woman was not the first woman I heard comment that US dominance was so prevalent that even discussions of racism had to be based on US agendas. Nor was she the only one to question the relationship of anti-semitism to racism.

As a facilitator, Bhuvana was very directive. She focused the topic and the type of conversation. Racism had been a source of conflict throughout the journey and Bhuvana made sure that the topic was discussed. Although she opened the meeting by suggesting the women talk about 'issues that divide us,' Bhuvana provided very clear direction by adding early on that racism was key to the discussion:

> Racism is an issue. It's an issue so important in this world in which we live. There are prejudices and biases against cultures, etc. Let us bring it out into the open rather than keep it with us. Also, if you are uncomfortable about the race question, please tell us why you are uncomfortable and so on.

She continued to bring the conversation back to racism throughout the community meeting.

Dialogue Content and Characteristics

The intent of the dialogue leaders was to keep the conversation at a personal level. A number of times, the participants brought up the definition of racism in reference to the conflict in Helsinki. Bhuvana asserted that the dialogue was not about defining a term. She explained that the UN had a convention devoted to that subject with many definitions of racism. 'Everybody knows what it is in every country because in the world it exists...Give me your views about this.' From her response, I had the sense that she was very knowledgeable on the subject and very aware of the complexity of coming to consensus on a definition of racism. However, as facilitator, she did not want this conversation to take place on an abstract, intellectual level. Some of the people present were hurting and she thought it necessary to respond to people's emotional needs. (What she missed, though, was that some women were still upset about the process by which the decision to accept the definition of racism into the WILPF mission statement was made.)

Bhuvana encouraged responses to the participants' experiences. At times, those responses were critical. Some women in the group felt a need to challenge the participant's feelings and/or experience. For example, a European American woman explained that she really appreciated it when people of color confronted her about her behavior—she learned a lot that way. Another European American woman responded saying she thought it was her responsibility to learn about her own racism—it was not the responsibility of people of color to teach her. Not everyone gave a sympathetic or supportive response, but rather than cutting off critical statements, Bhuvana encouraged further comments or responded herself.

In this setting, with the help of the Indian-US facilitation team, several of the participants felt safe enough to share their pain. As they talked about their personal experiences, differences became obvious among the women identified as white as well as the women identified as women of color. Some of the problems underlying their relationships began to be explored and initial solutions were suggested. Understanding of the problems and issues increased.

A number of the white European and North American women talked about how they had felt excluded or discriminated against in some way, on bases of age, disability, language, and nationality (e.g. Europeans commenting on US domination). As white women, they did not have the same experience on the train.

Maria, an Italian Canadian woman, confronted the participants with her theory on the cause of the group conflicts:

> It seems to me, and that's what's bothering me about the train, that we come to conclusions or some people come to conclusions rather quickly. 'Are you Samira?' for instance rather than asking, I'm sorry I don't remember your name, could you remind me of your name? Which would then allow the person to establish their identity. Or when we were in public sessions, and that is related, we say something that comes to our mind and in a furtive tone which is almost accusing rather than putting in a questioning tone which allows space to the other person to report. This is that element of going straight to something because I know I am right. It seems to me it creates a sense of fear, almost being accused.

Her theory pointed to the problem of actions based on assumptions and stereotypes about the other, rather than approaching the other in a curious mode, which allows the other to establish who they are.

Sonali was the first to give an example of how racism had affected her. She said:

> One of the issues on the train that has bothered me a lot even though I've enjoyed the train a lot, is being mistaken for other people that have the same skin tone as myself…What I've found myself doing on this train is no longer trusting people. That when I come up against somebody I haven't met before, I'm very withdrawn. I try and not like fully trust them just because I'm afraid of getting hurt.

Two white women responded saying they were forgetful of names but it had nothing to do with color. Bhuvana then restated the problem Sonali had raised, that is, not knowing how to recognize individuals within certain groups, said it was important, and asked for further comment.

Later, a white US woman put a question to the women of color caucus and the conversation shifted to a deeper level. The woman asked what the objective of the women of color caucus was (a good example of a question asked out of curiosity rather than a statement). There were three responses. One woman spoke briefly, saying they gathered to talk about issues that confronted them as women of color and how to deal with them. She added that it was 'not a conspiracy or anything of that sort.' Then Michelle, the young woman from Hong Kong responded:

> I think the reason why it was formed stems directly from what you said. After the WILPF conference and the very intense emotional feelings that people had there was not closure from that. And people got on the train with unresolved feelings. And I know that the women in the women of color support group felt that there were still incidents of racism on the train and that we needed a space to just air them to ourselves because there was nowhere else to talk about it. Because it seemed like we had done this in Helsinki and then we got on the train and nothing else happened. And so that is why the women of color support group came into being, I believe. To give ourselves a space that was just for us to say we're not crazy, it's really happening.

This interchange allowed for individual explanations of a position that increased the understanding of the issue. Bhuvana interjected as facilitator saying the issue was not the support group but learning to be sensitive, 'We are all hurt. Let's see what the hurt is about.'

Then Kathy spoke saying that there were some white women hurting and it would be good to hear from both sides. She had heard that some of these women felt they had not been understood. She added that to heal, the group needed to face the insensitivity on both sides. Her comments encouraged a white US woman to express her hurt:

> It's hurtful to a lot of us who have worked on race issues for a large part of our lives in that we are perceived as continuing racists which is not true. The other thing is I would like the support group at some point on this journey to be able to feel that they could

> come to some other people and build on what this woman was saying that they could feel safe with a lot of us so that they could air their views. I feel as long as they are separate then they are going to be talking among themselves and they are not going to be able to involve other people who really are sensitive to the issue of racism. And if we need to have our consciousness raised to a higher level then that needs to be addressed.

The woman communicated not only her pain but her perspective on what she felt were problems in the group's relationships. Her comment helped to start a discussion on underlying issues and led the way for another white woman to speak of her hurt.

In response to the woman's statement, another white US woman replied that she felt it was her responsibility as an oppressor, a racist, to take action and not to 'wait for others to teach us.' Bhuvana reinforced her point, commenting that it was a two way street, not a one way issue. Then the white Dutch woman, mentioned above, raised her voice and spoke angrily about how the definition of racism passed in Helsinki excluded Jews. She added that although there was racism in Europe, she did not like North American 'colored' people telling Europeans what to do.

After Bhuvana gave her explosive response as a facilitator, emphasizing the need to remain open to criticism, the tone of the conversation shifted again (some of the safety had been disturbed). A white US Jewish woman said she did not find her experience with anti-semitism to be similar to the racism that her black sisters experienced. Other white women talked about the desire for contact with people they didn't know. There was some discussion on how best to do this—someone suggested mealtimes. A woman spoke generally about the need to overcome ignorance of diversity and build on similarities.

Then Angela took a risk and spoke about her anger. She wanted to make it clear that she was not just talking about her perception of exclusion but concrete actions that had been taken. She called it rudeness, people saying 'mean and ugly things.' Her examples included someone waking up a woman of color with their foot. She was particularly angry that people had asked her, after her speech, if she had written it herself. The noise level started to rise, as people commented and protested among themselves. Bhuvana intervened to ask Angela to finish her statement and repeated loudly above the din that Angela felt offended by the question. Angela finished by saying she considered these to be hostile acts. Later a woman spoke up, saying the question regarding authorship was meant as a compliment because it was so beautifully written that her speech could have been written by a poet.

Toward the end of the meeting, several of the women involved in the conflict affirmed the importance of the dialogue, particularly the opportunities for changing relationships and for increased understanding. Geraldine felt that dealing with conflicts on the train served as a preparation for discussion of conflicts around agenda items. In her words:

> I'm coming here as a black activist and I want to put the issues for myself and my community on the political agenda. This peace train is not just about trying to be cozy

> and nice. If we want to change the world, we've gotta change ourselves. In order to change ourselves, that's not an easy process. And so there are going to be difficulties. I want us to be able to deal, really deal with some of those conflicts. Not walk away.

Geraldine connected dialogue and self-reflection with changing the dominant political agenda.

Barrie agreed that if their goal was to form global alliances, they needed to learn to work together. She maintained that:

> This progressive community represents the democracy and the world, the global world which we think we are trying to create. And if we can't figure out how to do it among ourselves, you know, the issue gets to be, how on earth are we goina change the world when we can't work internally, you know. What I'm hearing, is we're moving, you know, we're starting to move in that direction.

She felt that open dialogue was key to community building.

To summarize, WILPF members participated in three different sessions led with three different facilitator styles, but only one could be characterized as dialogue. The meeting in the Ukraine was led by a team of facilitators who made an effort create some safety for the participants, by giving them an indication they had been heard, and also encouraged confrontation and questioning that explored the complexities of issues. For the most part, the participants spoke as individuals and variation within identity groups started to become obvious. As a result, new information and greater understanding among the participants was gained. Furthermore, a few of the problems underlying the group relations were identified. Given the very short period of time, the dialogue process was just beginning before the group was forced to end the discussion.

SWVP

Conflict Resolution I: Sudanese Meeting at the NGO Forum '95 in China

During the FWCW conferences, the SWVP and other southern Sudanese made several attempts at dialogue and/or cooperation with women from the North. I observed two of the conflict resolution sessions. Both took place in China, one at the NGO Forum '95 and the other at the FWCW. The analysis of the following dialogue sessions is somewhat different than the meetings that the WILPF constituency held, for two reasons. First, the women involved with WILPF were not negotiating in the context of civil war, where the conflict had escalated to the point of armed conflict compounding the hatred and suffering. Second, the Sudanese groups were much more homogeneous and smaller in size (unlike the WILPF groups which may have included as many as twenty nationalities), so the focus on cultural practices is somewhat stronger.

The level of mistrust between the women participating was very high. SWVP initiated conflict resolution sessions in part because SWVP felt the women from the North were publicly attacking them. SWVP members were afraid of hidden agendas particularly since the Sudanese government directly or indirectly controlled the responses of the northern Sudanese women. Although they were interested in conciliation, they were not about to compromise or be intimidated. SWVP expressed a need for open and honest discussion about the problems between the Sudanese women. For example, women from both the North and South were interested in organizing groups of international women to visit the Sudan on a peace mission, but Lucia made it clear in an interview that SWVP would not be involved unless the Northern women discussed their objectives openly:

> But we don't want this kind of work, trying to collaborate but with a hidden agenda. We need the objectives to be very clear and the visiting, or mutual visiting should also be put across the line we are in.

SWVP wanted to work with women from northern Sudan but were not willing to be used as pawns in the process.

The first conflict resolution session I attended was the second meeting that had taken place involving women from northern and southern Sudan. Unfortunately, this conflict resolution session did not meet the needs of SWVP—it did not contain many elements of dialogue. As I described in chapter 5, during the African regional prepcom and in Hairou at the NGO Forum '95, northern Sudanese women made comments in public forums questioning both the right of the SWVP to speak and the credibility of their voices. In Hairou, SWVP called for women from northern and southern Sudan to meet together in the peace tent to discuss what had happened. The group of women that came together was fairly large, as mentioned in chapter 5, close to 20 people. However, the majority of the women came from the North. In the peace tent, the group sat and stood in a circle (Rachel stood the entire time). The conversation took place in English. Sayida, the young Sudanese soldier, brought along a video camera that she used at the beginning of the meeting—a potentially threatening move.

Meeting Facilitator

From my perspective as an observer, there was no facilitator. However, the male northern Sudanese government official who was present played a very important role in directing and controlling the conversation. The male government official participated in the meeting in order to reinforce state policies and to keep the northern women from publicly deviating from the party line (Garang Thieu Juac, conversation with author 27 June 2002). From the perspective of the government, as the weaker sex, the women would need assistance from a man to remain firm in their convictions.

The man spoke after about twenty minutes when the women began to discuss peace proposals. He called for pride in being Sudanese, saying that he was proud to gather together as Sudanese. He thought that the women had distinguished themselves at the conference. Next he praised the Sudanese minister of peace who was a woman. The official then went on to say that some Sudanese women were enjoying themselves outside of the country. He maintained that it was safe for them to return and yet they remained outside the Sudan.

Rachel was furious. The male official's comment was obviously aimed at her, a refugee. She spoke up, saying she was angry the minister had said there were women outside the country just for fun. Someone responded quickly denying what he had said rather than recognizing Rachel's feelings. His statement reinforced the position of some of the northern Sudanese women that SWVP was not credible. He implied that SWVP members were motivated by self-interest, not by any real danger or significant issues. His comments also served to divide the women. A northern Sudanese woman covered for him and agreed with him rather than reaching out to Rachel. His opening remarks drawing on national pride reflected the northern position—a united nation as opposed to self-determination for the South.

At the close of the meeting, the Sudanese government official took the opportunity to again sing the praises of the 'her excellency' the minister of peace, who was an advocate for peace. He mentioned that she had worked with former President Jimmy Carter during his visit to the Sudan. Moreover, he added, she shared the views of her sisters, not just as a minister but as a mother. An appeal to SWVP support the minister as a women, sister, and mother was made. However, from the feedback that Rachel gave me later, it was not effective. Moreover, his affirmation of the minister reinforced his obvious alliance with the state rather than the efforts of the grassroot groups present.

Meeting Content and Characteristics

With the official present, the northern women spoke most often. Much of their discussion centered on calls for greater involvement of women in the peace process. A number of women tried to build connections between women from North and South by referring to their roles as mothers and wives, stating that women are by nature more peaceful than men. They felt they needed to 'stand as one as mothers.' Others talked about how men forget the lessons they taught them as children, but they are still their sons and they should listen to their mothers. One woman argued that men cannot listen to each other but women, on the other hand, can agree.

Rachel did not join in the conversation on how women are better peacemakers. Instead, she emphasized a need for concrete proposals. In response, a number of women made suggestions. Several women talked about how arms sales fueled the war and those selling arms needed to be stopped. A couple of women validated government attempts to initiate peace talks. One woman explained the importance of teaching peace in our daily lives. This same woman maintained that women needed to work together as a pressure group to stop the warring parties.

At this point, Rachel tried to provide leadership for the session by changing the character of the conversation. She called for a just peace and challenged the women present, as intellectuals, to figure out how to stop the war. Rachel pointed out that, in terms of weapons sales, 'if there is a market, people will buy,' putting the responsibility back onto the warring parties. She went on to talk about 'transparency,' saying that unless the women talked about their problems, they could not resolve them. She urged the women not to attack other women in public. Rachel concluded by stressing the importance of networking and repeating the need for concrete proposals.

Rachel made a number of significant points that were never addressed by the group. First of all, Rachel talked about a 'just peace.' As I showed in chapter five, SWVP did not feel comfortable speaking of self-determination in front of critical audiences. Instead, they would use the less volatile term, 'just peace.' Rachel did not elaborate on her views on what it would take to achieve a just peace, nor did anyone ask. As a result, the group did not have a chance to talk about the problems or issues underlying north/south relations. Nor did they indicate that they had heard and understood what she said.

Second, Rachel felt it was very important to talk about the conflict that had taken place at the conference and how they would relate to each other. She was looking for some self-reflection or discussion on a more personal level. No one ever responded to her concern or even mentioned the conflict that had taken place in the African tent. The discussion remained at a very abstract level, leading Rachel to believe that the northern women were insincere in their reconciliation efforts. After the meeting, Rachel said to me, 'Those women say they are for peace,' but she did not feel they were sincere. The meeting did not provide an opportunity to discuss issues that were barriers to their cooperation and understanding. Proposals were discussed without having identified and agreed upon issues that needed to be dealt with.

As I mentioned earlier, it was important to Rachel that the northern women state their objectives clearly. She did not want to be manipulated. The meeting ended with a northern woman suggesting that they form two steering committees, one inside the country and one outside the country. A white woman present, who I later learned worked for an NGO based in the Sudan, raised the question as to how the two committees would stay in contact (Rachel had raised this issue earlier, asking the group how they would obtain visas to get into the country to meet together on this steering committee). Someone summarized the proposals suggested, mentioning the need to address the UN as well as the decision to write a letter to both the Sudanese government and the opposition that would be delivered by her excellency, the minister for peace.

I learned later that one of the main objectives of this meeting for some of the northern Sudanese women was to obtain signatures from SWVP on the peace letter to be delivered to the UN. This document would be a feather in the cap for the Sudanese minister of peace. Some of the women from the north did want a peace agreement, but on their terms as the dominant, state supported group. The discussion that took place in this conflict resolution meeting did not challenge their perspective in any way. In the end, SWVP did not sign the agreement despite pressure to do so. It did not reflect their agenda.

Meeting Feedback

After the conflict resolution session was over, Rachel debriefed the session with me. She continued to be angry at the man's comment that some women were out of the country for fun. She laughed harshly at this ridiculous notion. 'He says come on back but we can't come back!' she exclaimed. If she returned to any area outside the SPLM-controlled areas in the Sudan, she not be allowed to leave the country again and would be forced to follow Sharia Law. Rachel scoffed at the man's praise for the Minister of Peace. 'She has done nothing,' she said. Then she expressed her doubt at how sincere the women were in their desire for peace. To Rachel, talk about the need to involve women in peacemaking meant little in a context where she felt the northern women were attacking her publicly. It had not felt like an honest conversation to her. In all likelihood, she felt betrayed when the northern women came with the male official. She had expected the conversation to be woman-to-woman.

The male government official made open communication impossible. Not only was he biased, but his identity as a man and a representative of the state, with all its power, made it dangerous for the northern women to say anything that varied from the state position (Garang Thieu Juac, conversation with author 27 June 2002). They could safely talk about women as peacemakers and about methods of conflict resolution but mentioning injustice or self-determination would mean reprisal when they returned to northern Sudan. Using the video that the northern Sudanese soldier had filmed at the beginning of the session, the state could trace the women once they returned home. If the male delegate had not been present, the women would have felt free to speak honestly with one another.

Rachel's satisfaction with this meeting was very low. The Northern women tended to dominate. The conversation remained at an abstract level, and the discussion never reached the more personal, concrete level that Rachel was hoping for. General proposals were discussed, but the women were not able to lay the groundwork necessary for the further collaboration proposed by the northern women. Little understanding was gained during the session. It was an opportunity to restate positions and demonstrate loyalty to the state rather than a chance to exchange personal experiences, challenge stereotypes and find common ground. Although Rachel perceived her connection to the northern Sudanese women as a woman to be a starting point for further collaboration, she had had enough experience with her colleagues to mistrust them. This first conflict resolution session did not decrease the mistrust.

Dialogue: Mediation between Northern and Southern Sudanese at the FWCW in Beijing

The second attempt at dialogue between the northern and southern Sudanese women, which took place at the FWCW, was quite different in tone. This session was also initiated because women from the North had verbally attacked a woman from the South during a peace caucus meeting. During the meeting, a southern

Sudanese woman responded to a discussion concerning the appropriateness of war crimes tribunals; she did not think it was helpful to the peace process in the Sudan. The conflict erupted when the southern Sudanese woman explained that her daughter had been kidnapped and sold into slavery. The northern Sudanese women vehemently denied the existence of slavery and called her a 'liar.' This time, however, an international group of women intervened. They facilitated the meeting and did not allow the northern Sudanese women to take over. Coming from different cultural backgrounds, the impromptu team's methods were quite varied but effective. They succeeded in creating a moment of dialogue.

Once the Sudanese women had quieted down, Subhara, an older woman from India, offered to sit with the women later if they would like to talk to each other. Then she added, 'If we cannot talk with each other as women then we are no better than the men.' Members of the peace caucus applauded, and the Sudanese women agreed to meet.

When the peace caucus finished, a small group went with the four Sudanese to an adjacent room. I invited myself along. Subhara led the way, followed by a UNESCO employee from Senegal, two women from the USA who identified themselves as having international conflict resolution experience, and a Palestinian representative for the YWCA. As we went around with introductions, Sayida, the northern Sudanese soldier identified herself, along with another northern Sudanese woman associated with the Sudanese government, and a black African who worked in the Sudanese peace ministry. The southern Sudanese woman disclosed that she was a refugee in London with the NGO Africa Rights.

Dialogue Leaders

The spontaneous international team of conciliators worked very well with each other and the disputants. The techniques of the mediators might have clashed at another time but in this context, the mediators modeled cultural sensitivity towards each other despite different underlying assumptions about the process. For example, like Bhuvana, Subhara's decision to intervene may have been based on a cultural assumption that mediators in her society are elders or family members with authority based on cultural skills. Subhara, an older woman, had established herself as a leader within the caucus during the FWCW. Her rationale for taking action may have been very different from U.S. mediators who gain authority from their expertise or impartiality (Merry, 1987; Augsburger, 1992). The two US women who joined the group introduced themselves as international mediators. Subhara, on the other hand, did not talk about her credentials. Afterwards, she told me emphatically that she was not an expert.

During the mediation, the conciliators' assumptions about disputing as well as differing concepts of self came into play. Once everyone had gathered, the group sat and talked for a while. Then the two U.S. women suggested that we start by going around and talking about our individual goals for the session. At first Subhara ignored them, continuing to chat. Then she began to talk about how she hoped they could listen and build understanding between them, empathizing with how hard it was for them to be here, etceteras. Next she had us all go around and introduce ourselves.

This interaction illustrates some differences in cultural assumptions among the dialogue leaders. The U.S. women probably saw the attempt at conflict resolution as a distinct and scheduled event set up to form a contract based on individual interests. Subhara, on the other hand, may have conceived of conflict resolution as a subtle shift from normal interaction into conflict resolving based on the repair of relationships. As a result, the Americans did not see that the mediation had already started. Nor was the Indian dialogue leader comfortable beginning the mediation session by stating individual interests because she would tend to define the self in relationship to others (Merry, 1987; Augsburger, 1992).

Each member of the team of dialogue leaders played an important role. Subhara set the stage as a wise elder. She gave advice, told stories, and set some ground rules. For instance, when the northern soldier, Sayida, tried to interrogate the southern Sudanese woman, Subhara stated very firmly that there was no need to know each other's background or give last names, etc. She had to repeat herself a couple of times. Subhara told her own similar stories apparently hoping that the women could 'hear' what was said by their 'enemies' if it was coming from someone else. Her storytelling seemed to be effective. After Subhara told her own story of how difficult it was for her to acknowledge things she did not like in her own country, the northern women stopped attacking the southern Sudanese refugee when she talked about slavery. Moreover, Subhara's identity as an Indian woman might not have pushed buttons the way that the US women alone might have.

The US mediators used quite different techniques, but they also appeared to be helpful in generating dialogue. First, the two women reinforced the ground rules that Subhara set, saying directly that it may not be safe for everyone to give certain kinds of information during the meeting. Second, they asked the Sudanese women to reflect back what they had heard, a technique commonly referred to in the US as reflective listening. Sayida agreed to reflect back what the refugee had said about her daughter and how she was kidnapped. Once she had summarized the refugee's story, Sayida told her own story of suffering during the war, a significant shift in the meeting. The two women seemed to make a connection around their pain. Third, the US mediators did not challenge the authority of Subhara as the leader of the session. As a result, the dialogue leadership was not based on Northern cultural norms.

The Senegalese woman employed by UNESCO did not say much, but her presence was significant, particularly to the refugee. She sat on the couch in between the two southern Sudanese women, one a refugee and the other employed by the state. Most important, she provided some safety for the refugee, who was quite alone. Her physical presence created a buffer between the other Sudanese women. In addition, her identity as a Black African ally may have made the refugee feel more comfortable, given that the other mediators were from different continents.

Dialogue Content and Characteristics

Subhara reported to me later that the purpose of the dialogue was two-fold: 1.) to guide a 'safe' discussion between the women; and 2.) to facilitate learning and understanding. The first challenge of the facilitators was to limit Sayida's aggressive interrogation so as to create a safe space for the southern Sudanese woman, who was viewed by the soldier as a dissident. It appeared at first that the northern women came simply to pressure the woman from the South into signing a 'peace' agreement. Initially, the northern Sudanese women attempted to interrogate the woman from southern Sudan. As Subhara commented later, 'I felt that the women from the present regime were seeking more information rather than committing themselves in any way.'

The northern women were interested getting signatures from SWVP, particularly Rachel, on the peace agreement they had drawn up the third conflict resolution session. This would be a feather in their cap. Apparently, not only had Rachel refused to sign it, but she had flown back to the Sudan. At this session, the soldier Sayida tried to convince the southern Sudanese woman to sign the peace agreement, but she also refused. Once it was confirmed that Rachel had left, and the southern Sudanese woman had made it clear she would not sign, three of the women discussed leaving, in Arabic. (I learned this later from Subhara who understands Arabic.)

The group stayed, but continued to question the southern Sudanese woman about names, dates, and places, particularly where the woman's daughter had been sold into slavery. The dialogue leaders intervened throughout, trying to protect the southern Sudanese woman by insisting that nobody needed to give details, particularly if it affected their safety. Giving this type of information to the military and government representatives might have endangered the life of the refugee and/or her family. Subhara explained in her interview, 'My effort therefore was to see whether one could move them from that very confident position that they seemed to have that they could control and contain what the dissident (the southern Sudanese refugee) had said.'

Once the northern Sudanese women began to slow down their aggressive questioning, the dialogue leaders were able to draw out personal stories around the topic of loss during the war. The women spoke for a while about difficult issues that came up, like refugee status and slavery. Eventually the women calmed down somewhat and appeared to be more reflective. The conciliators affirmed the Sudanese women's efforts, some of the mediators and participants exchanged addresses, a conciliator took a picture of the group all together, and the session ended.

Dialogue Feedback and Analysis

Once the session had finished, I asked Subhara to reflect on the meeting. She had stressed, toward the beginning of the session, the importance of listening to different perspectives. She hoped that by listening the Sudanese women might gain some understanding. Specifically, Subhara felt that the attitude of the young soldier began to change when the women exchanged personal stories:

> But I felt encouraged when Sayida, the young and more outspoken woman talked about her mother's friend who had lost a son and who was unforgiving. And what the dissident said to her about the mothers in the South who had their lost sons and were unforgiving. There was some intellectual acknowledgment of the fact that the same suffering can afflict two bitterly opposing groups of people. And at root it is the same suffering...That, I thought was a movement in her thinking and her attitude...

She hoped they could see their common ground by listening to each other's experience of war.

The women confronted each other with their questions, positions, and stories of their personal suffering. The dialogue leaders tried to help the women listen to each other. For example, the northern Sudanese women insisted that the southern Sudanese woman could re-enter the country at anytime, implying that she must be benefiting from her refugee status. Subhara responded by telling the story of her own complex feelings about her nationality. She commented later:

> They were speaking from a position of wanting to dictate the terms of peace. The dissident, in her chance, insisted that she too had a right to dictate the terms of peace. And that was one reason why I spent time giving my personal example of how I feel about my nationality. I thought it was important for the regime to hear it. Nobody else should tell me that okay fine if you want to be a Sudanese, you can be a Sudanese. And the dissident independent of the regime spoke on what it meant to her to be a Sudanese.

Subhara challenged the northern Sudanese women to consider another point of view.

Subhara did her best to make sure the refugee, who was outnumbered, felt heard. Personally, she sided with the refugee but she did not disclose her bias to the group. However, in her interview, Subhara said she regretted that the facilitators may not have made it clear that they were there to support the southern Sudanese woman:

> I felt in some way that we had disappointed the dissident. My own attitude towards her, and I didn't get a chance to say this to her, was that I believed what she was saying. I wanted the others to believe it. Yet I realized that perhaps she needed reassurance that we were working in that group for her as well or for her primarily. Perhaps she did not get that impression.

The southern Sudanese woman told the story of how her daughter had been kidnapped and sold into slavery only to be questioned and challenged by the government women. Subhara responded to the high level of tension by saying that just because some things are hard to hear doesn't make them untrue, and she talked about activities that had taken place in her country. I thought her comments protective of the southern Sudanese woman but apparently, Subhara worried that they were not supportive enough.

During the dialogue, individual difference among the northern and southern Sudanese women representing the government became visible. The Sudanese woman from the peace ministry, Martha, a Christian from the South, spoke little during the meeting. Subhara thought her silence was significant:

> The one who puzzled me least, but concerned me most was the Christian woman from the present regime. Because I sensed that she had made a choice. And she had some opportunity, but she did not pursue the opportunity of explaining at all what lay behind her choice. Maybe she was not comfortable. It was not clear to me how confident the four women from the regime were with each other. I hope they go away and think about how freely they could or could not speak themselves, as a foursome. I think they were watchful of each other just as much as they were watchful of the whole encounter.

She concluded by saying Martha had compromised and that was why she was concerned for her.

Subhara was particularly interested in breaking down potential stereotypes of Sayida, perhaps as much for my benefit as a Northerner as for the other women. Subhara felt strongly that Sayida was on a liberation path even though 'she has not come to the point of acknowledging that the oppressed are oppressed.' In her opinion, Sayida was:

> part of the greater confidence that women in her country have been given by becoming part of the Islamic regeneration in that country. Because where else would she be holding such a position and be wearing a uniform and working as a soldier of the nation and the society. There has been a liberation of sorts of women. For all the veils and other things there has been a liberation of sorts and she is part of that liberation. So one has to understand her as well. She's very young. She never spoke about whether she had suffered any personal loss but she implied that there could have been personal loss in her life also. So who knows why she became like that but she has moved much further than many women of her society in being what she is today. So one shouldn't think her covered head means she's way back in the 17th century. She's not. She's the future of her country.

Sayida, who was the most aggressive to begin with appeared to make a shift during the meeting.

In her evaluation of the Sudanese meeting, Subhara seemed pleased with her offer to sit with the women while they talk over their disagreements:

> And the women from the regime I think had an unexpected experience. Perhaps they realized there are others to help them, not with expertise but just by presence and solidarity of presence. And this way if they wished to get into a genuine dialogue but I guess they also must have realized that unless there was greater sincerity on their part, that it was not to be again to be a dictated peace. They were speaking from a position of wanting to dictate the terms of peace.

She felt that it was important to bring people into a room to speak to each other, even if they could not agree on a single thing that was said. They at least had a chance to hear each other speak. Subhara replied that at the end of the session she had quizzed Sayida on whether she saw anything differently. Sayida replied she began to see things differently when Subhara suggested they sit together after the peace caucus.

At the same time, Subhara was aware of the limitations of the dialogue session. It was very difficult building even the most basic sense of safety or trust. She was concerned most for the southern Sudanese refugee. In regards to the refugee, Subhara said:

> I respect the caution she showed from start to finish. She was open to working together but she was cautious and I think she has had sufficient experience to have learned to be cautious...Perhaps she felt that she was being compromised into a kiss and make up position when the real issues couldn't possibly be addressed by any of us or even by them that kind of an encounter.

The group had begun to uncover and explore some of the problems in North/South relations, but the issue of the refugee's daughter remained unresolved. Nevertheless, the fight started when the refugee explained that rather than focusing on past injustice like Rwanda women who were not setting up war tribunals, her people were looking to rebuild for the future. The dialogue session may have been a symbol for the refugee of that forward-looking strategy.

To summarize, the first attempt by the Sudanese women to set up dialogue was not successful but the second session I described did contain characteristics and elements of dialogue. With the firm direction of the international team of dialogue leaders, the women spoke to each other about their personal suffering. Participants learned more about each other and about each other's situations, increasing the level of understanding of the problems they face and the obstacles they would need to overcome for a shared collaboration. Moreover, they had a glimpse of what it would be like to speak face-to-face and in depth about very difficult issues, e.g. slavery, that concern them all.

Beneath Paradise

Madelaine did not have the opportunity to take part in group dialogue like WILPF and SWVP did. The conditions present for the other two NGOs did not obtain for Beneath Paradise. First, although Madelaine was in conflict with several different groups of women, she was on her own as a NGO delegate in New York, making it difficult to hold a group dialogue session. Moreover, through her embarrassment tactics, Madelaine may have raised her adversaries' level of discomfort enough that they became alienated.

Madelaine made it clear that she distinguished between the French people and the French government. For instance, during her UN radio interview, she made a point of saying that the French people were not her enemy:

> We are still lucky we have our lives. And we can carry on and say to people 'They, hang on! Those who are those French are hypocrites'. When I say French, I wanna say that

> I'm talking about the government, not about the people. Because in France, themselves, we have our best Kanak solidarity in France, our best support. And the French themselves are totally opposed to their government who undermine them and oppress them as well. So that's what I want to say.

Had the French delegates given an indication that they would reconsider their response to Madelaine, I believe that she would have ended her campaign to expose their hypocrisy. Nevertheless, she publicly embarrassed her opponents and they did not express interest in dialogue with her.

Second, the community building or conflict resolution frame was not prominent in her situation, nor would it have been a priority for her given her goals and strategy for the conference. Madelaine used her resources to her advantage. Given the large number of women she was to represent and the many issues she had been asked to raise, she concentrated her efforts on gaining as much international attention as possible for her issues rather than opening up discussion with the French government delegates. Her strategy was to mobilize her many international allies to put pressure on the French government instead of trying to negotiate directly. She indicated that she had not had success speaking directly with the French delegates in the past. Media attention was more important for her than dialogue and she was partially successful in gaining the recognition she needed.

Third, no one took leadership. Neither Madelaine nor any of her adversaries took the initiative to set up a dialogue session. Given the large differences in status and power between Madelaine and the French delegates, it was very unlikely that the French or even the New Caledonian government delegates would voluntarily call for face-to-face dialogue. WILPF and SWVP did not have to face large differences in status among the disputants. Furthermore, on her own during the preparatory conferences, she called attention to herself and her cause in public forums that were not set up for dialogue. Someone would have had to take the time to organize and plan a specific meeting, but no one did. As a result, Madelaine did not participate in dialogue.

Conclusion

In this chapter, several group conversations are compared and contrasted in order to further understand what kind of international discourse assists building common agendas in transnational movements. Each of the conversations was useful to the participants in some way but the dialogue sessions exhibited the most potential for assisting the agenda-setting process. Kay and Geraldine's debate brought attention to the issue of racism but did not increase understanding among the participants or fuel a desire to work together. Angela's workshop increased understanding and explored difference, but did not probe issues problematic to participant relations. Although the SWVP initiated conflict resolution session allowed for face-to-face discussion and confrontation, it did not break down stereotypes, increase understanding or explore deep-rooted problems. Instead, it acted as a method of state control. In contrast, the moments of dialogue allowed participants to air their views, express their feelings, gain new insights, get difficult issues out on the table, and learn about their differences.

In theory, dialogue works well as a precursor to negotiations between conflicting parties because the participants develop both the will and the capacity to work together even as they explore their disagreements. Given the dialogue took place after much of the agenda was set and that the moments of dialogue were so short that the process never went past the beginning stages, there is little evidence to show that dialogue actually influenced agenda-setting in this context. However, from the data presented, one can speculate on the potential that dialogue has for the agenda-setting process more generally.

First, under the leadership of the facilitators, the dominant discourse was challenged, opening up space for alternate discourses. The international facilitator teams worked well in both the transnational dispute of the WILPF group and the intra-national conflict of the Sudanese women. Providing safety in these contexts meant making sure that one group did not dominate the other/s. In the US dominated setting of the WILPF dialogue, it was important that the US women helped to plan and facilitate the meeting but did not provide the main leadership. In this way, the US facilitators provided some safety and encouragement for the US women to participate without taking over the session. The Indian dialogue leader, on the other hand, created some safety for the women of color and/or Southern women by challenging dominant Northern assumptions and perspectives, and again, did not allow the white Northern women to dominate the discourse.

Opening up space for alternate discourse created a setting where relationships could be based on mutuality, respect and equal status. In the SWVP initiated session, the leader never questioned the dominance of the northern Sudanese women and in fact affirmed it, leaving the difficult political issues completely untouched. It reinforced asymmetrical power relations. In the Sudanese dialogue session, the international team put much of their effort into challenging the dominance of the northern Sudanese women and trying to establish even a little safety for the southern Sudanese refugee. Furthermore, the team symbolized the international attention and respect for the conflict in the Sudan that the southern Sudanese, in particular, so strongly desired.

Second, when transnational activist identities become more complex, they are more likely to mobilize. Dialogue is useful as precursor to negotiations because the participants obtain realistic not stereotyped information about each other. Accurate and more complex perceptions may result in more options and strategies. Empathetic sharing can build trust and lead to cooperative rather than unilateral moves. Further, when dialogue participants are able to see each other in a different light, they can identify problems that need to be addressed, and speak about needs that may not have been evident in the dominant discourse. Integration of the self without the restrictions of externally imposed definition allows for the fullest use of the individual's resources (Lorde, 1997). Dialogue facilitates the uncovering of difference and the integration of all aspects of self as the participant speaks as an individual. The expression and recognition of differences are important because without them, 'it is impossible to see the different problems and pitfalls facing us as women' (Lorde, 1997, p.376).

Third, by focusing on differences and personal experiences, the process of dialogue tends to break down identities and opens up the possibility of reconstructing them in more complex forms. According to Trinh T. Minh-ha, difference 'is that which undermines the very idea of identity, differing to infinity those layers of totality that form I' (1997, p. 415). The women who had been drawn together under the category of 'woman' saw that identity splinter into many pieces. The identity 'woman' had infinite meanings. However, as individual differences became visible in dialogue, new possibilities for expanding and rebuilding the category of 'woman' based on common issues and needs, were also revealed. Thus, dialogue had the potential to become part of the process of forming transnational activist identities.

Fourth, the dialogue provided bridging frames through which the women could speak about and potentially mobilize around any number of issues. The frame 'community building' was appealing to many of the women, who were disturbed by the conflict in their midst. Although they disagreed on what their priorities should be and/or were hurting from their conflicts with one another, most of the women believed that by uniting they would become stronger in their ability to make change. As Barrie said in her closing statement, 'If we can't figure out how to do it among ourselves, you know, the issue gets to be, how on earth are we going to change the world when we can't work internally?' Their own picture of themselves as progressive women provided social pressure to try to work with their differences and 'build community.' Similarly, the frame 'conflict resolution' mobilized the Sudanese women, who despite their deep mistrust of one another, under the watchful eye of the international community felt pressure to do what they perceived the men of their society had not been able to do—talk about peace.

In order to further understand the potential of the dialogue model for transnational NGO networks, the NGOs would need to meet the conditions for successful dialogue outlined earlier in this chapter. Preparation for dialogue intervention is essential. Advance preparation would include consideration of the impact of political and cultural context on participant attitudes and modes of interaction. By assessing both the different and shared needs of the different groups participating, dialogue facilitators can help to address power imbalances. For example, the silence of some of the nationalities present at the peace train dialogue may indicate a lack of comfort with Northern techniques of emotional explanation or with English as the main form of communication. In addition to advance preparation, the participants need more time with one another—at least enough to complete the stages of the dialogue process. With advance preparation, several position papers, not just one, could be developed for consideration as is common with public policy dialogue. Furthermore, the process needs a common task, such as agenda-setting, in order to make the results of their work together tangible.

Most of the conflict resolution endeavors contributed to the constructive approach to conflict within the NGO network. The women showed flexibility by trying different methods to address their difficulties as a group. Rather than consistently avoiding or escalating the conflicts in an uncontrolled manner, the NGOs developed strategies to try to come to an acceptable solution for all participants. These conflict resolution interventions helped to facilitate on-going relationships within the network and models for processing conflicts constructively in the future.

Chapter 6

Conclusion

This study of how diverse NGOs process conflicts over common agendas within transnational NGO networks focuses on the stories of individual activists. Conflict within transnational social movements is common. NGO networks experience conflicts regarding goals and means, common frames, and competition over resources. Within international women's movements, tension over power and representation have been a source of contention since the beginning of the International Women's Decade in 1975. Global conferences are common places for NGOs to uncover their disagreements. Studying the everyday experiences of NGO delegates at international events reveals some of the challenges they face and how they respond to those difficulties.

On the other hand, NGOs play a key role in resolving conflicts and building social relations within transnational social movements. Resolving conflicts is important to NGOs because they are interested in building connections with other NGOs to strengthen their lobbying power with governments or to develop global civil society or both. Without some level of agreement, NGOs cannot mobilize for global campaigns. Transnational social movements need social infrastructure to communicate ideas and practices. NGO collaboration is important to IGOs because IGOs rely on NGOs to find common ground on policy issues across national boundaries and generate options for resolving conflicts.

Conflict within social movement tends to be thought of as an obstacle to building social movements. However, this study shows how non-governmental organizations process conflict constructively. NGOs tended to approach the conflicts believing that all sides could reach important goals. The delegates showed flexibility using a wide variety of responses to reach an acceptable solution. Although they used some competitive tactics, they were also able to change their strategies if it would result in the best outcome. For the most part, the outcomes of the conflicts were constructive; that is, the outcomes facilitated an ongoing relationship among the NGOs in which future conflicts could be negotiated constructively.

NGOs use conflict to develop transnational social movements and build consensus around issues of common concern. Social movement conflict serves four purposes. Conflicts over NGO network priorities expose inequalities in large scale, non-governmental decision making. Contention arising from policy development increases understanding of regional, ethnic, racial and ideological differences and expands possibilities for collaboration. Deep-rooted, historical conflicts that surface become starting points for dialogue among NGO representatives. Attempts to resolve conflicts strengthen the network and facilitate the construction of transnational activist identities.

As a result, this study shows that NGOs would benefit from assuming the inevitability of conflict within transnational social movements and prepare for it. The NGO leadership offered various avenues for expressing difference, having voice and participating in many different forums. However, they did not sufficiently prepare for competition among NGOs, unequal power dynamics, and deep-rooted, historical conflicts. For example, the consensus process assumes symmetrical power relations. However, egalitarian relations were not evident among the delegates. If NGOs prepare for conflict at international events then they can design processes designed for processing conflict constructively in advance of international events.

As an analytic foci, conflict is useful for studying transnational social movements. Examining how conflict is negotiated among NGOs, deepens understanding NGO network decision making. Focusing on struggles for common meaning highlights the importance of social movement tools—strategic framing processes, repertoires of contention and activist identity formation—at an international level. Knowing more about the types of conflicts that NGOs experience is useful in itself but it also opens up opportunities to examine the potential of conflict resolution models for building common political ground within transnational social movements.

Agenda Setting: NGO Decision Making

The satisfaction that my informants experienced with their participation in the conference peace activities did not appear to have any connection to the consensus decision making process used by the peace caucus. WILPF chose a modified consensus process (as was the norm at the conferences) based on the assumption that all of the participants could participate equally. Consensus, in theory, is a non-hierarchical form of decision making. The women believed that the process would enable the expression of core values, that is, respect for difference and the empowerment of all participants.

Despite the good intentions, use of the consensus process resulted in the suppression of conflict and difference and the power of the Northern organizers was reinforced. The leadership ignored power inequity and difference and NGOs marginalized by the process struggled to make sure their own regional or local issues were at the top of the peace caucus priority list. The expression of difference became more difficult because consensus was required to move forward. Thirty minutes was not enough time to reach agreements based on an understanding of the issues important to other NGOs. Further, deep-rooted political conflicts were triggered by the agenda-setting process. Historical divisions were strengthened which was the opposite of what WILPF had intended. Most often, the Southern NGO delegates did not find their issues on the agenda and they struggled for visibility.

If NGOs utilize the consensus decision making process, they must become familiar with the limitations of the process, particularly at international events like the global UN conferences. The consensus decision making process itself does not erase hierarchical or asymmetrical power relations. As this research shows, without the proper conditions, consensus decision making may reinforce inequalities. In a setting with highly diverse participants, very little time, pressure to find unanimity, and relations characterized by deep-rooted conflicts and unequal access to power, a managed consensus was the most likely outcome. Conflict and difference were suppressed. If they understand the limitations of consensus decision making, NGOs can respond to the shortcomings of the process by modifying it or altering the conditions under which it is practiced. Deeper understanding of the process will also facilitate informed decisions about when consensus decision making is appropriate.

When choosing a decision making process, it is important for NGOs to be aware of their goals as well as their values. Is consensus necessary and, if so, how can it best be achieved? The Benchmark Environmental Consulting study reveals that only 17% of the NGOs were in favor of voting in plenaries for a common citizen's position before a governmental debate. This data may indicate that although NGOs are interested in unity and capacity building, they are unwilling to give up their own NGO position for a collective political voice to lobby governments (Benchmark Environmental Consulting, 1996).

The 1995 NGO consultation used consensus decision making to gain approval for the NGO generated Platform for Action (PfA). The two days allotted for the 1,200 delegates to reach consensus on the 250 page document was largely symbolic. The goal of the NGO leadership was to consolidate the power of the women's NGOs with a document that symbolized years of collaboration and commitment—not to reach a real consensus among the 1,200 delegates on the content of the document. (The consensus was that it was politically expedient for NGOs to have a single document.) When real consensus was not within the realm of possibility, participation was symbolic as well. The NGO delegates cheered when their leaders announced that they had achieved consensus.

Within the small gathering of peace activists (35), the NGO delegates expected that a real agreement on network priorities was possible and that their participation would count. The stakes for the NGO delegates were high; their specific concerns were more important to them than the NGO PfA (for some their survival was at stake). Tension arose when, through the consensus process, their issues were ignored or misunderstood. Clarifying the purpose of specific decisions and goals and the kinds of decisions to be made would help to determine whether consensus decision making would meet their needs. It is difficult for coalitions to come to anything other than a superficial consensus. If consensus was not necessary or desired then what was the goal of collective decision making?

Agenda Setting: Struggle for Common Meaning

During the conferences, the NGOs struggled to find common meaning and common political ground. This involved challenging dominant agendas and altering the agenda-setting process. Conflicts arising from agenda-setting processes point to four main issues. First, as the negotiations unfold, more about how the small, local, grassroots NGOs learn to engage other NGOs at the global level is revealed. Second, challenges to the agenda require not just strategic framing and identity formation but repertoires of contention to address power differentials. Third, transnational NGO networks experience not only issue-related disputes but deep-rooted conflicts. Fourth, a constructive approach to conflict encourages the growth of relationships within the network, despite all of the difficulties involved in collaboration.

Struggles with the agenda-setting process highlight the challenges that small, local, grassroots organizations face in a global context. At international events, NGOs are confronted with large, old/small, new divisions as well as North/South divides. The larger, older NGOs tend to conform more to the UN agenda than the smaller, newer NGOs that attend the conferences (Benchmark Environmental Consulting, 1996). Geraldine, who represented a local British NGO, SWVP, and Madelaine from Beneath Paradise never met and yet they had some common ground given their experience with deep-rooted conflict. All of these NGOs tended to target the larger, more powerful Northern NGOs primarily (although not exclusively). Small Southern NGOs attempt to link up with Northern NGOs in order to influence rich country governments (Uvin, 1996). Nevertheless, most NGOs attend international events to meet NGOs with similar concerns and yet they report having difficulty finding these NGOs once they arrive at the conferences (Benchmark Environmental Consulting, 1996). Would they have found more of the NGOs they hoped to meet if they had targeted them for mobilization?

As the small NGO delegates worked to gain attention for their issues, they experimented with various ways of framing their concerns so that they would have global appeal. A frame like the 'black agenda' was too localized, too identity-based, and did not clearly identify an issue. It did not succeed in a global context; if you were not black and British, it was difficult to ascertain what the frame meant. The frame 'anti-racism,' which appealed to the values of the target audience and, in a general way, identified the concern, did succeed. However, as the context changed so did the mobilizing power of the frame. When the target audience shifted from mostly European and North American representatives to a majority of Southern NGOs, the 'anti-racism' frame lost its mobilizing power. In a global context, racism was tied to many different frames from development to colonialism to militarism but many NGOs did not frame their key concerns as 'racism.' Although it resonated, the frame 'anti-racism' was too general to initiate action among large numbers of Southern NGOs.

Changes in the dominant transnational agenda required a combination of three social movement tools: strategic framing, identity formation, and repertoires of contention. During the agenda-setting conflicts, the NGOs developed frames, changed strategies depending on the context, and shifted and reconstructed activist identities. Within the peace caucus, Madelaine's frame 'De-colonization, De-nuclearization, and De-militarization' was the most successful challenge because it brought together familiar issues in a new way and it built on priorities of the target audience—de-nuclearization and de-militarization. Further, Madelaine's frame did not rely solely on the identity of the target audience for resonance.

SWVP faced special difficulties in engaging their target audiences because the armed conflict they were attempting to stop was hard for outsiders to understand and, given the lack of media attention, was relatively unknown. In Madelaine's case, it was clear that the large colonial power, France, was oppressing the small, indigenous population of Kanaky. The ethnic, racial, and religious conflict of the Sudan was more difficult for foreigners to comprehend. Nevertheless, SWVP succeeded in forming connections with international allies and to some extent with northern Sudanese NGOs using frames like 'just peace' and 'conflict resolution.' Both of these frames appealed to both the values and to the identity of their target audiences who saw themselves as peacemakers, although the specific issues implied in the frames were only clear to people very familiar with the Sudanese conflict.

Struggling to find frames that were meaningful to diverse constituencies with multi-layered identities was complex but even the most successful frames would not have been effective without strategy. Given the unequal power relations within the network, conflict escalation may have appeared to be the only way to push the more powerful delegates to acknowledge different frames. Simply presenting their issues without pressure was ineffective. The women of color affiliated with WILPF, Madelaine, and SWVP all developed strategies to gain attention for their strategic frames. Two of the three NGO delegations organized, disrupted, confronted, and embarrassed the other delegates in order to be heard. Madelaine and her colleagues organized a demonstration at the NGO Forum '95. They deliberately escalated the conflict using competitive tactics. On the other hand, SWVP did not use confrontation as a strategy, choosing instead to avoid triggering the anger of the northern Sudanese women. Their political context was different, however. The conflict in the Sudan had escalated to the point of violence and SWVP wanted to show that the women could address their problems without anger and violence. Either way, this study illustrates the importance of repertoires of contention in the strategic framing process that takes place within transnational social movements.

Activist identity formation was a significant factor in shaping frames and strategies, affirming the assumption that identity is key in mobilizing dynamics on a transnational level. The transnational activist identity 'woman' served to bring the women together. However, as conflicts arose, particularly around agendas, other aspects of their multiple-layered identities became more salient. Some of the women defined themselves in opposition to each other and attempted to organize around their difference. In-group differences were heightened. European and North American women of color started to organize separately. National and sub-national identities were reinforced. Southern Sudanese women found themselves at odds yet again with northern Sudanese women. Madelaine declared she had nothing in common with the French delegates as women. Furthermore, in a global context, the salience of certain identities like 'women of color' changed as the NGOs became more diverse and more international.

The effect of the strategic frames changed as identities deconstructed in the course of the conflicts. As such, this study shows that frames based too heavily on identity are less likely to succeed in settings where multi-layered identities shift. Many of the African women rallied around the identity-based frame 'women are peacemakers' until they came into conflict and then their racial and religious identities became more salient. However, the 'conflict resolution' frame appealed to their values, their roles as Sudanese women, to their identity as peace activists and referred to an issue that was important to them, i.e. the nonviolent resolution of the Sudanese war. It was this frame that brought many of the women together.

The evidence that deep-rooted conflict influenced the agenda-setting process reinforces the need for NGOs to prepare for conflict at international conferences. The conflicts that arose were not only about different perceptions concerning goals and means. Issue-based conflicts can be negotiated. However, deep-rooted conflict or conflicts that block the satisfaction of basic needs require a different approach. Racism in European and North American countries, French colonialism in New Caledonia, and the civil war in the Sudan are all on-going conflicts. When inequalities in decision making power became evident in the agenda-setting process, these conflicts were triggered. The focus shifted from discussion of issues important to women in armed conflict to the power to define discourse and to participate fully in decisions affecting the lives of their people. If NGOs recognize the presence of deep-rooted conflicts within NGO networks then they can design methods for processing those conflicts constructively.

Despite the limited success that the NGOs had in changing the dominant agenda, they were all willing to work together again because they chose a constructive approach to conflict. In the end, their goal was to find mutually acceptable frames that would resonate with and mobilize the peace activist alliance. They used competitive tactics and escalated the conflicts to make their positions known and to challenge the dominance of some of the NGOs. However, conflict escalation or harming other NGO delegates was generally not the objective as it would be in destructive conflict. Instead, the NGOs used the deep-rooted conflict to begin dialogue. WILPF responded by acknowledging and validating the concerns of the marginalized NGOs and made some small changes to the agenda. The delegates challenging the agenda changed their tactics when they received recognition. Each of the NGOs was satisfied with some of the outcomes of their interaction. By the end of the conferences, the constructive outcomes and productive approach to conflict reinforced their identity as transnational activists.

Agenda Setting: Transnational Dialogue

Although expressing difference played an important role in making deep-rooted conflicts visible, group discussion was utilized to increase understanding and foster cooperation between the NGOs. Of the various models of group discussion that the peace activists used, the dialogue model showed the most potential for resolving transnational network conflicts. All of the attempts at international discourse were useful to the NGO representatives in some way but the dialogue model, designed for assisting people with deep-rooted conflicts, was the most helpful in exploring underlying problems with the agenda-setting process in a constructive manner. Debate brought attention to the marginalized issue, racism, and helped to clarify participants' positions. However, the debate model did not increase understanding among the participants or create a desire to work together in the future. Prejudice reduction increased understanding and explored difference but did not delve into problems and conflicts between participants leaving the social infrastructure weak. The state controlled conflict resolution session between the Sudanese women brought the women together face-to-face but did not increase understanding, explore difficult relations or break down stereotypes.

In communal or inter-state conflict, dialogue is useful as a precursor to negotiations because parties develop the desire and the capacity to collaborate even as they explore their disagreements. In the context of transnational social movement conflict, dialogue serves to: 1) challenge the dominant discourse; 2) open up options for collaboration; 3) deconstruct and potentially reconstruct activist identities; 4) and provide a mobilizing frame for working through problems within the network. In this way, dialogue assists the NGO agenda-setting process.

During the conference dialogue sessions, the participants, with encouragement from the facilitators, challenged the dominant discourse and opened up space for alternate discourses. The international teams of facilitators helped to create norms where relationships were based on mutuality, respect and equal status. They did not allow the more dominant NGO delegates to take over the discussion. Further, as the women gained accurate, not stereotyped information about one another, they were able to identify problems that need to be addressed and speak about needs that may not have been evident in the dominant discourse. As a result, with more accurate and complex perceptions, the delegates began to formulate more options and strategies for cooperation. Moreover, multi-layered identities shifted as individual differences were revealed but in the process, new possibilities for expanding and rebuilding activist identities based on new connections opened up. Dialogue played a role in forming transnational activist identities. Finally, 'community building' and 'conflict resolution' were frames that motivated the women to come together and work out their problems. As women peace activists, they felt they could not expect the rest of the world to process their conflicts constructively and build positive relationships if they themselves could not.

Advance preparation for dialogue is essential pointing again to the need to assume NGO conflict. Planning for dialogue in advance requires a commitment not just to lobbying governments on issues but to building the social infrastructure of transnational social movements. The dialogue sessions at the conferences were set up in response to conflicts that arose after much of the network agenda had been set. These conflict resolution meetings were meaningful to the participants. Nevertheless, for maximum impact on the agenda-setting process, dialogue would precede or accompany the decision making. NGOs would need to plan ahead and schedule sufficient time for dialogue—at least enough to complete all of the stages of dialogue. To address power imbalances, advance preparation would include consideration of the impact of political and cultural context on the parties' attitudes and modes of interaction. Deciding on their lobbying priorities as a network could serve as the common task often used in dialogue to solidify participants' positive interaction. Choosing facilitators who are in a position to challenge the asymetrical power relations is also important.

Most of the conflict resolution efforts helped to strengthen the ties between the NGO delegates. Although the conflicts were not necessarily 'resolved', the NGO delegates noticed that other NGOs tended to take a constructive approach. Instead of constantly avoiding or escalating the conflicts as an end in itself, the NGOs attempted to find an acceptable solution for all participants. The positive outcomes resulting from their interaction empowered the NGO delegates. Many of them would continue to identify with the other women they met through the peace activities at the conferences. NGO conflict resolution helped to facilitate social relations within the network and offered models for processing conflicts constructively in the future.

This study contributes to the trend in conflict theory to highlight the positive potential that conflict brings. As Barrie, a dialogue participant said:

> This progressive community represents the democracy and the world, the global world which we think we are trying to create. And if we can't figure out how to do it among ourselves, you know, the issue gets to be, how on earth are we goina change the world when we can't work internally, you know. What I'm hearing, is we're moving, you know, we're starting to move in that direction.

NGOs play an important role in transnational social movements by resolving conflicts and building consensus among diverse organizations. Dissension reveals asymmetrical relations and deep-rooted conflicts within NGO networks as well as conflicts of interest. If they address these tensions, NGOs learn more about other NGOs, strengthen relationships, discover more opportunities for cooperation, and set up a strong basis for on-going collaboration.

Bibliography

Abu-Nimer, M. (1999), *Dialogue, Conflict Resolution, and Change: Arab-Jewish Encounters in Israel*, State University of New York Press, New York.

Acker, J. (1990), 'Hierarchies, Jobs, Bodies: A Theory of Gendered Organizations', *Gender and Society*, **4**(2), pp. 139-158.

Africa Rights (1995), *Facing Genocide: The Nuba of Sudan*, London.

Alexander, M.J. and Mohanty, C.T. (eds) (1997), *Feminist Genealogies, Colonial Legacies, Democratic Futures*, Routledge, New York.

Alexander, R. (1994), *Putting the Earth First: Alternatives to Nuclear Security in Pacific Island States*, Matsunga Institute for Peace, University of Hawai`i, Honolulu.

Allen, V.R., Galey, M. E., and Persinger, Mildred E. (1995), 'World Conference of International Women's Year', in A. Winslow (ed), *Women, Politics, and the United Nations*, Greenwood Press, New York, pp. 29-44.

Alonso, H. H. (1993), *Peace as a Women's Issue: A History of the U.S. Movement for World Peace and Women's Rights*, Syracuse University Press, Syracuse.

Amos, V. and Parmar, P. (1984), 'Challenging Imperial Feminism', *Feminist Review*, **17**, pp. 3-19.

Anderlini, S.N. (2000), *Women at the Peace Table*, United Nations Development Fund for Women, New York.

Anderson-Manley, B. (1991), 'Gender and State: A Caribbean Perspective', Reprinted in *Women Transforming Societies: Sub-Saharan Africa and Caribbean Perspectives*, (1994), Radcliffe College, Cambridge.

Antrobus, P. (1985), 'Changes in the Status and Position of Women in the Last Decade: Pointers for the Future', *Women and Development: Beyond the Decade, Proceeding*, Conference Report, Guelph University, Ontario, pp. 19-27.

Anzaldua, G. (1990), *Making Face, Making Soul Haciendo Caras: Creative and Critical Perspectives by Feminists of Color*, Aunt Lute Books, San Francisco.

Arnould, G. (1995), 'Dilemmas of Feminist Coalitions: Collective Identity and Strategic Effectiveness in the Battered Women's Movement', in R. Ferree and P. Martin (eds), *Feminist Organizations: Harvest of the New Left Women's Movement*, Temple University Press, Philadelphia, pp. 276-290.

Asian Women's Human Rights Council (1995), *Women in Black: A Gathering of Spirit*, Bangalore, India.

Augsburger, D.W. (1992), *Conflict Mediation Across Cultures: Pathways and Patterns*, Westminster/John Knox Press, Louisville.

Auvine, B., Densmore, B., Extrom, M., Poole, Shanklin, M. (1978), *A Manual for Group Facilitators*, Madison, The Center for Conflict Resolution.

Becker, C. et al. (1995), 'From Stuck Debate to New Conversation on Controversial Issues: A Report from the Public Conversations Project', *Journal of Feminist Family Therapy*, **7**(½), pp. 143-163.

Benchmark Environmental Consulting (1996), *Democratic Global Civil Governance Report of the 1995 Benchmark Survey of NGOs*, Royal Ministry of Foreign Affairs, Oslo.

Boulding, E. (1997), 'Peace-building Through Networking: Report of a Conference in Sweden', *International Peace Research Newsletter*, **15**(3), pp. 13-15.

Brock-Utne, B. (1989), *Feminist Perspectives on Peace and Peace Education*, Pergamon Press, New York.

Brown, C.R. and Mazza, G. J. (1992), *Peer Training Strategies for Welcoming Diversity*, National Coalition Building Institute, Washington.

Brown, H. (1992), *Women Organizing*, Routledge, London.

Buechler, S.M. (1990), 'Conceptualizing Radicalism and Transformation in Social Movements: The Case of the Woman Suffrage Movement', *Perspectives on Social Problems*, **2**, pp. 105-18.

Bulbeck, C. (1998), *Re-Orienting Western Feminisms: Women's Diversity in a Postcolonial World*, Cambridge University, Cambridge.

Bunch, C. and Carrillo, R. (1994), 'Global Violence against Women: The Challenge to Human Rights and Development', in M.T. Klare and D.C. Thomas (eds), *World Security: Challenges For a New Century*, St. Martin's Press, New York. pp. 256-273.

Burton, J.W. (1969), *Conflict and Communication: The Use of Controlled Communication in International Relations*, The Free Press, New York.

Burton, J.W. (1987), *Resolving Deep-rooted Conflict: A Handbook*, University Press of America, Lanham.

Cagatay, N., Grown, C., and Santiago, A. (1986), 'The Nairobi Women's Conference: Toward a Global Feminism?', *Feminist Studies*, **12**(2), pp. 401-412.

Cahn, D. (1990), 'Confrontaiton Behaviors, Preceived understanding and Relationship Growth', in D. Cahn (ed), *Intimates in Conflict: A Communication Prespective*, Lawrence Erlbaum Association, Hillsdale.

Carroll, B.A. (1971 September 1), 'Peace Research: The Cult of Power', Paper presented at the Annual Convention of the American Sociological Association, Denver, Colorado.

Carroll, B.A. (1989), 'Women Take Action! Women's Direct Action and Social Change.' *Women's Studies International Forum*, **12**(1), pp. 3-24.

Childers, M. and hooks, B. (1990), 'A Conversation about Race and Class', in M. Hirsch and E.F. Keller (eds), *Conflicts in Feminism*, Routledge, New York, pp. 60-82.

Chowdhry, G. (1995), 'Engendering Development? Women in Development (WID) in international development regimes', in M.H. Marchand and J.L. Parpart (eds), *Feminism/Postmodernism/ Development*, Routledge, New York, pp. 26-41.

Clark, A., Friedman, E.J., and Hochstetler, K. (1998), 'The Sovereign Limits of Global Civil Society: A Comparison of NGO Participation in UN World Conferences on the Environment, Human Rights, and Women', *World Politics*, **51**(1), pp. 1-35.

Clark, M.L. (1994), 'The Antarctic Environmental Protocol: NGOs in the protection of Antarctica', in T. Princen and M. Finger (eds), *Environmental NGOs in World Politics: Linking the local and the global*, Routledge, London.

Commission on Global Governance (1995), *Our Global Neighborhood*, Oxford University.

Cook-Huffman, C. (2000), 'Who Do They Say We Are? Framing Social Identity and Gender in Church Conflict', in P.G. Coy and L.M. Woehrle (eds), *Social Conflicts and Collective Identities*, Rowman and Littlefield Publishers, Lanham, pp. 115-132.

Cortright, D. (1993), *Peace Works: The Citizen's Role in Ending the Cold War*, Westview Press, Boulder.

Cortright, D. and Pagnucco, R. (1997), 'Limits to Transnationalism: The 1980s Freeze Campaign', in *Transnational Social Movements and Global Politics: Solidarity Beyond the State*, J. Smith, C. Chatfield and R. Pagnucco (eds), Syracuse University Press, Syracuse, pp.159-174.

Dalton, R.J. (1994), *The Green Rainbow: Environmental Groups in Western Europe*, Temple University Press, New Haven.

Davis, A.Y. (1990), *Women, Culture, and Politics*, Vintage Books, New York.

DeMars, W. (1997), 'Contending Neutralities: Humanitarian Organizations and War in the Horn of Africa', in Jackie Smith, Charles Chatfield and Ron Pagnucco (eds), *Transnational Social Movements and Global Politics: Solidarity Beyond the State*, Syracuse University, Syracuse, pp. 101-122.

Deng, F.M. (1993), 'Hidden Agendas in the Peace Process', in M.W. Daly and Ahmad Alawad Sikainga (eds), *Civil War in the Sudan*, British Academic Press, London.

Deng, F.M. (1995), *War of Visions: Conflict of Identities in the Sudan*, The Brookings Institution, Washington.

Deutsch, M. (1973), *The Resolution of Conflict: Constructive and Destructive Processes*, Yale University Press, New Haven.

Deutsch, Y. (1994), 'And Peace Shall Multiply Like Mushrooms', unpublished essay.

Devault, M.L. (1995), 'Talking Back to Sociology: Distinctive Contributions of Feminist Methodology', unpublished.

Donaldson, L.E. (1992), *Decolonizing Feminisms: Race, Gender, and Empire-Building*, University of North Carolina Press, Chapel Hill.

Donati, P.R. (1984), 'Organization between Movement and Institution', *Social Science Information*, 23(4-5), pp. 837-59.

Edwards, M. and Hulme, D. (1996), *Beyond the Magic Bullet: NGO Performance and Accountability in the Post-Cold War World*, Kumarian Press, West Hartford.

Eisenstein, H. (1991), *Gender Shock*, Beacon, Boston.

Elshtain, J. B. (1987), *Women and War*, Basic Books, New York.

Enloe, C. (1989), *Bananas, Beaches and Bases: Making Sense of International Politics*, University of California Press, Berkeley.

Epstein, B. (1991), *Political Protest and Cultural Revolution: Nonviolent Direct Action in the 1970s and 1980s*, University of California Press, Berkeley.

Ericson, J.M., Murphy, J.J., and Zeuschner, R.B. (eds) (1987), *The Debater's Guide*, Southern University of Illinois Press, Carbondale.

Ferree, M.M. and Martin, P.Y. (eds) (1995), *Feminist Organizations: Harvest of the New Left Women's Movement*, Temple University Press, Philadelphia.

Fisher, J. (1998), *Nongovernments: NGOs and the Political Development of the Third World*, Kumarian Press, West Hartford.

Fisher, R.J. (1990), *The Social Psychology of Inter-group and International Conflict Resolution*, Springer-Verlag, New York.

Fisher, R.J. (1997), *Interactive Conflict Resolution*, Syracuse University, Syracuse.

Folger, J., Poole, M., and Stutman, R. (2001), *Working Through Conflict*, Longman, New York.

Foster, C. (1989), *Women for All Seasons: The Story of the Women's International League for Peace and Freedom*, The University of Georgia Press, Athens.

Fraser, A.S. (1987), *The U.N. Decade for Women: Documents and Dialogue*, Westview Press, Boulder.

Fraser, N. (1989), *Unruly Practices: Power, Discourse, and Gender in Contemporary Social Theory*, University of Minnesota Press, Minneapolis.

Freeman, J. (1972), 'The Tyranny of Structurelessness', *The Second Wave*, **2**(1), p. 20.

Friedlander, E. (ed) (1996), *Look at the World Through Women's Eyes: Plenary Speeches from the NGO Forum on Women, Beijing 1995*, NGO Forum on Women, Beijing, '95, New York.

Galey, M.E. (1995), 'Women Find a Place', in Ann Winslow (ed), *Women, Politics, and the United Nations*, Greenwood Press, New York, pp. 11-27.

Gastil, J. (1993), 'Identifying Obstacles to Small Group Democracy', *Small Group Research*, **24**, pp. 5-27.

Gordon, H. (1986), *Dance, Dialogue, and Despair: Existentialist Philosophy and Education for Peace in Israel*, University of Alabama Press, Alabama.

Gould, M. (1980), 'When Women Create an Organization: the Ideological Imperatives of Feminism', in Dunkerley and Salaman (eds), *The International Yearbook of Organization Studies*, Routledge and Kegan Paul, London.

Gray, B. (1991), *Collaborating: Finding Common Ground for Multiparty Problems*, Jossey-Bass Publishers, San Francisco.

Gundelach, P. (1984), 'Social Transformation and New Forms of Voluntary Associations', *Social Science Information*, 23(6), pp. 1049-81.

Harris, A. and King, Y. (eds) (1989), *Rocking the Ship of State: Toward a Feminist Peace Politics*, Westview Press, Boulder.

Hartsock, N. (1990), 'Foucault on Power: A Theory for Women?', in L. J. Nicholson (ed), *Feminism/Postmodernism*, Routledge, New York, pp. 157-175.

Heinrich, W. (1997), *Building the Peace: Experiences of Collaborative Peacebuilding in Somalia 1993-1996*, Life and Peace Institute, Uppsala, Sweden.

Hirsch, M. and Keller, E.F. (1990), *Conflicts in Feminism*, Routledge, New York.

hooks, bell (1997), 'Sisterhood: Political Solidarity between Women', in A. McClintock, A. Mufti, and E. Shohat (eds), *Dangerous Liaisons: Gender, Nation, and Postcolonial Perspectives*, University of Minnesota Press, Minneapolis, pp. 396-411.

Hunt, S.A. and Benford, R.D. (1994), 'Identity Talk in the Peace and Justice Movement', *Journal of Contemporary Ethnography*, **22**, p.489.

Iannello, K.P. (1992), *Decisions Without Hierarchy: Feminist Interventions in Organization Theory and Practice*, Routledge, London.

International Fellowship of Reconciliation (1999), *Women Peacemakers in Consultation, Asia 1998*, [Videorecording] (Available from IFOR, Spoorstraat 38, 1815 BK, Alkmaar, The Netherlands).

Jaimes, M. A. with Halsey, T. (1997), 'American Indian Women: At the Center of Indigenous Resistance in Contemporary North America', in A. McClintock, A. Mufti, and E. Shohat (eds), *Dangerous Liaisons: Gender, Nation, and Postcolonial Perspectives*, University of Minnesota Press, Minneapolis, pp. 324-327.

Jaquette, J. S. (1995), 'Losing the Battle/Winning the War: International Politics, Women's Issues, and the 1980 Mid-Decade Conference', in A. Winslow (ed), *Women, Politics, and the United Nations*, Greenwood Press, New York, pp. 45-59.

Joseph, G.I. and Lewis, J. (1981), *Common Differences: Conflicts in Black and White Feminist Perspectives*, South End Press, Boston.

Karl, M. (1995), *Women and Empowerment: Participation and Decisionmaking*, Zed Books, London.

Keck, M.E. and Sikkink, K. (1998), *Activists Beyond Borders: Advocacy Networks in International Politics*, Cornell University Press, Ithaca.

Kelman, H.C. (1972), 'The Problem-Solving Workshop in Conflict Resolution', in R. Merritt (ed), *Communication in International Politics*, University of Illinois Press, pp. 168-204.

Kelman, H.C. (1986), 'Overcoming the Barriers to Negotiation of the Israeli-Palestinian Conflict', *Journal of Palestinian Studies*, **16**, pp. 13-28.

Kendrick, R. (2000), 'Swimming against the Tide: Peace Movement Recruitment in an Abeyance Environment', in P.G. Coy and L.M. Woehrle (eds), *Social Conflicts and Collective Identities*, Rowman and Littlefield Publishers, Lanham, pp.189-204.

Kirk, G. and Okazawa-Rey, M. (1998), 'Making Connections: Building an East Asia-U.S. Women's Network against U.S. Militarism', in L.A. Lorentzen and J. Turpin (eds), *The Women and War Reader*, New York University Press, New York, pp. 308-322.

Kleidman, R. (1993), *Organizing for Peace: Neutrality, the Test Ban and the Freeze*, Syracuse University Press, Syracuse.

Kriesberg, L. (1982), *Social Conflicts*, Prentice-Hall, Englewood Cliffs.

Kriesberg, L. (1997), 'Social Movements and Global Transformation', in J. Smith, C. Chatfield and R. Pagnucco, *Transnational Social Movements and Global Politics: Solidarity Beyond the State*, Syracuse University Press, Syracuse, pp. 3-18.

Kriesberg, L. (1998), *Constructive Conflicts: From Escalation to Resolution*, Rowman & Littlefield Publishers, Lanham.

Kriesberg, L. and Segal, D.R. (eds) (1992), *The Transformation of European Communist Societies*, JAI Press, Greenwich.

Kuol, M.A. (1994), 'Voice of the Women: Where it Pains', *The Displaced*, **1**(2), pp. 17-18.

Kuttab, J. (1988), 'An Exchange on Dialogue', *Journal of Palestine Studies*, **17**(2), pp. 84-108.

Leatherman, J., Pagnucco, R., and Smith, J. (1993), 'International Institutions and Transnational Social Movement Organizations: Challenging the State in a Three-Level Game of Global Transformation', *The Joan B. Kroc Institute for International Peace Studies Working Paper Series*, University of Notre Dame, Notre Dame.

Lederach, J.P. (1995), *Preparing for Peace: Conflict Transformation Across Cultures*, Syracuse University Press, Syracuse.

Lederach, J.P. (1997), *Building Peace: Sustainable Reconciliation in Divided Societies*, United States Institute of Peace Press, Washington.

Leidner, R. (1991), 'Stretching the Boundaries of Liberalism: Democratic Innovation in a Feminist Organization', *Signs*, **16**(2), pp. 263-89.

Lewis, D. and Wallace, T. (2000), *New Roles and Relevance: Development NGOs and the Challenge of Change*, Kumarian Press, Bloomfield.

Lorde, A. (1997), 'Age, Race, Class, and Sex: Women Redefining Difference', in A. McClintock, A. Mufti, and E. Shohat (eds), *Dangerous Liaisons: Gender, Nation, and Postcolonial Perspectives*, University of Minnesota Press, Minneapolis, pp. 374-380.

Mansbridge, J.J. (1980), *Beyond Adversary Democracy*, University Press, Chicago.

Marchand, M.H. and Parpart, J.L. (eds) (1995), *Feminism/Postmodernism/Development*, Routledge, New York.

Martin, P.Y. (1990), 'Rethinking Feminist Organizations,' *Gender and Society*, Vol. **4**(2), pp. 182-206.

Masdit, S. (1996), 'Opening Remarks', in E. Friedlander (ed), *Look at the World Through Women's Eyes: Plenary Speeches from the NGO Forum on Women, Beijing 1995*, NGO Forum on Women, Beijing, '95, New York, p. 3.

McAdam, D., McCarthy, J., D. and Zald, M. (1996), 'Introduction: Opportunities, Mobilizing Structures, and Framing Processes—Toward a Synthetic, Comparative Perspective on Social Movements', in Doug McAdam, John D. McCarthy, and Mayer Zald (eds), *Comparative Perspectives on Social Movements: Political Opportunities, Mobilizing Structures and Cultural Framings*, Cambridge University Press, New York, pp. 1-20.

McCarthy, J. D. (1997), 'The Globalization of Social Movement Theory', in Jackie Smith, Charles Chatfield and Ron Pagnucco (eds), *Transnational Social Movements and Global Politics: Solidarity Beyond the State*, Syracuse University Press, Syracuse, pp. 243-59.

McCarthy, J.D., Britt, D. and Wolfson, M. (1991), 'The Institutional Channeling of Social Movements in the Modern State', in *Research in Social Movements, Conflict and Change*, **13**, JAI Press, Greenwich, pp. 45-76.

McCarthy, J.D. and Zald, M. (1977), 'Resource Mobilization and Social Movements: a Partial Theory', *American Journal of Sociology*, **82**, pp. 1212-1241.

McClintock, A., Mufti, A. and Shohat, E. (eds) (1997), *Dangerous Liaisons: Gender, Nation, and Postcolonial Perspectives*, University of Minnesota Press, Minneapolis.

Melucci, A. (1989), *Nomads of The Present: Social Movements and Individual Needs in Contemporary Society*, (J. Keane and P. Mier, trans.), Temple University Press, Philadelphia.

Merry, S.E. (1987), 'Cultural Frameworks of Mediation', Paper presented at the Workshop on Transcultural Aspects of Dispute Resolution, University of Hawaii.

Meyer, D.S. and Marullo, S. (1992), 'Grassroots Mobilization and International Politics: Peace Protest and the End of the Cold War', in L. Kriesberg and D. R. Segal (eds), *The Transformation of European Communist Societies*, JAI Press, Greenwich.

Mies, M. (1986), *Patriarchy and Accumulation on a World Scale: Women in the International Division of Labour*, Zed Books, London.

Mies, M. (1991), 'Women's Research or Feminist Research? The Debate Surrounding Feminist Science and Methodology', in M. M. Fono and J.A. Cook (eds), *Beyond Methodology: Feminist Scholarship as Lived Research*, Indiana University Press, Bloomington, pp. 60-84.

Miles, A. (1996), *Integrative Feminisms*, Routledge, London.

Minh-ha, T.T. (1997), 'Not Like You/Like You: Postcolonial Women and the Interlocking Questions of Identity and Difference', in A. McClintock, A. Mufti, and E. Shohat (eds), *Dangerous Liaisons: Gender, Nation, and Postcolonial Perspectives*, University of Minnesota Press, Minneapolis, pp. 415-419.

Mitchell, C.R. (1981), *Peacemaking and the Consultant's Role*, Gower, Westmead, United Kingdom.

Mitchell, C.R. (1993), 'The Process and Stages of Mediation: Two Sudanese Cases', in David R. Smock (ed), *Making War and Waging Peace: Foreign Intervention in Africa*, United States Institute of Peace Press, Washington, pp. 139-160.

Mohanty, C.T. (1997), 'Under Western Eyes: Feminist Scholarship and Colonial Discourses', in C. Mohanty, A. Russo, and L. Torres (eds), *Third World Women and the Politics of Feminism*, Indiana University Press, Bloomington, pp. 51-80.

Mohanty, C., Russo, A., and Torres, L. (eds) (1991), *Third World Women and the Politics of Feminism*, Indiana University Press, Bloomington.

Moraga, C. and Anzaldua, G. (eds) (1983), *This Bridge Called My Back: Writings By Radical Women Of Color*, Kitchen Table/Women of Color Press, New York.

Morgan, R. (1970), *Sisterhood is Powerful: An Anthology of Writings from the Women's Liberation Movement*, Random House, New York.

Narayan, U. (1997), *Dislocating Cultures: Identities, Traditions, and Third World Feminism*, Routledge, New York.

National Coalition Building Institute, East Tennessee Chapter (n.d.) Retrieved 19 March 2000 from http//:www.korrnet.org/ncbi.

Ong, A. (1996), 'Strategic Sisterhood or Sisters in Solidarity? Questions of Communitarianism and Citizenship in Asia', [Electronic Version], *Indiana Journal of Global Legal Studies*, **4**(1).

Ounei-Small, S. (1996), 'The Struggle for Liberation in the Pacific', in E. Friedlander (ed), *Look at the World Through Women's Eyes: Plenary Speeches from the NGO Forum on Women, Beijing 1995*, NGO Forum on Women, Beijing, '95, New York, pp. 166-169.

Pietila, H. and Vickers, J. (1994), *Making Women Matter: The Role of the United Nations*, Zed Books, London.

Princen, T. and Finger, M. (1994), *Environmental NGOs in World Politics: Linking the Local and the Global*, Routledge, London.

Rahnema, M. (1997), *The Post-Development Reader*, Zed Books, London.

Ramos-Shahani, L. (1996), 'Toward the Twenty-First Century of Women: From Commitment to Action', *Women's Studies Quarterly*, **14** (1-2), pp. 135-140.

Rothman, J. (1991), 'Negotiation as Consolidation: Pre-negotiation in the Israeli-Palestinian Conflict', *The Jerusalem Journal of International Relations*, March.

Rothman, J. (1997), *Resolving Identity-Based Conflict*, Jossey-Bass Publishers, San Francisco.

Rothschild, J. and Whitt, A.J. (1986), *The Cooperative Workplace*, Cambridge University Press, Cambridge.

Rothschild-Whitt, J. (1979), 'The Collectivist organization: An Alternative to Rational-Bureaucratic Models', *American Sociological Review*, **44**, pp. 509-527.

Rucht, D. (1997), 'Limits to Mobilization: Environmental Policy for the European Union', in Jackie Smith, Charles Chatfield and Ron Pagnucco (eds), *Transnational Social Movements and Global Politics: Solidarity Beyond the State*, Syracuse University Press, Syracuse, pp. 195-213.

Ruddick, S. (1989), *Maternal Thinking: Toward a Politics of Peace*, Ballantine Books, New York.

Rule, J. (1981), 'With All Due Respect', in *The Outlander*, Naiad Press, Tallahassee.

Santiago, I. M. (1996), 'Opening Remarks', in E. Friedlander (ed), *Look at the World Through Women's Eyes: Plenary Speeches from the NGO Forum on Women, Beijing 1995*, NGO Forum on Women, Beijing, '95, New York, p. 13.

Sargent, L. (1981), *Women and Revolution*, South End, Boston.

Sather, T. (ed) (1999), *Pros and Cons: a Debater's Handbook*, Routledge, London.

Saunders, H. H. (1999), *A Public Peace Process: Sustained Dialogue to Transform Racial and Ethnic Conflicts*, St. Martin's Press, New York.

Saunders, H.H., and Slim, R. (1994), 'Dialogue to Change Conflictual Relationships', *Higher Education Exchange*, pp. 43-56.

Sen, G. and Grown, C. (1987), *Development, Crisis, and Alternative Visions: Third World Women's Perspective*, Monthly Review Press, New York.

Skevington, S. and Baker, D. (eds) (1989), *The Social Identity of Women*, Sage, London.

Slim, R. (1996), 'Redefining Conflict Resolution: Building Civil Society as an Essential Strategy for Preventing or Ending Conflicts', *Kettering Foundation Connections*, **7**(2), pp. 16-19.

Smith, D. (1987), *The Everyday World As Problematic: A Feminist Sociology*, Northeastern University Press, Boston.

Smith, J. (2001 February 23), 'Transnational Mobilization Against Global Trade Liberalization: Challenges for Global Institutions', Paper presented at the 2001 meeting of the International Studies Association, Chicago, Illinois.

Smith, J., Chatfield, C., and Pagnucco, R. (eds) (1997), *Transnational Social Movements and Global Politics: Solidarity Beyond the State*, Syracuse University Press, Syracuse.

Snow, D. A. and Benford, R. D. (1992), 'Master Frames and Cycles of Protest', in Frontiers in A.D. Morris and C. McClurg Mueller (eds), *Social Movement Theory*, Temple University Press, New Haven, pp. 133-55.

Snow, D.A., Rochford, E.B., Worden, S.K., and Benford, R.B. (1986), 'Frame Alignment Processes, Micromobilization, and Movement Participation', *American Sociological Review*, **51**, pp. 464-481.

Snyder, A. (2000), 'Peace Profile: Federation of African Women's Peace Networks', *Peace Profile*, **12**(1), pp.147-153.

Spalter-Roth, R. and Schreiber, R. (1995), 'Outsider Issues and Insider Tactics: Strategic Tensions in the Women's Policy Network during the 1980s', in R. Ferree and P. Martin (eds), *Feminist Organizations: Harvest of the New Left Women's Movement*, Temple University Press, Philadelphia, pp. 105-27.

Staggenborg, S. (1986), 'Coalition Work in the Pro-Choice Movement: Organizational and Environmental Opportunities and Obstacles', *Social Problems*, **33**, pp. 374-89.

Stephenson, C.M. (1995), 'Women's International Non-Governmental Organizations at the United Nations', in Ann Winslow (ed), *Women, Politics, and the United Nations*, Greenwood Press, New York, pp. 135-54.

Stienstra, D. (1994), *Women's Movements and International Organizations*, St. Martin's Press, New York.

Stoeker, R. (1995), 'Community, Movement, Organization: The Problem of Identity Convergence in Collective Action', *Sociological Quarterly*, **36**(1), pp. 111-131.

Stokes, G. (1993), *The Walls Came Tumbling Down: The Collapse of Communism in Eastern Europe*, Oxford University Press, New York.

Streek, W. and Schmitter, P. (1991), 'From National Corporatism to Transnational Pluralism: Organized Interests in the Single European Market', *Politics and Society*, **19**, pp. 133-64.

Susskind, L. and Madigan D. (1984), 'New Approaches to Resolving Disputes in the Public Sector', *Justice System Journal*, **9** (2), pp. 197-203.

Svirsky, G. (1998), 'The Impact of Women in Black in Israel', in L.A. Lorentzen and J. Turpin (eds), *The Women and War Reader*, New York University Press, New York, pp. 329-336.

Tajfel, H. (ed) (1982), *Social Identity and Intergroup Relations*, Cambridge University Press, New York.

Tannen, D. (1998), *The Argument Culture: Moving From Debate to Dialogue*, Random House, New York.

Tarrow, S. (1983), *Struggling to Reform: Social Movements and Policy Change During Cycles of Protest*, Cornell University Press, Ithaca.

Tarrow, S. (1992), 'Mentalities, Political Cultures, and Collective Action Frames: Constructing Meanings Through Action', in Aldon D. Morris and Carol McClurg Mueller (eds), *Frontiers in Social Movement Theory*, New Haven, Temple University Press, pp. 174-202.

Tarrow, S. (1995), *Power in Movement: Social Movements, Collective Action and Politics*, Cambridge University Press, New York.

Tarrow, S. (2001), 'Transnational Politics: Contention and Institutions in International Politics', *Annual Review of Political Science*, **4**, pp. 1-20.

Tilly, C. (1984), 'Social Movements and National Politics', in Charles Bright and Susan Harding, *Statemaking and Social Movements: Essays in History and Theory*, University of Michigan Press, Ann Arbor.

UN Fourth World Conference on Women (1996), 'Platform for Action', *Women's Studies Quarterly*, **14** (1-2), pp.159-290.

UN/WFP-Sudan, WFP/RLO (1993), 'Weekly Report for S. Sudan', June.

Uvin, P. (1996), 'Scaling up the Grassroots, and Scaling Down the Summit: The Relations between Third World NGOs an the UN', in T.G. Weiss and L. Gordenker (eds), *NGOs, the UN, and Global Governance*, Lynne Reiner, Boulder, p.59.

Vickers, J. (1993), *Women and War*, Zed Books, London.

Volkan, V.D., and Harris, M. (1992), 'Negotiating a Peaceful Separation: A Psychopolitical Analysis of Current Relationships Between Russia and the Baltic Republics', *Mind and Human Interaction*, **4**(1), pp. 20-39.

Volkan, V.D., and Harris, M. (1993), 'Vaccinating the Political Process: A Second Psychopolitical Analysis of Relationships Between Russia and the Baltic States', *Mind and Human Interaction*, **4**(4), pp. 169-90.

Washington Post (1990), 'Sudanese at Risk', January, p. A18.

Weisser, S. O. and Fleishner, J. (1994), *Feminist Nightmares: Women at Odds*, New York University Press, New York.

Williams, J. (1984), 'Gender and Intergroup Behavior: Towards an Integration', *British Journal of Social Psychology*, **23**, p. 313.

Wilmot, W. and Hocker, J. (2001), *Interpersonal Conflict*, McGraw-Hill, New York.

Winslow, A. (ed) (1995), *Women, Politics, and the United Nations*, Greenwood Press, New York.

Women Concern (1994), 'Voice of the Women: Sudanese Women's Voice for Peace Workshop: Ukweli Pastoral Centre, Kisumu 1-5 August, 1994', *The Displaced*, **1**(3), pp. 23-32.

Women's International League for Peace and Freedom (1996), 'Peace Train to Beijing: The 4th UN World Conference on Women', [Videorecording] (Available from WILPF, 1213 Race St., Philadelphia, PA, 19107-1691).

Young, I.M. (1990), *Justice and the Politics of Difference*, Princeton University Press, Princeton.

Index